STERLING
Test Prep

AP

U.S. Government
& Politics

Essential Review

3rd edition

www.Sterling-Prep.com

Our guarantee – the highest quality preparation materials.

Our books are of the highest quality and error-free.

Be the first to report a typo or error and receive a
$10 reward for a content error or
$5 reward for a typo or grammatical mistake.

info@sterling–prep.com

We reply to all emails – please check your spam folder

3   2   1

ISBN-13: 978-0-9977782-3-6

Sterling Test Prep products are available at special quantity discounts for sales, promotions, academic counseling offices, and other educational purposes.

For more information contact our Sales Department at:

Sterling Test Prep
6 Liberty Square #11
Boston, MA 02109

info@sterling-prep.com

© 2019 Sterling Test Prep

Published by Sterling Test Prep

Dear AP student!

Congratulations on choosing this book as part of your AP United States Government and Politics exam preparation!

Scoring well on AP exams is important for admission to college. To achieve a high score on AP U.S. Government and Politics, you need to develop skills and competence in American political culture, structures, and governmental functions, as well as an understanding of the relationships between the governing and linkage institutions on the exam.

This book provides a thorough and curriculum-oriented review of all content areas of the course per the College Board's most current AP USGP. The content is focused on a targeted and detailed review of all the important facts, concepts, and theories related to U.S. government and politics.

The information is presented in a clear and easy to understand style. This book can be used both as accompanying text during your AP course and as a review guide before the exam. By using it as your study tool, you will develop the necessary skills and will be well prepared for the course and exam.

The content is developed and edited by highly qualified political science teachers and researchers. The content was systematized and organized by education specialists to ensure the adherence to the curriculum and skills outlined by the College Board for the AP U.S. Government and Politics course. All content was examined for quality and consistency by our team of editors who are experts on teaching and preparing students for standardized tests.

We wish you great success in your future academic achievements and look forward to being an important part of your successful preparation for the AP exams!

Sterling Test Prep Team

181112gdx

Our Commitment to the Environment

Sterling Test Prep is committed to protecting our planet's resources by supporting environmental organizations with proven track records of conservation, ecological research and education and preservation of vital natural resources. A portion of our profits is donated to help these organizations, so they can continue their critical missions. These organizations include:

For over 40 years, Ocean Conservancy has been advocating for a healthy ocean by supporting sustainable solutions based on science and cleanup efforts. Among many environmental achievements, Ocean Conservancy laid the groundwork for an international moratorium on commercial whaling, played an instrumental role in protecting fur seals from overhunting and banning the international trade of sea turtles. The organization created national marine sanctuaries and served as the lead non-governmental organization in the designation of 10 of the 13 marine sanctuaries.

For 25 years, Rainforest Trust has been saving critical lands for conservation through land purchases and protected area designations. Rainforest Trust has played a central role in the creation of 73 new protected areas in 17 countries, including the Falkland Islands, Costa Rica and Peru. Nearly 8 million acres have been saved thanks to Rainforest Trust's support of in-country partners across Latin America, with over 500,000 acres of critical lands purchased outright for reserves.

Since 1980, Pacific Whale Foundation has been saving whales from extinction and protecting our oceans through science and advocacy. As an international organization, with ongoing research projects in Hawaii, Australia, and Ecuador, PWF is an active participant in global efforts to address threats to whales and other marine life. A pioneer in non-invasive whale research, PWF was an early leader in educating the public, from a scientific perspective, about whales and the need for ocean conservation.

With your purchase, you support environmental causes around the world.

Table of Contents

We want to hear from you

Your feedback is important to us because we strive to provide the highest quality prep materials. Email us if you have any questions, comments or suggestions, so we can incorporate your feedback into future editions.

Customer Satisfaction Guarantee

If you have any concerns about this book, including printing issues, contact us and we will resolve any issues to your satisfaction.

info@sterling-prep.com

We reply to all emails – please check your spam folder

Thank you for choosing our products to achieve your educational goals!

AP United States Government and Politics
Exam Information

The AP United States Government and Politics Exam is 2 hours and 25 minutes long and includes both a multiple-choice section and a free-response section. Student performance metrics on these two parts are compiled and weighted to determine an overall AP Exam score.

Section	Question Type	Number of Questions	Timing	Percentage of Total Exam Score
I	Multiple-choice questions	60 questions	45 minutes	50%
II	Free-response questions	4 question	100 minutes	50%

Given the number of questions and the time restrictions per exam section, it is advisable that students plan on devoting no longer than approximately 45 seconds per multiple-choice question and 25 minutes per free-response question. Following this recommendation should allow for the time needed to answer every question on the exam.

The content of the new AP United States Government and Politics curriculum and exam is divided into six topics. The table below lists the topics and their approximate presence on the exam. The coverage of the topics in the exam as a whole reflects the approximate weightings.

Topic	Approximate Percentage of AP Exam
Constitutional Underpinnings of United States Government	5-15%
Political Beliefs and Behaviors	10-20%
Political Parties, Interest Groups, and Mass Media	10-20%
Institutions of National Government	35-45%
Public Policy	5-15%
Civil Rights and Civil Liberties	5-15%

What (not) to Bring to the Exam

A no. 2 pencil is required for the multiple-choice section, while a black or blue ink pen is required for the free-response section. Please come to the exam prepared with both writing instruments and clear scratch paper. Calculators are not permitted during the exam. Any computations needed should be able to be completed either mentally or using paper and pencil. Multi-color markers and pencils are not accepted.

Assessment of Student's Learning on the Exam

Students are expected to demonstrate broad knowledge competence in American political culture, structures, and governmental functions, as well as demonstrate an understanding of the interrelationship between the governing and linkage institutions on the exam. They should also be knowledgeable regarding the rules governing elections and the structure and behavior of political parties and interest groups. To answer questions correctly, political behaviors, concepts, perspectives, politics, and processes must be satisfactorily defined, compared, explained, or interpreted.

The following are general parameters about the relationship between the components of the curriculum framework and the questions on the AP Exam. AP United States Government and Politics exam assesses:

- Students' competence in describing and comparing crucial facts, concepts, and theories related to U.S. government and politics.

- Students' ability to explain characteristic patterns of political processes and behavior along with their associated consequences.

- Students' skills interpreting basic information (charts, tables, etc.) relevant to U.S. government and politics

- Students' acumen concerning relevant concepts and theories and their ability to apply them appropriately with adequately developed connections.

- Students' proficiency in analyzing political relationships and evaluating policy changes using examples to buttress the argument.

Scoring

The multiple-choice section is graded electronically with points given for each correct answer provided. Missed questions and answers purposely left blank will be considered incorrect and will count against your final score. Therefore, it is important to leave yourself enough time to answer every question on the exam, even if this means guessing.

The free-response section is cross-evaluated and scored by multiple college faculty members and high school AP teacher participants of the annual AP Reading held each year in June. Fairness and consistency are monitored and enforced during the evaluation process through a system of checks and balances, with all evaluators strictly using shared scoring guidelines. A Chief Reader is also included in the process to ensure scoring standard accuracy.

The raw scores from both sections are then combined to arrive at the composite AP score. This score is represented as a 5, 4, 3, 2, or 1. This score is used to signify to colleges and universities the qualification level a student possesses in receiving either college credit or placement. Not all universities and colleges agree upon the same prerequisite scores, so it is important to check with their admissions offices directly to clarify their standards. Many universities and colleges will include this on their website. Located below is a chart illustrating each score and its associated recommendation as per College Board:

Composite AP score	Recommendation
5	Extremely well qualified
4	Well qualified
3	Qualified
2	Possibly qualified
1	No recommendation

Multiple-Choice Questions

The multiple-choice section consists of sixty questions with five (A-E) possible answer choices each. These questions sometimes require students to respond to data graphs, tables or maps and draw upon knowledge required by the curriculum framework. Each question addresses one of the learning objectives for the course.

Read all multiple-choice questions carefully. It is important to understand exactly what the question is asking for. If the correct answer is not immediately clear, fall back as best as you can to the process of elimination. Be sure to look at all the possible answer choices before selecting one. Eliminate as many incorrect answers are possible. Usually, there is at least one choice that is easily identified as wrong. Eliminating even one choice will greatly increase your chances of selecting the correct one. After eliminating the most obvious incorrect choice(s), eliminate any answers that strike you as "almost right" or "half right." You should consider "half right" as synonymous with "wrong." These answer choices are purposely included to catch test takers off guard. Only guess as a last resort.

Always remember that an unanswered question will lower your score since your score is based only on the number of correct answers provided (incorrect and skipped questions are weighed the same). Therefore, leave nothing unanswered.

Categorically speaking, the multiple-choice section is composed of six different types of questions: definition or identification questions, cause-and-effect questions, Roman numeral questions, except/not questions, Supreme Court case questions and graphic questions.

Definition or Identification Questions

These questions require test takers to recognize something and then appropriately describe or define it. For example, the following question from College Board appeared on exams in the past:

The Americans with Disabilities Act, which provides protections for the disabled, is an example of:

    (A) state supremacy
    (B) horizontal federalism
    (C) affirmative action
    (D) dual federalism
    (**E**) a federal mandate

Cause-and-Effect Questions

These questions require test takers to associate causes with their effects or vice versa correctly. For example, the following question from College Board appeared on exams in the past:

Which of the following is the most likely consequence of divided government?

    (A) Reorganization of the federal bureaucracy
    (B) Conflicts between states
    (**C**) Delays in confirmation of federal court nominees
    (D) Conflicts between national government and states
    (E) Elimination of the seniority rule in Congress

Roman Numeral Questions

These questions provide a question followed by a Roman numeral list of statements, phrases or words related to the question. The answers to choose among feature different combinations of Roman numerals correlating to the list featured immediately beneath the question. Choose the correct Roman numeral combination that fully answers the question (more than one Roman numeral may be correct). For example, the following question from College Board appeared on exams in the past:

Registered voters directly elect which of the following?

    I. The president and vice president
    II. Supreme Court justices
    III. Senators
    IV. The Electoral College

    (A) I only
    (B) IV only
    (C) I and II only
    (**D**) III and IV only
    (E) II, III, and IV only

Except/Not Questions

These questions are easily recognized by their inclusion of the all capitalized words "EXCEPT" and "NOT." Identify which four answer choices are correct. Then, select the one choice which is incorrect or does not fit with the others. For example, the following question from College Board appeared on exams in the past:

The Constitution and its amendments expressly prohibit all of the following EXCEPT

    (A) slavery
    (B) double jeopardy
    (C) cruel and unusual punishment
    (D) unreasonable searches and seizures
    (**E**) sex discrimination in employment

Supreme Court Case Questions

These questions present a particular Supreme Court case and then require test takers to identify, interpret or compare it correctly. For example, the following question from College Board appeared on exams in the past:

In *Brown v. Board of Education of Topeka*, the Supreme Court established which of the following principles?

    (A) A school official can search a student for drugs.
    (B) Everyone must go to school at least until the age of 16.
    (C) Tuition for private schools cannot be tax deductible.
    (**D**) Separation of students by race, even in equally good schools, is unconstitutional.
    (E) A moment of silent prayer at the beginning of the school day is allowable under the First Amendment.

Graphics Questions

These questions are identified by their inclusion of a graph, table or map that test takers must refer to answer the question. For example, the following question from College Board appeared on exams in the past:

OPINIONS ON AFFIRMATIVE ACTION FOR WOMEN

Age-Group	Men		Women	
	Favor	Oppose	Favor	Oppose
18-29	55%	22%	73%	9%
30-44	48%	35%	63%	24%
45-64	59%	31%	75%	9%
65 and older	40%	39%	71%	16%

The differences are shown in the table demonstrate which of the following?

    (A) Political efficacy
    (B) Women's greater political participation
    (C) Men's great political participation

(D) Age discrimination

(**E**) The gender gap

Free-Response Questions

The free-response section contains four questions that typically require students to both process information presented in the question into existing frameworks of understanding and to then respond. Being a free-response format, there is a wide degree of personal choice in how you write your answer response. These questions are representative of the varied content areas of the United States government and politics. Students might also be required to present and discuss relevant examples, clarify or appraise U.S. government and political principles or perform a detailed analysis of political relationships and events. As with the multiple-choice section, students may be required to respond to stimulus materials, including texts, charts, graphs, etc., in the process of answering the free-response questions. Categorically speaking, free-response questions appear on the AP U.S. Government and Politics exam in two different varieties: single-topic questions and multiple-component questions.

For free-response questions, it is important to answer questions in their entirety, not just partially. For example, some questions may ask test takers to both identify and explain. Performing only one of these required actions is inadequate and will be graded accordingly. A list of the possible actions questions require of test-takers includes: List/identify, define, describe, discuss, explain, compare/contrast, evaluate/assess and analyze. It is good practice to underline these directives as you see them so that these expectations are not forgotten or overlooked as you proceed to write your responses. Any additional work that goes beyond the question's stated directives does not earn you a higher score or result in extra credit. Therefore, in the interest of time management and keeping the content of your response purely relevant, answer all questions in their entirety but avoid being tempted into going further.

Before jumping immediately into writing mode, take a brief moment or two to brainstorm about the questions' topics. You are allowed to jot down notes or outline on scratch if this helps your composition process. Keep in mind though that there are roughly 25 minutes provided for answering each of the free-response questions. Be sure to find your balance between the time needed to brainstorm and the time needed to write.

Free-response answers should include specific evidence and avoid unsubstantiated claims. Long, meandering responses filled with loosely-related facts regarding specific concepts of phenomena are to be avoided. Only include information that is directly relevant and demonstrates the primary points of the argument which is made. This information should moreover be presented in a clear and concise manner. Terms should be used correctly. All claims should be directly stated. You do not want the readers who score your answers to infer or guess how something demonstrates a point. Regardless of whether they correctly guess your intentions or not, you will likely be graded more critically for including ambiguities.

Keep in mind when working on the free-response section that you are not bound to answer the questions according to the order in which they are presented. For example, if you immediately know how to write your response to the second question but not the first, by all means, skip to the second free-response question. This can help you avoid getting bogged down and frustrated, maximizing your time more efficiently. Additionally, devoting your allotted time first to those questions you are more knowledgeable on and confident in answering helps ensure that, if you run out of time, you run out of time on a question you are less confident in answering. Of course, if you do skip questions, be sure to go back and complete them as best as you can.

As you proceed through the free-response section, if you accidentally make a mistake writing in your answer booklet, simply draw a line through the error (strikethrough) to remedy the issue. Then, continue writing on as you normally would.

Practice Question Strategies

Locate and utilize as many practice questions (for both exam sections) as you can to quiz your knowledge retention and bolster the quality of your written responses. Questions from previous AP examinations are numerous and can be easily found online with a simple search. The more you practice, the better you'll perform. Additionally, it is helpful for your practice sessions to emulate the format of your upcoming exam as closely as possible. This means allotting yourself the same number of questions and time restrictions as the real exam includes.

Using free-response practice questions, train yourself to conceptualize your answer in your mind first before putting them to pen and paper. This aids in streamlining your response into a more fluid flow. Disconnected thoughts and poorly-organized writing will be graded accordingly.

Notes

Chapter 1

Constitutional Underpinnings of United States Government

The Constitution of the United States of America is a living document. This means that it can be changed and amended as the people and the country change. After the well-known Preamble, or introduction, the text of the Constitution is broken into seven sections called Articles. Each article deals with a particular section of the new government.

The state of modern United States politics is a reflection of the kind of federalism government established by the Constitution, the separation of powers and the system of checks and balances.

These developments were rooted in the historical context of the Constitutional Convention and the ideological and philosophical traditions on which the framers drew. These factors influenced the rationale for specific concerns and actions of the framers, such as James Madison's fear of factions or the swift adoption of the Bill of Rights. The United States Supreme Court's interpretation of key provisions of the Constitution sheds light and clarifies the theoretical and practical features of federalism, the separation of powers and the system of checks and balances. Theoretical perspectives related to the Constitution (i.e., democratic theory, theories of republican government, pluralism and elitism, etc.)

Notes

Considerations That Influenced the Formulation and Adoption of the Constitution

Influences

Modern government can be traced back to the philosophical traditions of the Enlightenment Age, a philosophical period in the 18th century that dominated Europe. During the Enlightenment Age, philosophers were beginning to rise against unicameral governments and absolute monarchism. Enlightenment Age philosophers promoted the idea that people innately possess liberty, the ability to progress, the ability to reason, and a capacity for tolerance. The philosophers believed that reason, rather than tradition, could lead to a better organizational structure of government.

Thomas Hobbes was a 17th century English philosopher and political theorist whose principal philosophy was based on establishing conditions in which man could create and sustain peace. Hobbes argued that by nature, humans seek to gain some advantage over each other rather than establish a community. He believed that this rapacious attitude could not sustain a society in the long term. As Hobbes stated "the life of man is nasty, brutish and short," which fundamentally represents his position on why the government needs to be established and maintained.

Thomas Hobbes, English philosopher, and political theorist

Due to this fundamental stance on the human condition, Hobbes believed that it was better for a man to be ruled by a tyrant than to live in a state of chaos and war. He wrote in his book *Leviathan* (1651) that the purpose of a governing body, which he calls the commonwealth, is to avoid war and allow peace to work for the benefit of all people. By war, Hobbes meant conflicting forces without a common authority. Hobbes specified three principal causes of conflict:

- competition for resources, which inspires conflict in pursuit of material gain;

- diffidence, which is the result of one's pursuit of safety; and

- glory, where conflict follows from the desire to protect or advance one's reputation.

Hobbes also believed that the people of the commonwealth are always subject to the powers of the commonwealth because of their desire for self-preservation and security. He stated, *"the only way to erect a common power [and secure the people] . . . is to confer all of their power and strength upon one man, or upon one assembly of men that may reduce all of their wills, by a plurality of voices, unto one will."*

John Locke was a 17th-century philosopher whose political theories greatly influenced segments of the U.S. Constitution. Locke believed in natural rights. He believed that with these rights, all men are born equal, free and independent, and have an inherent right to enjoy life, liberty, and property. Locke believed, concerning natural rights, that man's natural freedom requires that others be naturally obligated to respect that freedom. He stated, "The great and chief end, therefore, of men's uniting into commonwealths, and putting themselves under government, is the preservation of their property." It is the need to preserve man's right over their own lives, liberties, and possessions that form the basis for man's establishment of political authority. Locke believed that political authority or political power over natural rights might only be obtained by consent or through a social contract.

Concerning the revolution, Locke believed that unbridled power over the natural rights of man warrant and justified resistance by those subject to that power. He believed that a just leader is one that is bound by the laws of the legislative representatives of the people, and when one ceases to represent the people, he has become a tyrant. Locke believed that the only way to protect subjects from a reversion to executive tyranny by fiat is through the establishment of a system of checks and balances, where the legislative branch always has a say in the adoption of laws.

Charles de Montesquieu was an 18th-century aristocrat, author and authority on government who believed in the limited power of a monarch. While Montesquieu did not believe that there was a universal solution for political problems, he believed that law should be objective and evolve by society. He believed a monarchy, due to its inflexibility, could not properly serve a progressing society. He ultimately concluded that the powers of government should be separated between an executive, a legislative and a judicial branch of government to prevent the establishment of tyranny or absolutism in anyone. He stated, "If political liberty [or legal rights] is to be preserved for the individual, no one man or body in the state should have control of more than one of these functions."

Locke (left) and Montesquieu (right), French Enlightenment philosophers

Jean Jacques Rousseau was an 18th-century philosopher. He believed that human beings are naturally good, free and can rely on their instincts. He is quoted as stating, "Were there a people of gods, their government would be democratic." According to Rousseau, any contract whereby man alienates his freedom would be illegitimate, precisely because it is free will that constitutes man's moral nature. He believed, like Locke, that a state is made by a union freely formed by its members and that union must consent to a set convention or social contract.

Thomas Paine was an 18th-century political philosopher known for his pamphlet *"Common Sense"* which greatly influenced public opinion during the American Revolution. Paine viewed government as a necessary evil, required for the restraint of natural instincts and the preservation of larger social groups. He viewed the monarchy as a form of corrupt government tied to a hereditary succession that goes against biblical principles. He also viewed the monarchy as a threat to the future health of the nation because it gives any king the power to leave the throne to an incompetent successor. Paine believed that a representative form of government and a rotating annual presidency chosen by representatives of each state would be the most appropriate form of government.

Rousseau (left) & Paine (right), French Enlightenment philosophers

Continental Congress

As a precursor to the American Revolution and the establishment of an independent American government, the *Second Continental Congress* convened in 1775. This convention took place after King George II rejected the *Declaration of Rights and Grievances* which was a petition to King George III to restore harmony between Britain and the colonies after Britain passed punitive laws against the colonies. The purpose of the Second Continental Congress, which consisted of delegates from all thirteen colonies, was to replace legislatures dissolved by royal governors and to assume governmental duties, including the regulation of trade and issuance of paper money. Most importantly, the duty of the Congress was the organization of a continental army and developing an institutional structure to finance the war for independence. By 1776, a majority of the members of the Second Continental Congress voted to instruct all colonies to establish independent governments, secede from royal authority and approve a resolution calling for independence. Thomas Paine's pamphlet *"Common Sense"* is recognized for convincing the more conservative delegates to support independence. In July of 1776, the Second Continental Congress signed the *Declaration of Independence,* which is often called the blueprint for the American Revolution.

Declaration of Independence

One can find the segments of Locke's philosophy represented in the language of the *Declaration of Independence*. Both Locke and the Declaration of Independence espouse messages of equality, preservation of life, liberty and property, natural rights and revolution against monarchy. Locke and the framers of the Declaration of Independence talked about resistance against a tyrannical government. Locke states, "[w]hen any one, or more, shall take upon them to make laws whom the people have not appointed to do so, they make laws without authority. . ." The Declaration of Independence provides, "[w]hen in the course of human events, it becomes necessary for one people to dissolve the political bands that have connected them with another, and to assume, among the powers of the earth, the separate and equal state to which the laws of nature and nature's God entitle them [...]." The *Declaration of Independence* also set forth a belief in self-government, a position similar to Locke's belief that a sufficient government derives its powers from the consent of the governed.

One drawback to America's Declaration of Independence was the lack of an existing central government. The Second Continental Congress attempted to convince the colonies that reliance on Continental currency, as well as each colony's currency, was harmful to the national movement, harmful to the continued financing of the war against the British and would serve as a catalyst for inflation. By 1779, after the British began distributing counterfeit colonial currency to thwart the colonies' war efforts, Congress ceased issuing and honoring its national currency. The Second Continental Congress proposed a governing document in 1777 calling for a strong central government, but a majority of delegates did not favor this.

Drafting the Declaration of Independence

Articles of Confederation

The *Articles of Confederation*, which was the first governing document of the United States, was ratified by the Second Continental Congress on March 1, 1781. The initial purpose of the Articles of Confederation was to codify the procedures and powers of the Second Continental Congress. This document changed the name of the Second Continental Congress to the *Congress of Confederation*, appointed the temporary central government of the United States of America and established shared responsibilities between the states and central government. The Articles of Confederation also defined the relationship between the Confederation Congress and the sovereign governments of the states. The Articles of Confederation established a system in which the state governments had greater sovereignty and greater power than the central government. The powers delegated to the central government included the power to conduct foreign policy, the power to make treaties, the power to declare war, the power to maintain an army and navy, the power to coin money and the power to establish post offices. The powers delegated to the states included the power to collect taxes, the power to negotiate and enter into trade agreements with foreign countries and the power to control commerce. The Articles of Confederation and the Confederation Congress were vital to negotiating the *Treaty of Paris* between the United States of America and Great Britain in 1783 to end the American Revolution.

The Articles of Confederation were replete with problems. All amendments to the Articles of Confederation required unanimous consent by the colonies to avoid enhancing the powers of the central government, but due to the long travel time, it often took months to obtain consent. The central government lacked any power to tax, depended on the states for income and at the same time had no way of enforcing its right to collect revenues owed by the states. The value of state currency was in decline throughout this period. The states were always fearing the threat of other foreign enemies, and without a strong central government and a rising war debt, there was no way of drafting an army in the event of conflict. The central government could not regulate commerce between the states. Congress did not have law enforcement organizations or police power at their disposal. The Articles of Confederation lacked a system for amendment. The Articles of Confederation could not also adjudicate disputes between states and lacked a central executive power. Most importantly, the states were competing in the marketplace without a centralized and regulated market and were in need of a unified economic system.

Shays' Rebellion

Shays' Rebellion presents a perfect example of how the Articles of Confederation were weak. By 1786, the United States was suffering from a severe economic depression due to the Revolutionary War. States were battling over rights to land and sea, taxes were extremely high, unemployment was rampant, and wages were low. As a war tactic, the British sanctioned the colonies through curtailing trade. Daniel Shays, a war veteran and farmer, led a rebellion against courts in Massachusetts that were jailing debtors, confiscating property and declaring families bankrupt. The rebellion escalated into an armed conflict between Shays' "army" of over a thousand men and the Massachusetts militia across the Commonwealth.

Portraits of Daniel Shays and Job Shattuck, leaders of the Massachusetts "Regulators."

The Commonwealth sought the assistance of the federal government, but without the ability to tax, the federal government could not finance an army or enforce its laws. Even though Shays' men were ultimately defeated and disbanded, his rebellion demonstrated the weakness of a separate state and federal government. Rebellions similar to Shay's commenced throughout the United States. With rebellion and economic turmoil rampant through the United States, political leaders determined that the next course of action was to reshape the Articles of Confederation.

Constitutional Convention

Between May 25, 1787, and September 17, 1787, delegates from the thirteen independent states (Rhode Island did not participate) met in Philadelphia, Pennsylvania to revise the Articles of Confederation. Delegates to the Constitutional Convention included planters, bankers, businessmen, and lawyers. It was the intent of a group of delegates at the Convention, later to be called the Federalists, to replace the Articles of Confederation with a new set of governing documents. Opponents to the Constitutional Convention, many of whom did not attend, saw the attempt to revise the Articles of Confederation as a means of usurping the independent powers of state governments. American historian Charles Beard (1874–1948), who produced an interpretation of the Constitution from an economic standpoint, saw the Constitutional Convention as an attempt by the elite and wealthy leaders of government, persons like George Washington and James Madison (who were the wealthiest) to turn capital forces against the agrarian forces of the government. Beard contended that much of the controversy surrounding the Articles of Confederation involved property disputes between commercial business interests and owners of land property.

Federalist and Anti-Federalist

During the Constitutional Convention, the delegates were divided between Federalist and Anti-Federalist factions. The *Federalist* faction was the group of delegates, and eventually the political party, that advocated for a stronger central government. James Madison, John Jay, George Washington, and Alexander Hamilton were among the Federalists in attendance at the Constitutional Convention. The Federalists believed that a strong national government was essential to a state's ability to conduct foreign affairs, regulate disputes between states, collect taxes and defend the nation. This still allowed for most lawmaking to be designated by the states; however, they viewed a strong central government as essential to creating an environment where the individual states could thrive.

The *Anti-Federalists* believed that a stronger national government would tyrannize the people without restraint. Anti-Federalists, such as Patrick Henry (who refused to attend the Constitutional Convention), Samuel Adams, George Mason, and James Monroe, believed that a stronger national government would result in a monarchy and repress individual liberties and that stronger state governments would better preserve individual liberty. The Anti-Federalists were fighting on behalf of the small states to ensure that states maintained strong checks on the power of any central government, to usurp that power in instances where it would attempt to overreach. The Anti-Federalists insisted on the creation of a *Bill of Rights* to codify the rights provided to any citizen of the United States, and to protect them from the potential tyranny of an unchecked central government.

Virginia Plan

Key to the establishment of a new structure of federalist government was building a stronger, more organized central government to work in conjunction with the established state governments. James Madison, Edmund Randolph and other members of the Virginia delegation were the first to devise a plan for a new government. The *Virginia Plan*, as it was called, was a blueprint of a federalist system of government and has been defined as the blueprint of the *U.S. Constitution*. Delegates took the Virginia Plan seriously, believing that the plan would be the new government. The following decisions were taken from the Virginia Plan, agreed upon by the delegates and incorporated into the U.S. Constitution:

- Expansion of the federal government while granting state governments the power to self- govern

- Creation of a bicameral legislative branch of government consisting of an upper house and a lower house of the legislative branch, called Congress

- Creation of an executive branch to execute and enforce laws

- Creation of a judicial branch to review the laws and arbitrate disputes between the other branches of government

- Creation of a system based upon checks and balances

James Madison (left) and Edmund Randolph (right)

With respect to the legislative branch of government, delegates disagreed on the specifics of apportionment and the manner in which its members would be elected. In what is called the *Connecticut Compromise*, the delegates finally established the structure of the Congress. All delegates agreed that the voters of each state would elect the members of the lower house of the Congress and eventually agreed, after much dispute, that the members would be apportioned based on the population of the state. Although there was much dispute, the delegates eventually agreed that two individuals from each state would be elected to the upper house of Congress and that the state legislatures would elect them. The election of Senators by the state legislatures was abolished under the Seventeenth Amendment in 1913. Under the *Three-Fifths Compromise*, it was agreed that slaves would be considered three-fifths of a person to measure each state's population.

Amendments

Delegates agreed that there should be a difficult amendment process to the U.S. Constitution. Under Article V of the U.S. Constitution, the framers provided several mechanisms for ratification. There are currently 27 amendments to the United States Constitution. Most notable among the 27 amendments is the Fourteenth Amendment, which provides that all legal rights and protections granted under 5th Amendment Due Process Clause and the 14th Amendment Equal Protection apply equally to the states as they do to the federal government.

Other notable amendments include the 13th Amendment which abolished slavery, the Fifteenth Amendment which expanded the right to vote and the 16th Amendment which allows the Congress the power to levy an income tax without apportioning it among the states or basing it on the United States Census.

According to Article V of the U.S. Constitution, the U.S. Constitution may be amended if:

- the amended language receives a two-thirds majority vote from each house of Congress, as well as ratification by three-fourths of each state's legislature, or

- the language receives two-thirds majority vote from each house of Congress as well as ratification by a convention in at least three-fourths of the states, or

- a national convention is requested by at least two-thirds of state legislatures and three-fourths of state legislatures vote to ratify the amendment or the language is proposed by a national convention and ratified by a specially called convention of at least three-fourths of the states vote in each state. (This mechanism has never been used to date)

Bill of Rights

The framers of the U.S. Constitution attempted to expedite the passage of the *Bill of Rights* to make good on their promise to opponents of the U.S. Constitution. The ten amendments, which make up the Bill of Rights, were passed and ratified to appease the fears of the Anti-Federalists who believed that a strong federal government would oppress individual freedoms and liberties. Without the crucial additions and promises present in the Bill of Rights, key states might not have ratified the U.S. Constitution. The Bill of Rights, which are guaranteed to protect individual freedoms and rights, were added in 1791. The Bill of Rights espoused rights not set forth in the Articles of the U.S. Constitution. These rights include:

- freedom of religion

- freedom of speech

- a free press

- free assembly

- the right to keep and bear arms

- freedom from unreasonable search and seizure

- security in personal effects

- freedom from warrants issued without probable cause

- guarantee of a speedy trial

- guarantee of a public trial with an impartial jury

- prohibition of double jeopardy

Other plans were introduced at the Constitutional Convention by both proponents and opponents of a federal system of government. The *New Jersey Plan* was introduced by William Paterson. The plan proposed revising the Articles of Confederation so that each state would receive equal representation in a unicameral legislative branch of government. The New Jersey Plan also granted the United States the power to levy taxes, established a multi-person one-term executive branch of government to be elected by Congress and a judicial branch of government. Also, the New Jersey Plan proposed that national law would take precedence over state law.

William Paterson, Supreme Court justice and pioneer of the New Jersey Plan

Alexander Hamilton proposed a government blueprint inspired by the British parliamentary system. The *Hamilton Plan* proposed elimination of state government sovereignty, the establishment of a bicameral legislature, the creation of a national governor with a lifetime appointment and the creation of state governors. The delegates of the Constitutional Convention rejected both plans.

39 delegates from eleven states signed the final draft of the U.S. Constitution. Delegates from Rhode Island (who did not participate in the Convention) and New York were not present to sign the document. The U.S. Constitution was ratified by nine of the thirteen states as was required by Article IV of the Constitution. The Bill of Rights was not included in the draft of the Constitution signed by the 39 delegates in 1787. The Bill of Rights was drafted by Congress as amendments to the Constitution and put into effect on December 15, 1791.

The Federalist Papers

To encourage ratification of the U.S. Constitution by the states, James Madison, John Jay, and Alexander Hamilton wrote the *Federalist Papers*. In *Federalist 10*, James Madison argued that factions exist in society as a derivation of passion and political interests. He believed that a larger united republic would better protect the interests of the majority against a minority faction. He also posited that in a representative democracy, individual liberty is protected from majority rule where the interests of the majority act as a detriment to public interest. He stated, "[t]he smaller the society, the fewer probably will be the distinct parties and interests composing it; the fewer the distinct parties and interests, the more frequently will a majority be found of the same party." He further stated that the smaller the number of people in the majority, the more easily the majority will be able to work in concert to execute their plan of oppression. "Extend the sphere and you take in a greater variety of parties and interests; you make it less probable that a majority of the whole will have a common motive to invade the rights of other citizens; or if such a common motive exists, it will be more difficult for all who feel it to discover their own strength and to act in unison with each other." *Federalist 10* argued that the principles of the U.S. Constitution guard against the tyranny of the majority in a direct democracy to protect the interests of the public.

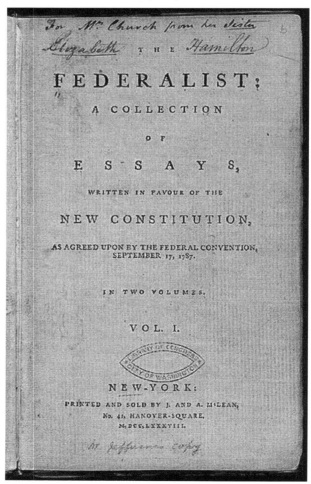

Title page of the Federalist Papers *by Alexander Hamilton, James Madison, and John Jay*

The issue of majority rule was important to the framers of the U.S. Constitution. The framers implemented the *Electoral College* so that a majority in the more populous states could not have excessive influence in the election of the president. The framers established scattered election terms for the Congress and the Senate to reduce the potential of factions to develop and influence policy. They created the Bill of Rights to protect the minority against the majority and to protect the people from the government and established the separation of powers to limit the power of the national government.

Madison began an argument for separate branches of government in *Federalist 48*. In *48*, Madison stated that while the three branches of government should remain divided, they should not be so divided that they diminish their control over each other. He warns against those with encroaching power and their attempt to control everything. Madison also argues that merely defining the branches of government is insufficient as a means to guard against executive encroachment. He states, "[t]he legislative department is everywhere extending the sphere of its activity, and drawing all power into its impetuous vortex."

Madison wrote in *Federalist 51* that the safeguards implemented by the U.S. Constitution establish three separate and independent branches of government and restrict them from usurping power. He writes, "[t]he framers recognized that, in the long term, structural protections against abuse of power were critical to preserving liberty." Madison wrote in *Federalist 51* that if men were angels and chaos did not exist, the government would not be necessary. He stated the "great security against a gradual concentration of the several powers in the same department consists in giving to those who administer each department the necessary constitutional means and personal motives to resist encroachments of the others." *Federalist 51* seems to be the basis for a bicameral form of legislative government as Madison stated, "The legislative branch is the strongest, and therefore must be divided into different branches, be as little connected as possible and render them by different modes of election."

Alexander Hamilton was the author of *Federalist 78*, in which he attempted to explain to Anti-Federalists the importance of a federal judicial system that is not beholden to political interests and is therefore not elected. According to *Federalist 78*, the federal courts must interpret and apply the Constitution and to disregard any statute that is inconsistent with it. The judicial branch of government may be considered the weakest branch because it lacks the power of the purse, the power to declare war and does not set policy. The judicial branch, however, could be seen as the most influential branch of government because the judges are appointed for life, and their decisions can last decades into the future.

Alexander Hamilton, political theorist and author of the Federalist Papers

Hamilton states that the judicial branch has the power of judicial review, the power to determine whether acts of Congress or acts of the executive branch are constitutional. Hamilton also defined the role of *stare decisis*, or precedent, in the judicial branch. Hamilton stated, "[t]o avoid an arbitrary discretion in the courts, it is indispensable that they should be bound down by strict rules and precedents, which serve to define and point out their duty in every particular case that comes before them." Hamilton believed that the reliance on precedent would prevent the imposition of judicial activism or the independent principles of the judges. In contrast, the U.S. Supreme Court stated in *Obergefell v. Hodges* that under the Constitution, judges have the power to say what the law is, not what it should be. Citing *Federalist 78*, the U.S. Supreme Court stated, "[t]he people who ratified the Constitution authorized courts to exercise 'neither force nor will but merely judgment." Judges are not subject to the will of the people or the will of politicians but subject to the will of the U.S. Constitution.

One can find elements of Hobbes, Locke, Rousseau, and Montesquieu throughout the text of the U.S. Constitution. Some state that the framers of the U.S. Constitution did not align their principles completely with the egalitarian harmony espoused by the political philosophers Hobbes, Locke, Montesquieu, and Hume, but were rather inspired by those philosophies to establish a functioning government.

Thomas Paine wrote that "government even in its best state is a necessary evil; in its worst state, an intolerable one." Hobbes placed a great emphasis on the need for the state to limit its concerns to the matters of peace and common defense; his influence can be seen in the language of the U.S. Constitution. The primary goal of the framers of the U.S.

Constitution was to establish a unified government for the common defense of the thirteen states. This is why the framers placed the role of Commander in Chief in the hands of the president, and the power to declare war in the hands of the Congress instead of delegating the duties of defense to the state governments.

Hobbes believed that man's passion is the foundation for war, which is why the framers of the U.S. Constitution placed a great emphasis on dividing the power over the military among two branches of government, the legislative and the executive.

Locke's beliefs can be seen throughout the U.S. Constitution. Locke believed that each person is entitled to life, liberty and property that inspired the framework of the 5th Amendment Due Process Clause and the 14th Amendment Equal Protection Clause and Privileges and Immunities Clause. Locke's belief that the power of government may only be obtained by the consent of the governed is replicated in the framers' decision to make the United States of America a representative democracy in which the people elect government officials. Locke and Montesquieu's belief in a checks and balances system of government is equally reflected in the language of the U.S. Constitution, evidenced by the Senate's power to ratify appointments and treaties executed by the president and the power of judicial review.

Notes

Separation of Powers

Inspired by Charles de Montesquieu, the framers of the U.S. Constitution believed that the power of the U.S. government should be divided based on administrative duties. As set forth in *Federalist 51*, the United States government is divided into three branches, the executive, the judicial and the legislative.

The legislative branch is charged with the power to make the laws, the executive branch is charged with the power to execute the laws, and the judicial branch is charged with the power to review the laws. The framers divided national powers among three branches of government to prevent an abuse of power by one person or one group and safeguard freedom for all Americans. The framers sought to establish a cautious and deliberative system of government, not an impulsive government ruled by one. Therefore, they wanted three independent branches of government, each governed by its own rules, elected or appointed by independent laws set forth by the Constitution, and holding power for varying time periods or terms.

Legislative Branch

Article I of the U.S. Constitution established the legislative branch of the United States government. Article I established the *Senate* and the *House of Representatives* who are charged with creating the laws, regulating interstate and foreign commerce, the power to investigate the executive branch of government, taxing and spending, the power to raise an army and the power to declare war. Both houses of Congress are granted the authority to subpoena and to oversee laws being implemented by demanding that members of federal agencies appear before them. All bills related to revenue are initiated in the House of Representatives. The Senate is uniquely charged with the power to consider and consent to executive appointments, charged with the power to ratify treaties and charged with the power to remove an executive or judicial officer from office after impeachment by the House of Representatives. Congress also has the authority to make all laws necessary and proper for executing its duties.

Seals of the House of Representatives (left) and Senate (right)

Members of the House of Representatives are elected every two years. Each member must have attained the age of twenty-five, be an inhabitant of the state in which he shall be elected and have been a citizen of the United States for seven years before the election. Senators are elected every six years. Each member of the Senate must have attained the age of 30, be an inhabitant of the state in which he shall be elected and have been a citizen of the United States for nine years.

The U.S. Constitution is a continually evolving document. It provides a blueprint for the government, but it is only in a skeletal form. The genius of the U.S. Constitution is its ability to evolve and allow the government to interpret, review and amend the language of the document over time. Powers specifically set forth by the language of the U.S. Constitution are considered to be express or enumerated powers of the national government. Implied powers are those powers established by case law. One such mechanism is the power of judicial review granted to the U.S. Supreme Court by its case law.

Under Article I of the U.S. Constitution, Congress has the power to create all laws necessary and proper for the carrying out of its duties. In *McCulloch v. Maryland* (1819), James McCulloch of the First Bank of the United States sought review of a decision of the State of Maryland to levy taxes on the federal bank. Even though Article I of the U.S. Constitution did not grant Congress the power to establish a bank, the U.S. Supreme Court held that the federal government could establish a bank under the Necessary and Proper Clause of Article I. Justice Marshall, writing for the majority, stated that Article I is not dispositive of Congressional authority but provides a mechanism for the expansion of its authority. He stated that for Congress to seek an objective that is within its enumerated powers, it is natural for Congress to be able to interpret those powers as long as the interpretation is rationally related to the objective and not forbidden by the Constitution.

Chief Justice John Marshall of the McCulloch v. Maryland case

In *Gibbon v. Ogden* (1824), the U.S. Supreme Court held that Congress has the authority to regulate interstate commerce. Article I provides Congress with the power to regulate commerce with foreign nations and among the several states and Indian tribes. The purpose of the *Commerce Clause* was to curtail state-imposed discrimination on commerce that arose under the Articles of Confederation and remedy the absence of any federal commerce power under the Articles of Confederation. In *Gibbon*, Justice Marshall held that the power to regulate interstate commerce not only relates to economics but also expands to the regulation of interstate navigation, which impacts commerce.

The Commerce Clause is a key function of Congressional power. The Commerce Clause of the U.S. Constitution, as well as case law like *Gibbon v. Ogden,* have expanded the powers of the U.S. government over the powers of the state by directly regulating the distribution of commerce between the states, a power specifically enumerated in the U.S. Constitution. Also, the Commerce Clause has been used to limit state policies that discriminate against out-of-state motorists or establish monopolies. The Commerce Clause has also been used to enforce the protection of civil liberties and civil rights violations against protected classes of people.

In *Heart of Atlanta Motel, Inc. v. United States* (1964), the U.S. Supreme Court determined whether Congress may regulate the actions of private businesses that were in clear violation of the 1964 Civil Rights Act. The Heart of Atlanta Motel carried out racial discrimination policies despite the implementation of the 1964 Civil Rights Act which banned discrimination in places of public accommodation by refusing to rent rooms to African Americans. The motel filed suit against the United States on the grounds that Congress exceeded its regulatory authority to regulate interstate commerce. The U.S. Supreme Court held that the policies of the motel were in violation of the U.S. Constitution and infringed on interstate commerce through impeding the ability of African Americans to freely travel, pointing out that 75% of the motel's clients were from out-of-state and that the motel was in a strategic location for business.

Executive Branch

Article II of the U.S. Constitution established the executive branch of the United States government. The executive branch consists of the president and the vice president who hold office for a term of four years. The U.S. Constitution charges the executive with the duty to execute the laws passed by Congress, to enforce the laws, command the military as its Commander in Chief, make treaties (with the advice and consent of the Senate), appoint ambassadors, appoint executives to government agencies, appoint judges to federal benches, and advise Congress on the state of the union. In addition to these charges, the executive has the authority to propose legislation to Congress, the authority to call a special session of Congress, the authority to veto legislation passed by Congress, the authority to remove executive appointments, the authority over all foreign affairs, the authority to enter into treaties, the authority to enter into agreements with foreign governments, and the authority to deploy troops once Congress has declared war.

The president also has the power to enter into executive agreements without ratification by the legislature. These agreements are solely agreements between the president and another nation over issues of foreign policy, the president's power as Commander in Chief, or a prior act of Congress. These agreements are politically binding but not legally binding on the United States because the Senate does not ratify them. Under the *Case Act*, the president is required to notify Congress about the implementation of an executive agreement within 20 days of the execution of that agreement. The Article II powers are unique in that they fail to delineate the specifics of any power of the president. For example, the president is the Commander in Chief of the armed forces, but the U.S. Constitution fails to define his role or authority. It seems as though the powers of the president not enumerated within the U.S. Constitution are left to the interpretation of the courts.

Under Article II of the U.S. Constitution, the president must be a natural born citizen of the United States. The U.S. president must have attained the age of thirty-five years to be eligible for the Office and must have resided in the United States for the previous 14 years. The president may not be elected to office more than twice under the 22nd Amendment. Each term is four years. If the president is removed from office due to death, resignation or inability to discharge the duties and powers of the office, the office shall devolve to the vice president. Congress enacted the Presidential Succession Act, which says that if the vice president is unable to accept these duties, the office of the president will devolve to the Speaker of the House, the president *pro tempore* of the Senate and the Cabinet.

Under the elections clause of Article II of the U.S. Constitution, each state must appoint electors equal to the number of Senators and Representatives to which the state may be entitled in Congress. The number of electors is also based upon the population of the state. These electors shall meet in their respective states and vote by ballot for the president and the vice president. In the event of a tie, the House of Representatives will choose the president and vice president. The candidate with a majority of electoral votes is elected to office. This system is known as the *Electoral College*.

The U.S. Supreme Court limited the power of the president during the Korean Conflict in the case of *Youngstown v. Sawyer* (1952). The U.S. Supreme Court held that the president's issuance of an Executive order to seize and operate steel mills during a labor strike in the steel industry was unconstitutional. The Supreme Court held that the act of taking dominion over property is a legislative act granted solely to Congress.

In *United States v. Curtiss-Wright Export Corporation* (1936), the U.S. Supreme Court upheld the plenary authority of the executive branch over foreign relations. In this case, Curtiss-Wright was indicted for violating a federal embargo by sending arms to Bolivia. Curtiss-Wright argued in defense that the embargo was an unconstitutional delegation of legislative authority to the executive branch. The U.S. Supreme Court stated that while the Constitution does not explicitly say that all ability to conduct foreign policy is vested in the president, it is nonetheless given implicitly and by the fact that the executive, by its very nature, is empowered to conduct foreign affairs in a way that Congress cannot and should not.

In the case of *United States v. Belmont* (1937), the president of the United States agreed with the Soviet Union to confiscate Soviet corporations' wealth being held on U.S. soil. Belmont, who held funds on behalf of the former Soviet corporations, sued the United States to recover those funds. The U.S. Supreme Court determined that the president has the authority to enter into executive agreements with a foreign government without the advice and consent of the Senate. The U.S. Supreme Court further held that these executive agreements preempt state constitutions, laws and policies under the federal government's exclusive authority over foreign policy.

Judicial Branch

Article III of the U.S. Constitution establishes the judicial branch of the United States government. Article III established one court, the U.S Supreme Court, which holds original jurisdiction over the adjudication of cases involving ambassadors, public ministers, cases in which a state is a party to the lawsuit, controversies between a state and the United States government and cases between two states. The U.S. Constitution does not define the number of justices on the bench, as that is determined by statute, but it does state that the court should be presided over by one chief justice. The U.S. Supreme Court has appellate jurisdiction to review cases from the highest state courts and the federal appellate courts.

The U.S. Supreme Court is also charged with the duty to review the constitutionality of legislation and executive action by reviewing decisions of lower federal courts or a state's highest court. If the U.S. Supreme Court intends to review the decisions of a lower, it is deemed to have granted a writ of certiorari. *Certiorari* is granted if four of the nine justices determine that a case arising from a lower court satisfies case and controversy. In writing about the powers of the judiciary over the national government, Thomas Jefferson believed that strict construction was important for narrowly construing federal powers. Congress has plenary power to establish, terminate and delegate the duties of all other federal courts. State courts are autonomous from federal courts except that federal courts have the power to review a state court decision where the constitutionality of the state court decision is under review. *Marbury v. Madison* (1803) is a U.S. Supreme Court case famous because it defined the U.S. Supreme Court's power of judicial review over a decision of the legislative branch, a power not delineated in the U.S. Constitution.

Thomas Jefferson, U.S. president, and political theorist

Constitutional interpretation of statute, powers, and policies are concerned with the justification, standards and methods by which courts exercise judicial review. The problem of constitutional law is that it permits majorities to rule in wide areas of life because they are in the majority. The dilemma is that neither the majority nor the minority can be trusted to define the proper spheres of democratic authority and individual liberty. Over time it has been realized that balancing the wishes of the majority with the rights of the minority lies in the hands of the judiciary. One form of judicial review is known as *constitutional absolutism*. This mode of review rests on the premise that there is no necessary inconsistency between the practice of judicial review and the principles of democratic government because the American system is a constitutional system.

In *Fletcher v. Peck* (1810), the U.S. Supreme Court reviewed the constitutionality of a state statute. The state of Georgia enacted a law claiming possession of Native American lands and then selling the tracts of land to developing companies. Peck brought suit against Fletcher after a tract of land sold by Fletcher to Peck did not have a clear title when it was sold. The Georgia legislature repealed the law after Peck's purchase. The U.S. Supreme Court ruled that the repeal of that state law was an unconstitutional invalidation of a binding contract. The case is known both as the first instance in which the U.S. Supreme Court ruled on the constitutionality of a state statute and as a precursor to the contract clause that restricts states from invalidating or interfering with contracts.

Notes

Checks and Balances

The separation of powers doctrine establishes the needs and desires of the Federalists to establish a set of independent administrations. In *Federalist 51*, Madison makes the argument that in a constitutional system it is important to make each institution autonomous, that is, independent of one another. However, there must be a balance. Madison states that to avoid the tyranny of any one branch of the government it is essential that the other branches be diligent in assuring that they focus on the actions of the other two at all times.

Checks and balances is a system whereby each branch of a government regulates the actions of the others. It provides a system whereby each branch must cooperate in order to accomplish a task of great importance. For example, Article I of the U.S. Constitution states that Congress has the power to override a presidential veto power by a two-thirds majority vote in both houses of Congress. Article III provides that the President has the authority to veto legislation passed by both houses of Congress. The judicial branch has the power, although not enumerated in the Constitution, to review the laws passed by Congress. Other checks and balances in the system include, but are not limited to:

- Presidential treaty power requires the advice and consent of the Senate.

- Presidential appointment power requires the advice and consent of the Senate.

- Congress has the sole power to declare war and raise an army, while the president is the Commander in Chief.

- Congress has the power to investigate the actions of the executive branch of government.

- Congress has the power to delegate legislative powers to the executive agencies as long as Congress maintains oversight over those powers.

- The President has the power to nominate judicial appointees, while the Senate has the power to consider presidential judicial appointments.

- The House of Representatives has the power to impeach an executive or judicial officer; the Senate has the power to try and, if convicted, to remove that executive or judicial officer, with the Chief Justice of the U.S. Supreme Court presiding over the trial.

The U.S. Constitution does not specify the appellate jurisdiction of the judicial branch of government, that is, the judicial branch's power of judicial review. *Marbury v. Madison* (1803) is a U.S. Supreme Court case famous because it defined the U.S. Supreme Court's power of judicial review over a decision of the legislative branch. In *Marbury*, the U.S. Supreme Court held a congressional statute expanding the original jurisdiction of the U.S. Supreme Court and requiring that the U.S. Supreme Court issue a writ of mandamus to federal officers is unconstitutional. The Supreme Court stated that the court must ascertain and resolve a conflict between the two branches, as well as the meaning of any particular act proceeding from the legislative body.

Supreme Court building

In the U.S. Supreme Court case *Clinton v. City of New York* (1998), the Court held that the president's line-item veto was an unconstitutional grant of legislative power to the executive branch. Article II of the U.S. Constitution grants the president of the United States the power to advise Congress on the state of the union and recommend legislative measures to Congress. Article II also grants the president the power to veto bills passed by Congress as a part of the checks and balances power. In 1996, Congress passed the Line-Item Veto Act authorizing the president to veto portions of a fiscal bill, and the City of New York sought review. The Supreme Court held that the president of the United States is authorized to approve or reject bills, in whole, as a member of the executive branch, but the President is not authorized by the Constitution to enact, amend or repeal legislation, as that lies solely within the authority of the legislative branch.

In *INS v. Chadha* (1983), Jagdish Chadha, who was born in Kenya to Indian parents, was deemed by the United States, Kenya, and the United Kingdom to be a stateless person after Kenya was declared independent of the United Kingdom. Chadha sought suspension of his deportation proceedings due to hardship. The Attorney General granted his request. The U.S. House of Representatives, however, unilaterally overruled the Attorney's General's suspension of his deportation proceedings. The U.S. Supreme Court held that the House of Representatives could not enact a statute that permitted it to unilaterally overrule or veto the decision of the executive branch of government because it is inconsistent with the bicameral principle of government established by the U.S. Constitution. The U.S. Supreme Court stated that the bicameral system of government was established to hinder encroachment by the legislative branch of government.

Notes

Federalism

Federalism is a system of government whereby the national government works in conjunction with state and local governments to execute the powers of government for the welfare of the people. The idea of federalism was central to the creation of the U.S. Constitution and the American political system. Unlike unitary governments, federal governments are much more democratic and are much more effective in protecting the rights of its citizens. Under the confederal system of government, like the government under the Articles of Confederation, state governments hold greater power over the national government. This confederation of sovereign states believed that the states should be able to act independently of the national government.

Under federalism, some government powers are exclusive to the national government, some powers are exclusive to the state governments, and some powers are shared. The modern U.S. system of government is very much an amalgamation of the federal and confederal systems of government where the powers are often shared or at least intertwined. This concept is known as dual federalism. One such example of dual federalism is the role state government plays in the national electoral process and the design and amendment process of the U.S. Constitution. The power to operate courts of law, build roads, regulate traffic and collect taxes are powers shared by both the national and state governments.

Grants

State governments, through block or categorical grants from the federal government, have the sole authority to regulate and implement programs for the poor, programs to clean the environment, improve education and protect the disabled. A block grant is a grant of funds by the federal government given to state and local governments with only a general indication of how the money is to be spent by the state or local government. These grants are distributed in blocks to state and local governments and are generally supported by local governments due to their transferability.

Categorical grants are given to state government with a specific provision in mind. Medicaid, the Food Stamp Program and Head Start are examples of categorical grants given by the federal government. Many of these grants required that the states match the funds provided by the federal government. In the 1980s, President Ronald Reagan set forth a plan to move much of the spending power for these programs to the states by his Anti-Federalist stance. His approach was called the "New Federalism." While Reagan's program reduced federal subsidies to these programs, it did not eliminate federal funding of these programs. Some might construe Reagan's movement as devolution of federal power to shift the decision-making authority to the state and local level.

Mandates

The federal government also sets mandates on state governments. These mandates require that states comply with certain federal rules and guidelines by limiting certain activities. Often these limits on activities and mandates are tied to federal grants. Other rights apply to civil rights regulations or environmental protections. For example, the federal government may place restrictions on grants given to state and local governments where those governments fail to establish anti-discrimination protections, environmental protection or emissions regulations. Mandates include the Social Security Amendments, the Hazardous and Solid Waste Amendments, the Highway Safety Amendments, the Asbestos Emergency Response Act, the Drug-Free Workplace Acts, the Ocean Dumping Ban Act and the Clean Air Act Amendment.

Enumerated and Reserved Powers

Under the doctrine of enumerated powers, certain powers remain exclusive to the federal government. Under these powers, the federal government holds an operative power and responsibility over its citizens without regard to the particular state in which they reside. The national government holds the exclusive authority to print money, regulate interstate commerce, declare war and enter into international trade and foreign policy agreements. These specific powers are known as enumerated powers because they are specifically set forth in the U.S. Constitution. The federal government does not, however, have the power to grant titles of nobility, spend without passage and approval of an appropriations bill, impose export taxes or pass *ex-post facto* (i.e., retroactive) laws.

State governments have independent governing powers. Under their reserved powers, state governments have the exclusive power to issue licenses, the power over intrastate commerce as long as that commerce does not interfere with interstate commerce, the power to run local, state and federal elections and, per the Tenth Amendment, all other powers not specifically granted to the national government under the U.S. Constitution. Other reserved powers include the power to establish local governments and regulate trade within the state. States also have police power and the authority to legislate for the protection of the health, morals, safety, and welfare of the people. The state government has the responsibility of regulating social, moral and family policies. State governments do not have the authority to regulate or enter into treaties with foreign nations, declare war, print money, interfere with contracts, maintain a standing army and impose import or export duties.

The national government does have some authority over the state governments in the Federalist system. Under the Full Faith and Credit Clause of Article IV of the U.S. Constitution, states are obligated to accept the court judgments, laws, licenses, contracts and other civil acts that are granted in another state. States are prohibited from subdividing or combining without Congressional consent. States may not abridge the privileges and immunities of any state citizen by restricting their ability to obtain police protection, their ability to access state resources or their ability to access state courts. Conflicts between state law and a federal law are resolved in favor of the federal law.

As previously stated, certain laws defining federal versus state powers are enumerated by the specific language of the U.S. Constitution. Other laws defining these powers have been created by case law through the doctrine of judicial review. One of the consequences of federalism is that courts can enhance the powers of the federal government or diminish the powers of the federal government because the legislative boundaries on this issue are always evolving and the powers of the state and federal governments are always in conflict. Therefore, one will find that at one time the Supreme Court will favor states' rights over federal rights and at another time will favor federal rights over states' rights.

Many conflicts between state and federal government arise where there is a state law in conflict with federal law. Under the Supremacy Clause in Article VI of the U.S. Constitution, "this Constitution, and the laws of the United States which shall be made in pursuance thereof; and all treaties made, or which shall be made, under the authority of the United States, shall be the supreme law of the land; and the judges in every state shall be bound thereby."

In *Martin v. Hunter's Lessee* (1816), the U.S. Supreme Court held that its power of judicial review expanded its authority to review a decision from the highest court of a state where a federal law or the federal constitution conflicted. In this case, Denny Martin sought review of a Virginia law that permitted the confiscation of property owned by foreigners after the American Revolution. Martin argued that his property rights were protected by U.S. treaty, not subject to Virginia law. While the Virginia Supreme Court held that the U.S. Supreme Court lacked the authority to review a Virginia law, the U.S. Supreme Court held that it had appellate jurisdiction and therefore the right to overrule any state law that conflicted with a federal treaty.

In *McCulloch v. Maryland (*1819) the U.S. Supreme Court held that where there exists a conflict between federal law and state right or law, federal law shall prevail. In this case, James McCulloch of the First Bank of the United States sought review of a decision of the State of Maryland to levy taxes on the federal bank. Even though Article I of the U.S. Constitution did not grant Congress the power to establish a bank, the U.S. Supreme Court held that a state government could not tax a federal agency.

Gibbon v. Ogden (1824) is also known as a federalism case. The U.S. Supreme Court held that Congress has the authority to regulate interstate commerce by preempting state regulations on interstate travel. In this case, the State of New York, among others, had awarded exclusive licenses to navigate rivers in each state to specific steamboat lines. Article I provides Congress with the power to regulate commerce with foreign nations and among the several states and Indian tribes. The purpose of the Commerce Clause was to curtail state-imposed discrimination on commerce that arose under the Articles of Confederation and remedy the absence of any federal commerce power under the Articles of Confederation. In *Gibbon*, Justice Marshall held that the power to regulate interstate commerce not only holds in matters of economics but also expands to the regulation of interstate navigation which impacts commerce. The court determined that while states and the federal government have concurrent power over the navigation of its waters, federal licenses to navigate take precedent (i.e., judicial decision) over any similar licenses issued by the states.

In *U.S. v. Lopez* (1995), Alfonso Lopez sought review of a federal regulation declaring schools to be gun-free zones on the grounds that the act was an unconstitutional regulation of education, a regulation under the exclusive authority of the states. The federal government argued that the statute was enacted under Congress' power to regulate commerce because guns in an educational environment cause violence, raise insurance rates and relegate educational institutions to unsafe environments.

The U.S. Supreme Court held that while there are certain extensions to the commerce clause, the regulation of the carrying of handguns where there is no evidence that carrying them would affect the economy on a massive scale is an invalid extension of the commerce clause. The Supreme Court stated, Justice Rehnquist for the majority, that "to uphold the

Government's contentions here, we have to pile inference upon inference in a manner that would bid fair to convert congressional authority under the Commerce Clause to a general police power of the sort retained by the States."

In reviewing these cases, what are the advantages and disadvantages of a federalist system? Scholars have determined, as an advantage, that federalism mobilizes political activity among the people because it nationalizes political issues. However, the system confuses political issues for those uninformed about the functions and issues important to the government. A federalist system diminishes the power of special interest groups due to the size of the national government. Federalism also provides a system where policy ideas can be challenged on a smaller level before being implemented on a larger scale. The dual court system can be considered a disadvantage of federalism, because it confuses the populace about legal issues and laws, making it difficult for people to remain abreast of the laws.

Notes

Theories of a Democratic Government

The notion of democracy dates back to Ancient Greece. The term itself means the rule (*kratos* or *cratos*) of the populace (*demos*), thereby creating the Anglicized version, democracy. Plato believed that philosophers were the natural rulers of their time, rivals to the actual monarchs, and revolutionaries in the case of a regime where man cannot live free and happy. Although they were not necessarily proponents of a democratic government, these philosophers believed in the power of the people to rise against tyranny. Tyranny occurs when absolute power is placed in the hands of a unitary and corrupt leader.

Plato, philosopher of ancient Greece

Plato lived in a democratic regime where all males could directly participate in legislative action and had a voice in deciding important government positions. In that government, the legislature excluded women, children, slaves, and foreigners from making decisions in government. Plato thought that democracy was an unjust form of government replete with disorder and desire for excessive liberty and that the needs of the people could never be met in this form of government because the democratic government would focus on excess, not moderation.

Democracy is a form of government that places the ultimate political authority in the hands of the people as opposed to an individual authority. Democracy espouses the theory of popular sovereignty, a policy similar to the theories of Locke in which power to govern belongs to the people who are governed by consent. Direct democracy is derived from the philosophies of ancient Athens wherein the citizens debated and voted directly on all laws. Democracy is an effort to bring about a compromise between the power of majorities and the power of minorities.

In a *direct democracy*, citizens debate and vote directly on all of the laws of the community. The difficulty with direct democracy is that it requires a high level of participation and is based on a high degree of confidence in the citizens. Democracy often leads to majoritarianism, a system in which the government is ruled by solely by the decision of the majority. This rule by the majority at the behest of the others living in a democracy can lead to a system of governance known as the "tyranny of the majority," whereby a slim majority of the population can mandate the decisions of the government as a whole.

The members of the Constitutional Convention believed that a *representative democracy*, in which the people elect representatives to govern and make laws, is the most efficient form of government. The framers of the U.S. Constitution established a representative democracy out of fear that the majority would overly influence policy, to counter the influence of factions and to reinforce federalism. There are benefits and detriments to establishing a representative government.

Constitutional Convention of 1787

Representative democracy is a more efficient form of government because it allows people who are knowledgeable about the issues the opportunity to make the decision instead of relying on the decisions of uninformed individuals. Some of the pitfalls to a representative democracy are the inability of constituents to effectively control the actions of their representatives. Representative democracies increase the chances that elected officials will succumb to the influence of factions to the detriment of their constituents' interests. The oversight of representative democracy is performed by the people who hold the ultimate power to remove an elected official from office through the election process. There are two schools of thought on whether representative democracy is efficient.

The belief that representative democracy is not a democracy but a system in which an elite class, not a representative body, makes decisions of the nation is known as the *elite theory* of democracy. The belief is that large corporations, policymakers and financial foundations are in a position to exert significant power over the policy decisions of the government. What sets elites apart from the general populace are their resources, intelligence, skills and having a vested interest in government decisions. This type of governance is often classified as an oligarchy, where the government is controlled by a select few, or a plutocracy, where the government is controlled by those who have access to resources (such as those listed above) that are not within reach of the populace as a whole.

Pluralism, the second theory, is the belief that the members of a representative democracy base decisions on the will of a group to protect the interests of the individual. It is the belief that in a diverse society, too many interests exist to allow one cohesive group to decide the interests of the populace. Pluralism is based on a dialogue and a spirit of compromise necessarily entailing various concessions on the part of individuals or groups of individuals which are justified to maintain and promote the ideals and values of a democratic society. Theorists believe that autonomy only exists when the governing body is made up of members from disparate functional and cultural groups within society.

Notes

Chapter 2

Political Beliefs and Behaviors

Individual citizens hold a variety of beliefs about their government, its leaders and the U.S. political system in general. Taken together, these beliefs form the foundation of U.S. political culture. The formation, evolution and transmission processes of these beliefs are important. Equally important are the reasons why U.S. citizens hold certain beliefs about politics and how families, schools and the media act either to perpetuate or change these beliefs. Political culture affects and informs political participation on a profound level. For example, individuals often engage in multiple forms of political participation, including voting, protests and mass movements for a variety of reasons. This participation may affect the political system.

What leads citizens to differ from one another in their political beliefs, behaviors and their views about the political process, and the political consequences of these differences is the subject of constant analysis. Demographic features of the American population can inform understanding of these differences.

Notes

Beliefs That Citizens Hold About Their Government and Its Leaders

The United States is a large and diverse country where people hold a wide range of political views and beliefs about their government. The Bill of Rights guarantees freedom of conscience, which means that every American is free to hold whatever political beliefs they choose. The consequence is that there is no official belief system that people must hold. An American citizen cannot be jailed because of their political views. The fact that citizens are free to believe whatever they wish enables a wide range of views or "plurality." The political theorist Hannah Arendt argued that plurality is a part of the human condition, as each person born into the world is unique, meaning each person will have their own set of views and beliefs about the world.

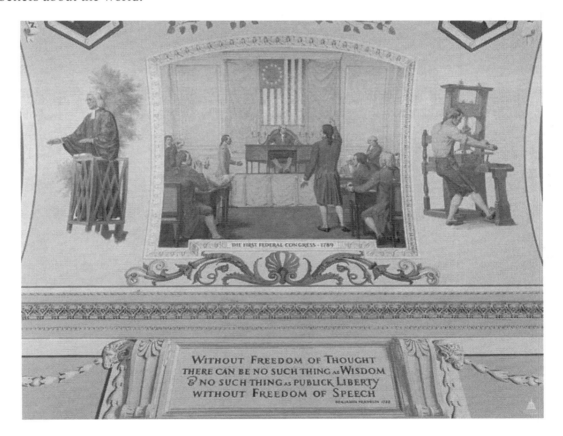

The First Federal Congress, 1789, where the Bill of Rights was created

While many factors can affect different people's beliefs about politics (which will be discussed further in this chapter), there are general groups of ideas people tend to associate with broadly. These general groupings are often called ideologies and include things such as liberalism, conservatism, socialism, and libertarianism. Someone who identifies as a libertarian, for example, may do so because they generally agree with the idea of less government involvement in the economy and one's social life, but one libertarian may have very different views from another libertarian about specific details. In many cases, someone identifying with a major ideology may do so because one agrees with one or two major aspects of the ideology while disagreeing with another major aspect. This means that even within ideologies, there is a plurality of views. Thus, viewing political beliefs solely in terms of ideologies can be complicated, as people rarely agree with every aspect, making lumping people together into groups problematic.

Due to the two-party system in the United States, there tends to be an oversimplification of the range of views people believe. In the mass media, it is presumed that one is either a liberal or a conservative, each corresponding with a political party. Due to human plurality, it can be difficult to lump people together into broad ideological groupings in general; to narrow those groupings into just two ideologies is a gross simplification. One may be a liberal on one issue but a conservative on another. At the same time, there are many more broad political ideologies besides liberalism and conservatism. While every person has a different set of opinions, studying broad ideologies is mainly important for their relation to what type of government a person would prefer.

Political theorists as far back as Aristotle in ancient Greece have sought to classify the different types of government to determine which type might be best. For Aristotle, there were only three types of government, and each could be either good or bad, making a total of six potential political structures. According to Aristotle, the government was either ruled by one person, a few people or many people. When one person ruled it, it was either a monarchy (if it was good), or a tyranny (if it was bad). When the government was comprised of a few people, it was either an aristocracy (if it was good), or an oligarchy (if it was bad). The government of the many was a polity (if it was good), and democracy (if it was bad). The reason Aristotle defined a pure democracy as bad is because he believed "rule of the people" meant that the poorer masses would have the use and the control of state resources, but the rich would need to be taxed heavily in order for the system to work; thus, the rich would be exploited by the poor. He found that a polity (or politeia), in which all citizens were bound by a governing constitution that served the interests of both the rich and poor, to be the most favorable. Except how "democracy" is defined in today's vernacular, these governmental classifications are still useful today, as they inform much of the discourse around positive and negative governance in the modern world.

Aristotle, ancient Greek philosopher

A monarchical system is a mode of governance where a monarch rules on behalf of his people, whereas a tyrannical mode of governance occurs when the "governance of one" turns into governance in the interests of only the monarch and his inner circle. An aristocratic mode of governance is one in which a select segment of society is chosen to govern the population as a whole. This group is assumed to be representative of the wisest members of the given polity. If this select group begins governing in its interests and explicitly against the interests of its constituency, the aristocratic form of governance has become an oligarchy.

The United States Senate was designed to represent the ideals of the aristocratic mode of governance. Since the few are the rich, accusing the government of being an oligarchy is generally meant today to say that the wealthy have too much influence. In terms of a "government of the many," Aristotle believed that democracy represented a bad form of governance because of its tendency towards the tyranny of the majority. Aristotle argued that having a mixed regime (polity), which combined a king, an aristocracy and a democracy was the best form of government due to the ability of each of the constituent parts to balance against the other two. This corresponds directly to the arrangement of the American political system, with a single president, a Senate theoretically composed of the wisest few and the House of Representatives as a democratic institution meant to be representative of the many. Aristotle would likely approve of the American system of government, although he did think that a monarchy is the best and, at the same time, the most dangerous form of government because it could easily turn into a tyranny, which he considered to be the worst form of government.

Generally, those who believe in a certain type of government also believe in a corresponding set of ideological beliefs. These beliefs, however, may not support their type of government. For example, a liberal might support monarchism, and one in favor of democracy might be a communist. Different ideologies can mix and correspond to different forms of government. Consequently, there are seemingly countless combinations of major ideologies and types of government. For the sake of brevity, the next section will deal with five major ideologies and the most common type of government that each ideology endorses. Again, it is important to remember that each person will have a different interpretation of the ideology, and thus even two people who claim to support the same ideology could have very different beliefs regarding details.

The Five Major Political Ideologies

Before looking into the major political ideologies, it is important to understand that all politics exist on a right-left spectrum. Right-wing policies tend to be more conservative, and left-wing policies tend to be more liberal. However, this spectrum should be seen as a circle where the further one goes on the spectrum of either side, the closer they get to authoritarianism. Therefore, though Fascism and Soviet Communism are extreme representations of the left and right on the political spectrum, they should be seen as "touching" due to their authoritarian nature. Most political ideologies are not as extreme as the above examples; however, it is always important to understand the characteristics of ideology and where it falls on a circular spectrum.

Further, it is important to realize that ideologies existing on the left-right spectrum may be better indicators than the common American descriptors of conservative-liberal. These interpretations are inherently subject to narrative and therefore are often not truly representative of the beliefs of an individual or party. For example, the Democratic Party is considered liberal in the modern American political lexicon; however, some of its policies may be slightly right of center on the political spectrum. Also, if one looks back to the presidency of the Republican Dwight Eisenhower, many of his policies were slightly to the left on the political spectrum. It is important to take the actual policies of politicians into consideration when thinking about their ideology.

U.S. President Dwight D. Eisenhower

The most basic type of government is a monarchy. Monarchists believe that one person should be in charge of all decisions and legislation. This was the predominant form of government during the Middle Ages; people believed that kings and queens had a divine right to rule. Divine right means that the monarch was believed to derive his or her authority directly from God, and thus the monarch would rule society subject to no outside control. It was then extrapolated that due to their divine mandate, questioning the monarch was not only an act against the government but against God himself. Since it was accepted that the monarch was essentially chosen to rule by God, monarchies tended to be hereditary, meaning that the son (or sometimes the daughter) of the monarch would take over after the current monarch died.

While very few Americans today would consider themselves monarchists, it is an important historical ideology in the development of American political society. The American Revolution was a categorical rejection of monarchism as an ideology. To posit the idea that society should be founded on a secular principle of government that is not grounded in the authority of God, but the authority derived from the consent of the governed is called republicanism. Republicanism, as an organizational principle for the government, is almost universally accepted in the United States. Due to the republican revolutions in the United States and France, which overthrew monarchies and led to the increase in secular ideas, absolutist monarchism as an ideology has largely died out, except for some notable exceptions in the Gulf States, Swaziland, Brunei, and the Vatican. The most prevalent form of monarchy that can be observed today is a constitutional monarchy. The most well-known constitutional monarchy is in the United Kingdom, where the role of the monarch has become largely ceremonial.

General Washington in the American Revolution

According to its supporters, the main advantage of monarchy is that it gives the king the ability to act quickly without having to jump through the hurdles of pluralistic modes of governance. Monarchists claim that this makes government more responsive to the people than a democracy with its slow procedures of legislation and debate. However, the absolute power of one person can be the worst aspect of the monarchy. If the king is unpopular and engages in destructive policies, there is no mechanism in place to stop him or her, and the monarch can quickly turn into a tyrant.

The principle of having a government ruled by one person or one grouping without any provision for the opposition is not exclusive to monarchism. Advocates of various forms of absolutism all agree that government should be decisively united. Absolutism can come in many forms, including dictatorship by one person or political parties, such as Adolf Hitler's Nazi Party in Germany in the 1930s and Joseph Stalin's Communist Party in Soviet Russia. Both parties were the only ideologies allowed in government, allowing them to rule without debate or opposition.

Absolutism can further be divided into authoritarianism and totalitarianism. Authoritarian governments are concerned primarily with making sure that everyone follows his or her rules at whatever cost. In contrast, a totalitarian government wants to control how people think, not just how they act. One can disagree with an authoritarian government and not be persecuted, so long as one does not act against the government. A totalitarian government insists citizens believe in it and agree with it. Both the Soviet Union in Russia and the Nazi Party of Germany were totalitarian, as they wanted to control people's beliefs. Examples of authoritarian governments that were overthrown more recently are the dictatorships in Tunisia and Egypt.

While very few people would openly identify their political views as totalitarian or even authoritarian because of their association with destructive regimes of the past, these are important ideologies in the context of American political culture. Many people continue to believe that government should rule unopposed or that holding certain political views should be outlawed. It is important to understand how authoritarian and totalitarian thinking may exist in American political culture even if people do not identify with these terms.

Presidential portrait of George W. Bush

For example, after the 9/11 terrorist attacks, President Bush declared that "you are either with us, or you're with the terrorists," implying (to some) that Americans had to agree with everything the president was doing unquestionably. Otherwise they were enemies of the American government. While this is not to say that President Bush transformed the country into a totalitarian mode of governance, he was implicitly referencing that only through adhering to a set of principles (that he defined) could one be considered an American.

Another example of such totalitarian rhetoric was that of Senator Joseph McCarthy in the 1940s and 1950s, who headed the House Un-American Activities Committee, which sought to target the thousands of "communists" living in the United States. Again, during the McCarthy era (1950-54), the United States was not governed on the principles of authoritarianism, but McCarthy's rhetoric was that of an authoritarian.

If absolutism is one extreme of government, the other extreme is anarchism. Anarchists believe that government is inherently oppressive, and people can only be free when there is a very limited form of government or no government at all. While on the surface this may sound ridiculous or simply unrealistic, anarchism tends to advocate self-government as opposed to the traditional government. Within the United States, there are two main branches of anarchism: one that endorses capitalist economics and one that endorses socialist economics. Anarchist capitalism usually referred to as libertarianism, is the more popular variant in the United States. Libertarians believe that the government is oppressive by nature and tend to advocate for a policing government reduced to the smallest size possible, for example, one which should only provide for the security of citizens from foreign or domestic threats.

Many libertarians call for what they term a "night watchmen state," meaning the government's role is only to intervene in cases of crime. Libertarians tend to support liberal social policies because of their distrust of government and are in favor of same-sex marriage, drug legalization, and are pro-choice on abortions. Libertarians see government regulation on these issues, as promoted by conservatives, as taking away free choice from individuals. On economic matters, libertarians tend to take a very pro-capitalist and right-wing point of view, believing that corporations should be free to do whatever they please. This means that on economic issues, libertarians tend to align with what Americans would call a conservative economic view, as they oppose environmental regulations, are against unions, oppose minimum wage and workplace safety laws, and generally do not believe the government should regulate the economy.

Anarchist socialists (sometimes called libertarian socialists) agree with libertarians on social issues but believe that corporations themselves are a form of oppressive government. Anarchist socialists believe that workplaces should be run through democratic committees and that the large-scale federal government should be replaced by small-scale democratic councils which form governments at the local level. Unlike Soviet communism, which was economically left-wing, but politically right-wing and totalitarian, socialist anarchists oppose government control of the economy while supporting socialist and sometimes communist principles of collective ownership. Libertarians such as Ron Paul have recently become more popular, while socialist anarchists like Emma Goldman were instrumental in their time in influencing American political culture. Their activities in the late 19th and early 20th centuries eventually led to the shortening of the standard workday from twelve to eight hours.

Liberalism is one of the main political ideologies in contemporary American political culture. However, as with conservatism, liberalism has evolved. Originally liberalism was a less extreme version of Libertarianism. Liberals generally believed that governments were a restriction on freedom, but a necessary one. Thus, liberalism originally meant limited government which was to be kept in check through the American system of checks and balances. In the light of President Franklin D. Roosevelt's New Deal, American liberalism shifted and came to regard the government as a source of progress whose job is to help people.

U.S. President Franklin Delano Roosevelt

Today, liberals generally want less government regulation on social issues such as drugs, marriage, and abortion, but want more government regulation of the economy. Liberals want the government to use its power to promote the social good, but in a way that still encourages and maximizes the space for capitalism. One of the main contrasts between liberalism and conservatism is that liberals tend to believe that change will result in progress, whereas conservatives are skeptical about change (especially that imposed by the federal government) and feel that traditions are generally superior.

The American version of liberalism tends to promote a progressive income tax system, welfare programs to help the poor, programs to help reduce unemployment, increased spending on education, equal opportunity programs to help minorities and immigrants, and a general expansion of civil rights. Liberalism differs from anarchism in that liberals believe the government can be a force for good and is not inherently oppressive. It also differs from socialism in that liberals support a capitalist organization of the economy; however, they believe that there should be checks on its ability to function without oversight and regulation from the government. It should be noted that this notion of liberalism only relates to the modern context of liberalism in American politics, as the term liberal has a different meaning in the sphere of economics (i.e., a theory that argues that economic decisions should be made by individuals, not by institutions).

Conservatism has also evolved and is more complex in the American context. The original conservatives in Europe were almost all exclusively monarchists, whose goal was conservation of the monarchy and against growth in Republicanism after the American and French Revolutions. After Napoleon's sweep across Europe, most absolutist monarchies had to give some power to legislatures due to the widespread demand for constitutional monarchies. Concomitant with this growth in the demand for constitutional monarchies, there was also a growth in industrialization and urbanization. Conservatives were deeply skeptical of this trend as the new industrialists were beginning to amass power outside of the traditional means of acquiring assets from family holdings. Therefore, though these conservatives often grew to support legislative checks on the monarchy, they were not willing to support all the changes that were occurring in this era.

In the United States, the meaning of conservatism was different and has evolved with time. Some of the first conservatives were those who wanted to conserve the institution of slavery in the South. These large landowners were the equivalent of European aristocrats and believed the radical change of ending slavery would disrupt the entire economic and social fabric of the American South. These were the first real conservatives in the proper sense in American history.

With the rise of the New Deal in the early 1930s, conservatism in the United States shifted in position, seeking to conserve the traditional conception of American liberalism (in an economic sense) which promoted limited government. Beginning in the Cold War and finally reaching full steam in the 1980s, American conservatism again remade itself into an ideology which promoted government regulation on social issues at the urging of conservative Christians and urged government deregulation of the economy as a means of conserving classical American liberalism. Today, the American version of conservatism tends to support increasing the influence of Christianity in government, traditional social and family structure, lower taxes, and a strong military.

Since the new millennium, there have been two main movements in American conservatism, the neo-conservatism of George Bush and the fundamentalist conservatism of the Tea Party. The former was centered on foreign policy and was largely accepted in the wake of the 9/11 attacks. The American people were looking for a response from the government; George Bush and his inner circle of advisors provided this through their interventionist foreign policy.

Traces of this legacy can even be seen in the foreign policy of Barack Obama, particularly at the behest of the former Secretary of State Hillary Clinton, who proposed intervention in many conflicts around the world, though President Obama did not always act on her recommendations. The latter movement is primarily domestic, taking many of its cues from nativist and libertarian ideologies.

U.S. Secretary of State Hillary Clinton

The modern Tea Party groups arose as a spontaneous movement in response to several government programs, including economic stimulus package of 2009, healthcare reform legislation, and government bailout of the banks in the wake of the 2007-2008 financial crisis.

One of the main quirks in the American interpretation of political ideology is the confusion between what the terms mean in an academic sense and what they mean in practice. In the academic world, the definition of liberalism is closer to that of non-interventionism in all spheres of life. According to this ideology, there should be a limited government that looks out for the general welfare of citizens; however, the people under the jurisdiction of a liberal government should generally be allowed to make their way, both personally and economically.

This confusion dates back to the New Deal era when a large portion of the socialist programs enacted by Franklin D. Roosevelt were not termed "socialist" to make a distinction between New Deal activism and the Soviet Union. Since this time, when the government has proposed socialist ideas, such as a mandatory minimum wage, taxation for the creation of the interstate system, Obamacare and any number of other projects, these programs have tended to be called "liberal" as opposed to "socialist." In the realm of conservatism, the American definition is closer to the academic definition, as conservatism is inherently harkening to return to a past era.

One example of a peculiar confusion between the liberal and conservative party ideologies (Democrats and Republicans) in the mainstream American political media is the issue of gun control. While most Americans know that conservatives tend to be more inclined to support the right to own a gun and liberals tend to be more inclined to want the government to regulate gun ownership, these positions are seemingly the opposite of what one would expect from these two ideologies.

Since liberals usually want less government control on non-economic issues and a general expansion of civil liberties, it would seem that liberals should be pro-gun-ownership. At the same time, since conservatives want the government to regulate social issues and argue that security and law and order should be more important than individual liberties, one would expect that conservatives would want to regulate guns in the name of security and public order.

While most of the political ideologies present in America are largely similar to those in the rest of the world, the one area where American political culture is truly unique is on the issue of gun ownership, in part because of the uniqueness of the Second Amendment.

The issue of gun ownership also demonstrates how ideologies are not consistent in their stances on political concepts such as the freedom of the individual in relation to public order and security.

The next main ideology is socialism. As previously mentioned, socialism has played an important role in American politics, though often under a different name. There are many different varieties of socialism, but the general idea is that the government should be used to counterbalance the harmful effects of capitalism. Socialist governments generally see their primary goal as promoting economic equality and fairness, which means trying to limit the power of corporations. Social democrats and democratic socialists promote programs such as universal healthcare which is meant to ensure that corporations cannot profit from human sickness and injury. They also promote strong legislation protecting workers, social welfare programs to help the poor and see their role as correcting the excesses of capitalism.

Socialism is different from communism in that socialists generally do not promote government ownership of the economy but believe the government should focus on promoting equality and helping the poor. Communism, on the other hand, involves the state assuming ownership of the entire economy and attempting to plan the economy rather than use markets. Furthermore, socialists recognize that there are "public goods" (e.g., transportation infrastructure, power provision infrastructure, etc.) and there is a need for the government to provide these goods and services which are often not profitable if one according to the strict logic of the market.

An example to illustrate this point would be on international treaties which give corporations the power to change government laws. The Trans-Pacific Partnership (TPP) and North American Free Trade Agreement have clauses which allow corporations to force member countries to change their laws if the corporation feels that the new law will harm their profits. Liberals (and conservatives) generally support these corporate rights treaties because they believe that capitalism is generally beneficial, even if it has a few bad side effects that the government needs to fix. Socialists believe that these sorts of treaties are anti-democratic and give too much power to corporations, and they oppose signing them. The recent TPP agreement was negotiated and supported by President Obama, while Senator Bernie Sanders strongly opposed it.

While communism has had very limited influence in American politics, Democratic Socialism and Social Democracy has played a role. Some Democratic Socialists, such as Vermont Senator Bernie Sanders, one of the first mainstream political candidates in

American history to openly tout his ideology as that of Socialism, argue that President Roosevelt's New Deal was an example of social democracy.

U.S. Senator of Vermont, Bernie Sanders

Sanders and other socialists see some of America's major social assistance programs that came out of the New Deal, such as social security and minimum wage laws, as proof of America's unacknowledged socialist tendencies. Socialists differ from liberals in that socialists generally see corporations and capitalism as problematic and needing to be heavily regulated and from which people need protection. Much of the socialist agenda is now practiced in the United States, though it usually exists under a more acceptable name.

Ideologies can have a tremendous amount of impact in determining people's political beliefs. Many people do not spend much time thinking about their political beliefs. This means that their beliefs on one issue may lead them to identify as part of a certain ideology, even if they have not thought about the other beliefs within that ideology. Individuals may defer to the overall ideology rather than thinking for themselves.

For example, if a person feels strongly that the government should not be involved in regulating social issues because this person believes that marijuana should be legal, they may come to identify as a libertarian. If this person has no clear beliefs about what they think about the economy, then he or she may defer to standard libertarian thinking when asked about economic questions. When such a situation occurs, it means that not only is ideology a general description of what people believe, but it is also something which can determine what people believe.

Many political theorists have sought to engage in a critique of ideology in general, as they see ideology as more like brainwashing than as a simple description of what people believe. These critics of ideology are not opposed to people having their own set of political beliefs, but their goal is to get people to arrive at these beliefs through thinking for themselves rather than simply buying into a system without questioning it. These critics often point out how easily the Nazi ideology swept across Germany, allowing Hitler to come to power with popular support, as an argument that not thinking for oneself and simply subscribing to a popular ideology can be extremely dangerous.

Portrait of Hitler at an SS meeting during the German occupation of WWII

To encourage independent thinkers, many political scientists argue that political beliefs should not be categorized by lumping people into the five major ideologies, but instead by examining the opinions of people on certain important aspects of politics. Ideology in this negative context is something that can make people believe in political causes that harm their self-interest.

Many political scientists seek to uncover how ideology causes people to vote for a political party that would seemingly harm them. For example, while the states in the South are on average much poorer than the others, they also tend to overwhelmingly support the Republicans whose economic policies tend to favor the rich. According to economic theory, people are supposed to act in a self-interested fashion, so the poorest states should have the least support for the Republicans, not the most. Political theorists know that ideology can play a role in shaping people's political actions in such a way as to make their choices seem strange. It is always best to be critical of everything that one hears about politics and try to form opinions based on one's thinking rather than relying on what others say.

Political Beliefs and Concepts

Since no two people will have the same political views, even if they both identify as part of the same broad ideological grouping, it can be more informative to analyze how people feel about concepts of politics and government. For example, we can learn more about the average American by asking what they think should be the role of the government should be in regulating the economy, regulating social issues and taking in immigrants, than we can by simply asking if they are a liberal or a conservative.

While a person may identify as part of one ideology their actual beliefs may orient them to something completely different. Instead of asking if someone is a conservative, we can instead ask what they believe the role of the government should be in maintaining law and order, what they think the place of religion should be in society and government, and how much they value freedom relative to equality. By asking more specific questions, political scientists are better able to find out what people believe rather than asking them to answer in terms of liberal or conservative, which can often result in misleading answers.

In American political culture, certain positions on major issues have changed with time and have either become dominant or divisive. Concepts such as freedom, equality, and democracy are often taken for granted as the pillars of American political culture, in that everyone believes in these three concepts. If someone is asked what he or she think freedom is, and he or she talk about the right to own guns, while another person answers that freedom means voting and participating in government, it is easier to deduce a lot more than by simply relying on ideological labels. This is the inherent problem with the transient terms listed above: they fit into a category of their support being "trivially true."

This means that the real knowledge of the individual's political beliefs stem from asking them what this concept means to them. Freedom can have many interpretations; the gun owner may say that they are free because the government cannot take away their guns, while at the same time believe that governments should take away the freedom for people to marry whom they choose or to have abortions. Freedom can also mean the ability to participate in government, to criticize authority and to hold any political opinion, all of which are unconnected to whether guns, abortions or gay marriage are legal. Another person may interpret freedom in economic terms, like the ability to start one's own business or to quit a job when one chooses, which can happen regardless of whether there is much social or political freedom.

Similarly, equality can have multiple aspects. The term "equality" also shares the position of being "trivially true." This is a term which has been popular since the onset of American democracy. At one stage, equality among the states meant that in determining proportional representation, one slave was counted as 3/5 of a person. Equality is transient just as freedom is, and to understand one's position relative to this concept; it is similarly important to ask base-level questions to ascertain what one believes.

Most Americans believe in political equality, in that every person should have one vote, but economic equality is more controversial. Many people do not believe that the government should engage in welfare programs to help the poor, believing instead that everyone must compete in the market. Someone making this claim is probably a conservative, while a socialist would complain that the government spends too much money helping corporations and ignoring the poor, thus unfairly increasing inequality.

Economic inequality has skyrocketed since the mid-1980s and is increasingly becoming an issue thanks to protest movements, such as "Occupy Wall Street." Currently, according to some studies, the top 0.1% of people in the United States control as much wealth as the bottom 90% (though many economists disagree with this number). From 1929 to 1980, Americans progressively became more equal in wealth. Issues of social equality are also very controversial, especially concerning race. African Americans are disproportionately incarcerated, unemployed and not able to afford a home. While these issues are strongly linked to economic inequality, many people argue that discrimination remains a real problem at a structural level. By asking people about their opinions on concepts of equality or freedom in relation to political, social and economic issues, a much better picture of their opinions can emerge.

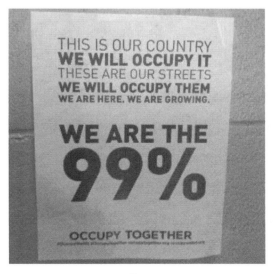

Occupy Wall Street poster

The same is true for democracy, which in itself is a very vague term and has many possible implementations. Two people may both claim to be strong believers in democracy, but one might see voting in elections every couple of years as democracy, while another might see that as hardly democratic at all and argue that real democracy means that people must be more involved in government through direct participation.

Someone else may argue that democracy is a great ideal that should be applied to the economy as well, as socialist anarchists argue that workplaces should be democratic and that the workers should elect the bosses, rather than appointed by the owners. Again, political beliefs are complex, and various ideologies and political concepts can be mixed in a plurality of ways. Thus, any sort of talk about universal political values that define America is inherently misleading, because what defines America is a plurality of different opinions guaranteed by the 1st Amendment.

Democracy is the final "trivially true" terms. The vast majority of Americans believe in democracy; however, many people do not understand what this entails. Some express a minimalist view, where simple ability to participate in free and fair elections is enough to declare the polity a democracy. While others are maximalists, who believe that democratic principles should be expanded to include all aspects of political participation, with far more regular inherent mechanisms for the public to voice their opinion.

Processes by Which Citizens Learn About Politics

The first exposure to political beliefs and viewpoints usually comes through one's family. From a young age, children will hear their parents talking about politics, and this is often the start of a child's political education. Some parents may seek to teach their children about politics and the political system actively, and some may try to ensure that their children have the same political views that they do. For the most part, family political identification is a very strong factor in forming someone's political beliefs. If one's parents are both liberals and strongly support the Democrats, chances are their child will be a liberal and support the Democrats as well.

Even though children and teenagers cannot vote, political scientists are often very interested in studying the political opinions of these groups, as it can help them understand the political socialization process and measure how much of a role family plays in shaping one's political views. In a major study conducted in 2005, researchers found that 71% of Americans aged 13-17 said they held the same political views as their parents. 7% said they were more right-wing, and 21% said they were more left-wing. It is often popularly assumed that young people would be more liberal than their parents, but in general, teenagers have the same views as their parents, which indicates that for young citizens, the family is the predominant means of political socialization.

This continuation of the political views and alliances of parents and children is also seen in politicians. The Kennedy family, for instance, were all liberal Democrats through multiple generations. George H.W. Bush and George W. Bush were both conservative Republicans, and Bill and Hillary Clinton share similar political views.

Young voters, broadly classified as those twenty-four years of age and younger, tend to be much less attached to a single political party than older voters. This is partly because young citizens are still figuring out what their political views are and are thus less inclined to choose one party. While family conditioning can play in a role in leading a young voter to identify with one party rather than the other, young voters are much more likely to switch parties than older voters.

As young people leave high school and go to college or move into the workforce, they usually move out of their parents' home, diminishing the influence of their parents' political views. Also, young people find themselves in a new social situation which leads to a variety of new influences which can affect their political beliefs. For older citizens, especially once they retire, there is a tendency toward partisan stabilization. This means that once a voter retires, they tend to vote for the same party without regard for the specific circumstances of the election.

Education is an extremely important aspect of the political process for new citizens. Thomas Jefferson is famous for stating that an educated citizenry was a requirement for America to survive as a free democracy. Through the education system, young citizens come to learn about the workings of the government and their role in the political process. For most Americans, this education comes in high school, so many people may forget these lessons later in life. Often young people fresh out of a high school politics course are some of the most knowledgeable citizens on the technicalities of government. However, if these young citizens do not continue to engage with the political process and continue learning about the function of government, they become gradually less informed.

Students who go onto college also tend to absorb more information about the function of government, even if political science is not their primary field of study. Citizens with higher levels of education are less inclined to be swayed by emotional pitches from politicians, such as fear-based politics, and more likely to analyze the statements of politicians critically. As Thomas Jefferson pointed out, educated citizens are essential to a well-functioning democracy because they use their vote to make an informed choice on the future direction of the country. Those with less education are more likely to vote irresponsibly by being swayed by attack ads, voting for a party without considering the campaign issues or simply voting for superficial reasons such as which politician they would most like to have over for dinner. Jefferson feared that if the population were politically uneducated, the government could become tyrannical and take advantage of the population instead of governing for the benefit of the population.

Once a citizen is out of school, their primary means of learning about politics comes through the news media. Citizens who pay attention to the news tend to be better informed than those who do not. Reading the news in a newspaper or online or watching it on TV is critical to ensuring that citizens stay informed. This means that the media has an extremely large responsibility to educate the public about political issues in a sensible manner. While the news cannot be objective because the truth is always filtered through the bias of individual people, it can strive to present multiple sides to an issue and ensure balanced news coverage.

Those who own the media can use their control of news to shape what citizens know and think. Media can shape what people know about politics by neglecting to report certain stories altogether or by presenting commentators and opinion from only one side of an issue. While the media rarely lies outright, as this would cause the public to lose all trust, they do engage in subtle manipulations.

However, with the rise of the Internet and an individual's ability to select which news media one consumes, there has been a shift in the direction of individuals seeking out media sources which support the views an individual already holds. This is often called confirmation bias, in which an individual seeks out facts which support their previously held conception of a particular issue or set of issues.

One example of confirmation bias comes from a study conducted in 2005 comparing the beliefs of people regarding whether or not the U.S. had found weapons of mass destruction in Iraq after the 2003 invasion. In reality, the U.S. did not find weapons of mass destruction (WMD), so researchers analyzed the percentage of people who falsely believed WMDs were found. The study found that people who got their news from certain sources were much more likely to believe that WMD were found than others. 33% of people who got their news from Fox News believed incorrectly that WMD were found, while 11% of people who got their news from PBS and NPR had this incorrect belief. This study demonstrates that the news can play a critical role in informing Americans about what is happening politically or play a critical role in misinforming Americans. As in all aspects of politics, people need to be aware of the biases inherent in the news media and critically think about what is presented.

With the emergence of the 24-hour cable TV news networks, such as CNN, Fox News, and MSNBC, some political scientists have argued that these news networks can lead to people becoming less informed due to how one-sided they have all become. In many ways, these news outlets are more like ideological apparatuses meant to convince viewers of their point of view rather than to inform viewers of what is happening and provide commentary from multiple angles and multiple opinions. It can be very important to analyze the bias of a news source to determine the validity of its reporting and the opinions it is presenting.

For example, it is widely recognized that Fox News has a conservative bias and MSNBC has a liberal bias, thus Fox News commentary that defends a conservative politician and MSNBC commentary that defends a liberal politician should be taken with a grain of salt; it is presumed that each of these networks will simply defend its side. Alternatively, if Fox News is criticizing a conservative or MSNBC is criticizing a liberal, then there ought to be more attention given to that commentary because the networks are not simply following their standard partisan lines.

Thus, it is important always to understand the bias of news sources, especially since most news networks are not forthcoming about their bias. Politics can never be neutral, so any claims of a media source to be neutral or objective must always be met with skepticism, as humans who write or report the news are almost always biased. By acknowledging the bias, one can determine if the commentary is simply an expression of that bias or is contributing something unique and interesting.

Recently, studies have shown that younger Americans are learning about political issues from social media and comedy programs, such as The Daily Show and The Colbert Report. Through social media, friends can help others learn about political issues by sharing links to news stories and articles. Given how much people now use sites like Facebook and Twitter, the reach of these stories on social media has become extremely large. With overall trust declining in the American news media, the popularity of comedy programs which make fun of the news has increased. Although these shows are not news in the proper sense, they can educate citizens about important political issues. For example, comedian Stephen Colbert won a Peabody Award in 2012 for making Americans aware of the issues surrounding the Supreme Court's *Citizens United* ruling and the establishment of Super PACs which allowed unlimited, anonymous spending during an election campaign.

Stephen Colbert at the 71st Peabody Awards

Taken together, the many ways in which Americans learn about the political system is called "political socialization." This process is most intense when citizens are younger and learn about politics for the first time but is a continual process which occurs throughout life. Especially when experiencing a major change, such as moving to a new city, changing jobs or finding a new circle of friends, a person can be introduced to a new set of political beliefs previously unconsidered.

The process of adapting to new beliefs of acquaintances can be positive or negative but is still an example of political socialization. The more people have the opportunity to encounter different and new viewpoints, the more likely they are to be open to changing their opinions. Those who do not encounter contrasting views tend to keep the same opinions they have always had. Sometimes people actively seek out new means of political socialization because they are interested in challenging their own opinions and seeing what other people think. All too often, however, people actively avoid hearing opinions they may disagree with because they do not want to have to think about and reconsider their political views.

Notes

Nature, Sources, and Consequences of Public Opinion

Public opinion is complex and continually evolving. The first question to consider is whether or not public opinion exists. While it is quite obvious that individuals have opinions, it is more contentious to consider whether or not a group of people can have a collective opinion. An opinion is formed through the processes outlined in the previous section, namely through education, consuming the news media in any of its various guises and by discussing politics with other people. An individual can easily do this, but it makes less sense to think of a group forming an opinion unless every single member of that group is the same. Some political scientists prefer to talk about public moods or public interests because they see opinions as reserved for the individual.

Further issues of trying to measure public opinion or the public mood relate to issues regarding knowledge and change. A complex political issue that requires a lot of thought and study may be outside of the realm of public knowledge. If the public is asked their opinion on something about which they know nothing, the answers they will give are not an expression of public opinion but of public ignorance. If "public opinion" is reframed as "the public mood," it can be useful in gauging the general attitudes of the public.

Take the example of the Electoral College and its procedures of electing the president. If one tried to determine the public's opinion on the Electoral College was, we would likely get unreliable answers since most people do not know how it works or what its purpose is. If instead one considered the public's mood toward the Electoral College, one might be able to discern whether or not there was a general desire to change the way the Electoral College works or keep it the same. The latter does not require one to have an informed opinion, but only a vague sense that either something is broken with the Electoral College or that it works well.

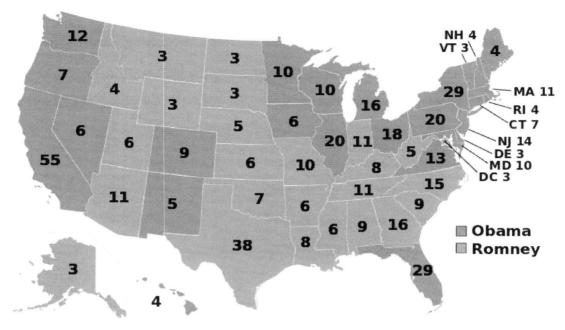

Electoral College map of the 2012 United States presidential election

The concept of public opinion is also problematic because as an aggregation of many individual opinions, it is constantly in flux. Even on matters as simple as whether or not same-sex marriage should be legal, public opinion has continued to change. A politician ten years ago who said that public opinion was on his or her side in opposing same-sex marriage might be just as correct as a politician today who said that public opinion was on their side in supporting same-sex marriage. Politicians on different sides of an issue who appeal to public opinion can often both claim to have the public on their side, which often has no basis in fact. However, due to the prevalence of confirmation bias, there is a likelihood that the base to which this individual is appealing will have their view(s) reinforced with such statements.

Public opinion and public mood are also difficult to measure. The usual method is through opinion polling. A certain number of people are called, usually at least 1,000, and asked their opinion. If the sample of people called is representative of the wider public, the principles of statistics dictate that the answers given by those called in the sample will reflect the answers of the wider public. People often criticize polling by saying that they were not asked for their opinion. Therefore the poll is not accurate. This is not an accurate statement as not every person needs to be asked to get a reasonably accurate picture of the wider views of the population. That being said, there are issues regarding how public opinion is measured through polling.

The wording of questions in a poll can have a dramatic effect on the results. If the questions are worded in a way that is biased towards one response over another, responses may not truly reflect what the person being polled believes. For example, a poll with the aim to discover public opinion on the issue of whether or not to accept refugees from a war-torn country needs to frame questions in a very neutral way to get an accurate result. If the question is biased, then it can change the results. If the question was framed in such a way as to imply the refugees were violent or possible terrorists, then this will lead people to oppose accepting refugees. If the question is worded to emphasize the suffering of the refugees, it will influence people to give answers that are more inclined to support allowing refugees into the country. Thus, when one sees an opinion poll being cited, it is a good idea to look at what questions were asked to make sure the questions were not biased toward one response over another.

Another issue with measuring public opinion through polling relates to creating a representative sample. Those who are contacted must be representative of the entire American public. If they are not, then the poll will not tell us anything about the views of the wider public. The most famous example of a political poll using an unrepresentative sample was the poll conducted by the magazine Literary Digest for the 1936 presidential election. The poll sampled 2.4 million people, which is a massive sample which should have given extremely accurate results. The poll predicted that Republican candidate Alfred Landon would win the election easily with 50% of the vote and win 32 of 48 states in the Electoral College.

In the actual election, Democratic candidate Franklin Roosevelt won a landslide victory with over 60% of the popular vote, winning all but two states in the Electoral College. This poll got the results spectacularly wrong because the sample was not representative of the wider American public. The poll only asked subscribers of the *Literary Digest* magazine whom they planned to vote for. The problem was that *Literary Digest* subscribers were overwhelmingly wealthier than the average American, especially during this period in the Great Depression, causing the opinion poll to overwhelmingly favor the Republicans when in reality Americans overwhelmingly favored the Democrats that year.

A second problem related to representative sampling relates to the issue of evolving technology. Traditionally, polls have been conducted by randomly selecting numbers from the phone book. By using random selection, the problems of the *Literary Digest* poll would be avoided. Today, however, fewer people have landlines as more people shift to cellular phones. While many polling firms are beginning to adapt by calling cell phones and using online questionnaires, some polling firms still use the random phone book method. Since people with landline telephones tend to be disproportionately older, their polling sample is not representative as it is made up of people mostly over the age of fifty.

There are also considerations of how random these polling samples are. While they may be able to contact people at random, many people will refuse to answer the questions. This means that polls are already biased toward the type of people who want to give their opinion on political matters, which are usually those individuals who have already formed strong opinions. This means that those who do not feel strongly about political issues are often not properly represented in polling.

There are multiple consequences of public opinion and the public mood. Public opinion is most notable during elections where pollsters closely monitor public opinion to try to predict who will win an election. Politicians running for office often campaign on issues which they think the public supports, and thus public opinion can shape the election platform of parties and candidates. Once in office, public opinion is often polled on specific issues to inform politicians.

While politicians do not always do what public opinion suggests, they do closely monitor it at all times. If a politician is going against public opinion, he or she may try to keep this policy out of the media and make it less visible. If a politician believes he or she has public opinion on his or her side, then the politician will often make an effort to try to talk to the media as much as possible to ensure the public has a favorable opinion of them. Public opinion is also important for the general attitude of what people think about the president and Congress. This is called "approval rating," and if it drops too low, then the president will take measures—perhaps even reverse course—to appeal to the public to win reelection or leave a positive legacy.

In addition to simply using polling to figure out what percentage of the population is for or against a certain action on a certain issue, there are also other characteristics that can be measured. Saliency measures how important an issue is and is often measured in relation to targeted groups. For example, if the president is trying to win votes from young people, his or her team may conduct saliency polling to try to figure out what issues are most important to young people. If the polling finds that young people care most about education and do not care at all about social security, then the campaign can focus its material aimed at young voters on education issues.

Intensity polling is like saliency but measures how strongly people feel about an issue rather than how important they feel it is. Again, this is usually conducted on targeted groups.

An intensity poll about gun ownership might reveal that NRA members feel strongly about this issue, while the rest of the population might feel it is an important issue but not have strong opinions on it.

Friends of NRA logo

Finally, stability polling measures how susceptible a group is to change its opinions. Stability polling is especially important for political parties, as they want to identify districts held by the opposition in which the electorate might change their minds and vote for another party. If a stability poll finds that the majority of voters in a district have already made up their minds and are not open to changing their vote, then political parties will generally dedicate less time to campaign in that district. They know that places, where opinion is less stable, provide better opportunities to convince people to change their minds.

Notes

How Citizens Vote and Otherwise Participate in Political Life

There are many ways to participate in politics, and voting is the most common way to participate in the official process of government. While the federal government has jurisdiction over federal elections, individual registration laws vary by state. The Constitution has three major amendments dealing with voting rights upon which states cannot infringe. The 15th Amendment guarantees citizens the right to vote regardless of their "race, color, or previous condition of servitude." This amendment was passed in the wake of the Civil War and was meant to prevent voter registration discrimination against former slaves. The 19th Amendment, passed in 1920, eliminated sex as a basis of discrimination in voting and allowed women to vote for the first time in federal elections. The 26th Amendment, passed in 1971, eliminated age as the basis of discrimination and lowered the minimum voting age from 21 to 18.

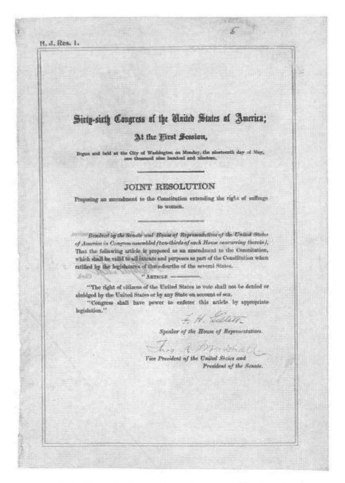

Nineteenth Amendment, passed in 1920

To vote, citizens must first register (except in North Dakota where registration is not required). Unlike much of the rest of the world, people of voting age are not automatically registered, and thus registration is an extra step in voting in the United States. Until the National Voter Registration Act of 1993, citizens had to go to a government office to register. After this act, citizens in most states could register to vote when they renewed their driver's license or interacted with certain other government services.

In 2015, Oregon became the first state to make voter registration automatic upon receiving or renewing a driver's license. Registration laws vary between states, and six states even allow citizens to register to vote on Election Day, while some other states only have a limited window during the campaign when one can register. To make voter registration more convenient, seventeen states now allow users to register through the internet. The extra step of registering to vote is a significant factor in why voter turnout tends to be lower in the United States as compared to other similar countries. Approximately 25% of the voting age population of the United States are not registered to vote.

In some states, those convicted of a felony are not allowed to vote for the rest of their lives, while in other states they can vote once they are no longer on parole. In some states, one can choose to declare a party affiliation when voting which allows one to vote in the primary for that party. Thus, if one registers as a Democrat, one can vote in the primary elections that decide which Democrat will be the candidate to run for president. In other states, anyone can vote in primaries, and in others, those who register as independents can vote in either primary, but those who register with a party cannot vote in the other party's primaries. The rules are different in each state, and thus voters must be aware of how their state operates to ascertain their eligibility.

In addition to voting in municipal elections, state elections and national elections for president and members of the Senate and the House of Representatives, citizens can vote in primary elections. Primaries are the means by which voters choose who will represent a given political party in the general election, where they will be pitted against rivals from other parties. In states that are solidly in support of one particular party, the primaries are often the main path to general election victory, as support for the other party is below the level needed to win. Given that the United States has a two-party system, voting in primaries is often just as important as voting in the national elections because it is an opportunity to choose who the candidate for each party will be.

Primaries run on a state-by-state basis and are staggered so that not all states vote at once. Each state is assigned a certain number of delegates who are pledged to support whomever their state voted for. There are also superdelegates who are unpledged, meaning they can vote for whichever candidate they want, regardless of whom people voted for in the primaries. After all the primaries have been conducted, the pledged delegates and superdelegates get together and vote to determine their party's presidential candidate.

The existence of the superdelegates is controversial because they tend to be party insiders and establishment figures who can sway the result against the wishes of the primary voters. The further problem is that the number of superdelegates can vary from election to election, meaning the party can essentially stack the deck in favor of a certain candidate, even if voters in the primary would prefer another candidate. For this reason, many political scientists have criticized the system of superdelegates as undemocratic.

Once the primaries are decided, and national elections are held, citizens can vote for whom they want to be president, who their local representative in the House of Representatives will be and, in rotating years, who their U.S. Senators will be. The presidential election is by far the most visible, as it is national, and the president holds a great deal of authority. For this reason, the voter turnout in the presidential election is much higher than voter turnout in Congressional elections, even when they are held on the same day. Many people feel that the president has the real power, so it does not matter whom they elect to Congress.

The assumption that the president has the most political power is erroneous; Congress is responsible for legislation and thus has a great deal of power in both passing laws and limiting the authority of the president. Also, one's representative in the House is a local person whose job is to respond directly to those in his or her district (however, this is often more of a theory than practical reality). The president cannot respond to every complaint or suggestion an American sends him or her, but the local representative's job is to do precisely this.

Voter turnout is an important aspect of an election. Political scientists measure voter turnout as a way of determining how legitimate a government is. If many people vote, then it is assumed that the government is legitimate in that it represents the people well. If very few people vote, then the government has legitimacy problems, as it was only selected by very few people. A major trend in both the United States and in mature democracies around the world is a significant decrease in voter turnout levels from what they were in the 1960s. In the 1960s, American presidential election turnout averaged in the 60-70% range; today it has fallen to the 50-60% range with just 49% turnout in the 1996 election.

U.S. voting booths

The determining factors that lead individuals to participate or refrain from participating in the democratic process is a major branch of political science. Demographics provide some clues, as wealthier Americans are more likely to vote than poorer Americans, and older Americans are much more likely to vote than younger Americans. Whites are more likely to vote than blacks and Hispanics, though this difference disappears when you factor out wealth. People who are more educated are more likely to vote, but again, more education corresponds to more wealth, again making economic differences the primary demographic factor in voting patterns.

Beyond demographics, there are many reasons why people choose to refrain from exercising their right to vote. In the popular media, people who do not vote are often portrayed as apathetic, meaning they are too lazy to vote on Election Day. Studies have found little evidence to support this claim, and in reality, many people who do not vote are simply uninterested in politics and feel that they are not informed enough to use their vote to make a responsible choice.

Another major factor in not voting is that many people feel that neither of the two parties can represent their views, and thus they choose not to vote rather than voting for someone with whom they disagree. In some cases, voting or not voting becomes a habit, and people who have always voted continue to vote, while those who have never voted continue not to vote. When voting is a habit, elections are simply a thing in which one either participates without thought or does not participate without thought.

Many political scientists, however, return to the issue of legitimacy when looking at voter turnout. Rather than trying to figure out why people are voting less often and blaming this problem on individuals, they argue that governments, in general, have become less responsive to the public and overall less democratically legitimate. These scholars argue that if the government did a better job of engaging the American public and delivering on its promises, then Americans would trust the system more and thus be more inclined to vote. This position is supported by polling on the question of how much Americans feel they can trust the government to do the right thing. Until the mid-1970s, Americans overwhelmingly believed that they could trust the government to look out for the general well-being of the people, regardless of which party was in power. In the 1980s, opinion shifted, and the majority answered that they did not trust the government to act in the best interest of the people, regardless of which party was in power.

This lack of trust is especially prevalent concerning Congress. Public trust in Congress has been in steady decline since 2000, and in 2014 reached an all-time low, with only 14% of Americans feeling that Congress was doing a good job. This shift, which perhaps explains a decline in voter turnout, can be traced to some causes. The Watergate scandal, which led to President Nixon's resignation as a result of the cover-up of his agents spying on opponents and breaking into Democratic headquarters to steal information, shook the public's faith in the government in general. If the president could not be trusted to obey laws, the whole political system falls into disrepute.

At the same time, the Vietnam War led to massive public protests, and at Kent State University in 1970, the Ohio National Guard opened fire on a crowd of unarmed student protesters, killing four of them. This incident contributed to Americans viewing the government with distrust. A further shift came in the 1980s as President Reagan reoriented economic policy toward deregulation and budget cutbacks. Whereas the government had previously been seen as an entity which built or enabled things, it now became an entity that tore things down, leading to a shift in perspective and distrust. All of these factors, which decreased people's trust in government, can help explain why voter turnout has plummeted.

Watergate Complex

In addition to general concerns about the legitimacy of the system as measured by voter participation rates, the voter turnout rate is increasingly becoming a factor which may decide elections. Given that a significant number of Americans do not currently participate in the electoral process, tapping into these groups who do not vote can often lead to electoral success. Rather than simply trying to get people to switch parties, which can be difficult, candidates increasingly realize that if they can inspire people who are disillusioned with the political system to vote for them, they can win.

The best example of this was the 2008 Presidential Election won by Barack Obama. Obama campaigned on an inspirational message that focused on targeting people who normally did not vote at all. Voter turnout in that election increased by nine million votes, and Obama beat McCain by just over nine million votes in the popular vote total. By convincing those who normally did not vote to show up and vote for Obama, the Democrats were able to win the presidential election. Rallying non-voters to vote is quickly emerging as an important campaign strategy in an era when significant numbers of people do not vote. Canadian Prime Minister Justin Trudeau accomplished a similar task in 2015, as he increased his party's vote by six million and voter turnout increased by six million, allowing him to win the election.

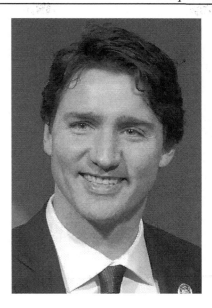

Canadian Prime Minister Justin Trudeau

There have been many proposals meant to increase voter turnout, which differ depending on what a group or person believes explains the cause of low voter turnout. Groups like FairVote blame the electoral system for low turnout, arguing that the winner-take-all system in Congressional elections is biased against third parties and that the Electoral College distorts the actual will of the people in the presidential vote. FairVote argues that the president should be elected directly by the people in a popular vote and that Congress should use proportional representation to decide who gets a seat. Proportional representation is the electoral system used in most other countries, and it means that if 30% of Americans vote for Party A, then Party A will get 30% of the seats in the Senate or House of Representatives. In the current system, Party A could get no seats with 30%, or it could get 45% of the seats. FairVote argues that because the electoral system distorts how the people voted, people become disillusioned and decide not to vote. They also point to studies which show that countries using proportional representation have a significantly higher voter turnout compared to countries that do not.

In 2015, the Brookings Institute published a book outlining a plan to increase voter turnout by focusing on the current generation of youth and getting them involved. They suggest that political parties need to take the first step by recruiting younger candidates. The minimum age to run for the House of Representatives is 25, and the Senate is 30, yet the average age is 57 in the House and 62 in the Senate. By recruiting younger people to run for office, Brookings argues that government will represent Americans better. Young people will be more likely to vote when they do not think of the government as being run almost exclusively by older people. They also recommend making political awareness a factor in college admissions and developing more mobile phone technologies to make political participation easier.

Another popular proposal is to develop a system to allow people to vote online. While many Americans are worried that this could lead to corruption or security problems, making people able to vote online would significantly enhance access to voting and in all likelihood increase voter turnout. While people often claim that online voting could be "hacked," the entire infrastructure of the banking and financial system is online and is not easily "hacked."

Getting elected as a politician is the most direct way to participate in government. However, there are many financial barriers to even being considered a viable candidate. While democracy is premised on the idea of equality of opportunity in that anyone can run for office and win if he or she can convince the public of their views, many political scientists have criticized the fact that running for office has become extremely expensive as replacing democracy with a plutocratic oligarchy.

A plutocratic oligarchy is a system whereby access to the necessary capital to convince others of their viability as a candidate is a necessary condition to run for most offices. Since the 2000 Presidential Election, candidates from the two major parties have needed to raise one billion dollars to remain viable. Before 1971, there were no regulations of any sort on campaign finance, but in 1971 Congress passed the Federal Election Campaign Act to try to regulate spending and make campaign donations more transparent. This act required candidates to disclose who donated to their campaigns and how much they donated. The act was amended in 1974 to create the Federal Elections Commission which established limits on how much a candidate could donate to their campaign, put limits on how much Political Action Committees (PACs) could donate, placed donation limits on individuals and set in place overall spending limits.

In 1976, the Supreme Court struck down parts of this act; campaign spending limits were ruled unconstitutional and also removed limits on how much a candidate could donate to their campaign. In the 1990s, the issue of "soft money" became a problem. While donors were limited in how much they could give to a political party as part of an election campaign, they could give unlimited amounts of "soft money," which were donations to a party meant to fund its operations that were not related to election campaigns. Even though this soft money was not supposed to be used for campaigning, parties used it indirectly to help candidates win elections by running general ads or spending it on registering potential voters. By 2002, the two main parties had raised and spent over $400 million of soft money.

In response, Congress passed the Bipartisan Campaign Reform Act of 2002 which more expressly outlawed the use of soft money for political campaigns. The act also opened up the ability to use what are called "527 organizations," which are not directly part of a political party but can spend unlimited money running ads to promote their cause during an election. As a result, much of the soft money that was now outlawed was channeled into these organizations, who spent it indirectly campaigning for their preferred candidates.

Election finance laws became even more controversial with the Supreme Court's *Citizens United* ruling, which allowed the formation of Super PACs. These PACs allowed unlimited, virtually anonymous contributions by anyone, including corporations, which could be spent during a campaign in any way, so long as they did not directly coordinate with a political party. In reality, the same people who ran the campaigns of the political parties served as chairs of Super PACs, and thus Super PACs are seen by many as fundamentally undermining previous restrictions on campaign finance. For all of these reasons, it can be difficult for anyone who is not wealthy and connected to run for office.

Since donating money is another way of participating in an election, campaign finance and spending is an important issue. If ordinary people pitching in with a few small donations end up not mattering because a Super PAC can spend unlimited corporate money, then the democratic intent of elections is undermined. As of 2016 federal election, corporate donations directly to parties are banned but instead, are funneled through Super PACs. Individuals may donate $2,700 per year per candidate. An individual may donate an additional $5,000 to a PAC, a total of $10,000 to a local or state political party, and $100,200 per year to a national political party. These numbers reflect the maximums as of 2016 and are periodically adjusted.

Also, there is no longer a limit on the total amount of donations one can make to candidates. If someone had enough money, he or she could donate in one year $2,700 to every candidate in each of the 435 districts that make up the House of Representatives and an additional $2,700 to every candidate in each of the 100 Senatorial candidates. Previously there were limits on the total aggregate amount of money one person could spend, but these limits were struck down in 2014 by the Supreme Court ruling in *McCutcheon v. FEC*.

Seal of the Supreme Court of the United States

Other Forms of Political Participation

While voting is the only official means of participating in government, there are plenty of other ways to participate in politics in a non-official capacity. Beginning with the aspects which take the least amount of effort and involve a minimum amount of participation, citizens can participate politically by sending letters or emails to their local representative. While a representative may not read every letter he or she receives, someone on their staff will. This person will then provide summaries to the representative to give him/her an idea of what issues their constituents are concerned about. Thus, by writing letters and sending emails, one can push one's representative to consider a certain issue. If an email or letter is particularly persuasive, it may be passed on to the representative who will read it and write a reply. Similarly, one can sign petitions which can be sent to politicians to demonstrate that the public cares about an issue enough to sign their name to it.

If one has more time and feels very strongly about an issue to the point that writing a letter does not seem to be enough, one can join an interest group and attempt to lobby the government. Many interest groups which defend the public interest rely on volunteers and run periodical lobbying campaigns. These groups are always looking for supporters to help with their activities. Another way to participate politically is to talk about political issues with people. Since some people may be off-put about controversial political topics, a good place to find an in-depth discussion on political issues is often on the Internet, where debaters can remain anonymously. There are many websites where people can find vigorous discussions of political issues among people who want to talk about politics. Participating in these discussions can help one to develop more informed opinions, and it also gives one the opportunity to try to convince others of one's political opinions. Democracy in its purest sense involves discussing and debating politics with other people.

During an election campaign, the best way to participate in politics is to work on the campaign team of the candidate one supports. Candidates rely on a support team for various roles. They always need people to call potential supporters and ask for donations, to drive people to the polling station on election day, to go door to door with the candidate, to hand out flyers and campaign material and to convince other people to support the candidate. Candidates also often need scrutineers to go to a polling station and make sure the voting happens without any problems. Both parties will send a scrutineer to make sure that the election workers are not doing anything which may lead to support for one party over the other.

The most involved someone can be in politics is by becoming an activist and joining a group dedicated to a cause. Activist groups often engage in a diversity of tactics to promote their cause, including writing material to convince others to support their cause, holding information sessions, organizing people to support their cause and participating in protests and demonstrations. A protest is often the most democratic form of participation as it opens politics up to everyone, allowing anyone to participate.

Protest movements have been significant in leading to major advances in American history, from winning the eight-hour workday, to allowing women to vote, through to the civil rights movement. When the government refuses to act, political participation through protest can be one of the most effective means of participating directly in political change. Recently, protests such as Occupy Wall Street have made the issue of economic inequality part of the national conversation. Increasingly, these sorts of protest movements are being organized online, making them easy to find and join.

Civil Rights movement protest

There are some reasons why activists hold a public protest. The first is to make an issue visible to the wider public. When thousands of people show up to protest and cause a disruption, the media shows up and covers the event. This means the cause of the protest will be discussed and the public can learn about issues to which they may not have otherwise been exposed to. Before the major protests in Seattle in 1999, almost no one had heard of the World Trade Organization. After the protests became national news for weeks, anyone who watched the news knew about the treaty and how it was problematic for workers' rights and the environment.

Seattle Ministerial Conference in 1999

The second reason to protest is to demonstrate and create power. When the government sees thousands and thousands of people marching in the street, all united for a cause, it demonstrates that people are serious about an issue and that the government must do something about it. In 2006, when the House of Representatives passed a bill that called for the deportation of undocumented migrant workers, massive protests were organized by pro-immigrant and Hispanic groups and their allies. Half a million people marched in Los Angeles, and 300,000 people marched in Chicago. The House of Representatives took notice of these demonstrations and realized that if they went forward with this bill, they would be in much trouble with voters. As a result of the protests, the deportation bill was thrown out in the committee phase of the legislative process.

The third reason for protests is to demonstrate solidarity. Sometimes something happens which is perceived as an injustice, and people want to show that they care and support the victims of injustice. In 2014, solidarity-based protests occurred in Ferguson, Missouri, as people took to the streets to show their support for a young man who was shot and killed by police under suspicious circumstances. One can also join a protest on a specific issue out of solidarity. When gay and lesbian groups organized protests against bans on same-sex marriage, many people who were not gay joined the protests in a show of solidarity because they believed everyone should be treated equally under the law.

Related to solidarity is the fact that joining a protest can form political networks which can lead to other forms of action. Politics is an inherently collective activity; one cannot simply engage in politics alone, it must always be done with and against others. Protests can help people establish the connections for future forms of non-protest related activity. For example, after the WTO protests in Seattle, many people got connected, leading to the establishment of environmental lobbying groups and even an online news website geared towards political activists. Those non-protest political activities would not have happened if political networks were not established by individuals joining up with each other at a protest.

Finally, protests are exciting and energizing. Marching in the street and joining up with thousands of people is exhilarating. The feeling of actually participating directly in political action is something that can inspire people to go on to do other political activities later in life. Many of the activists who marched with Dr. Martin Luther King Jr. during the time of the civil rights movement went on to become prominent politicians and community leaders. Many people who are part of major protest movements report that being involved in those protests changed their lives and made them better people.

Civil Rights leader Martin Luther King Jr.

Even if a large protest does not achieve its immediate goals, the inspiration that many individuals take from becoming politically engaged in such a direct way ends up having lasting effects. While the current media discourse tends to portray mass protests as ineffective, this view ignores the above factors and tends to see protests as only about marching around holding signs. Protests can take various forms, including direct action and civil disobedience. General strikes were once the primary form of protest, in which everyone would not show up for work for a day, thus shutting down the whole economy. Considering that mass public protests in Egypt and Tunisia in 2014 were able to overthrow dictatorships, it seems pretty clear that protests of every sort remain an effective tool of democratic participation.

Factors That Influence Citizens to Differ From One Another in Terms of Political Beliefs and Behaviors

Given that there are a variety of ways to participate in government and an almost inexhaustible range of opinions people can have on any political topic, what are some of the factors that lead people to hold one set of opinions over another? As noted earlier, the family often plays a large role, as children tend to adopt political views similar to those of their parents. The strong influence of the family demonstrates how people tend to absorb the views of those around them. When political scientists study these environmental factors, which influence what people believe, it is called demographics.

Many demographic divisions are important factors explaining differences in political views. While demographic factors tend to do a poor job of explaining participation, they can provide information on what groups of people are more likely to believe. When political scientists analyze demographics, they do not view these relationships as causal, but as correlational. For example, if it was found that black people are more liberal than white people, political scientists do not assume that one's skin color is what determines one's political views, but instead, view this as a correlation, not a causation.

One of the major demographic factors which can lead to differences in belief is religion. Sometimes the actual content of one's religious beliefs can form a causal relation with one's political views, but often the connection between religion and political views is merely correlational and is explained better by other factors. Over the years, political scientists studying the correlation between religion and political views have found some general correlational trends.

They have found that Roman Catholics tend to tilt to the left on economic issues while Protestants tend to tilt to the right on economic issues, with both groups being correlated to right-wing social views. They have also found that Jews tend to lean more to the left on both social and economic issues than either Catholics or Protestants. Again, it should be emphasized these are general trends, which means not every single member of these religions hold the same political beliefs, only that it has been observed that more than half of these groups tend to gravitate toward similar beliefs on these issues.

Many studies of opinion polling on social and economic issues have identified a strong connection between one's political views and the intensity of religious beliefs. These studies argue that the main factor of this connection is not which religion one belongs to, but how intensely one believes in it. Greater intensity of belief has been consistently linked to more right-wing views, and less intensity of belief is strongly linked to more left-wing views.

There are also noticeable differences in the voting patterns between the sexes. Since the 1960s, women have increasingly moved to support the Democrats, while men's voting patterns have stayed the same. As a result, today women disproportionately vote for the Democrats as compared to men. Studies have also shown statistically significant differences on key social issues between men and women. Women are more likely to favor some gun control regulations and less military spending, and they tend to support legislation against workplace harassment. Interestingly, many other issues which would seem to be more important to women, such as abortion, show no statistically significant difference in opinion between men and women in most studies.

Another major source of demographic differences relates to skin color. On issues related to affirmative action and bias treatment by police, racial differences can be significant in what political views people have. On other issues though, such as the length of prison sentences and whether one would vote for a black president, there were no significant differences in opinion. Age is another significant demographic factor, as young people and older people tend to diverge on many issues. Part of this is explained by the fact that younger and older people have different concerns, but much of it relates to the fact that older people became politically socialized in an earlier era with different political values, which makes their views seem more conservative by comparison.

In addition to analyzing the traits of groups of people, the second major aspect of demographics is the study of where people live. There is an extremely strong correlation between being more right-wing and living in a rural area, whereas living in a very large city is correlated with being more on the left of the political spectrum. The region in which one lives is also a significant demographic factor for predicting what the majority of people might believe. The South tends to be more conservative, whereas the west coast tends to be more liberal.

Regional factors can change over time as well. At the turn of the 19th century, rural areas were much more likely to support left-wing economic causes, as rural farmers formed the base of support for the Progressive Party and William Jennings Bryant. With time this has changed, and today farmers tend to be more conservative. The same is true for what parts of the country tend to believe; while today the American South is staunchly conservative and overwhelmingly Republican, it used to be the main base of support for the Democrats.

Therefore, although factors like where someone lives can be strong indicators of their political views, their beliefs, and allegiance to political parties may shift over time.

Campaign poster for William J. Bryan, American politician

One of the reasons why a similar group will shift from one belief to another over time is related to demographic changes. If the demographic makeup of who lives in a region changes, then quite clearly the dominant beliefs in that region will change. At the same time, if someone is a member of a certain demographic group that tends to believe in a certain set of political values, those values may differ from the values of the region in which they live. For example, if one lives in Texas, there is a significant chance they will support the Republicans. If someone is black or Hispanic, he or she are probably more likely to support the Democrats. However, a black or Hispanic person who lives in Texas is less likely to support the Democrats than a black or Hispanic person in California.

After personal traits and geography, the other major demographic factor is wealth. How wealthy someone is, usually measured by their tax bracket or the socioeconomic class of their profession, tends to be one of the strongest indicators of political views. Very wealthy Americans tend to be more conservative while working-class Americans tend to be more left-wing on economic issues. Wealth and class tend to be more causal factors in political beliefs, as, the Republicans tend to favor tax cuts and programs that benefit the wealthy, thus leading wealthy and upper-class people to support the Republicans. Working class people are more likely to support redistributive progressive tax policies and programs which help people down on their luck.

One major exception includes people who strongly identify as "very religious." Even if they are relatively poor, the religion factor tends to be more important in pushing their beliefs. Thus, people who identify as "very religious" but are also working class tend to be much more conservative than those who are working class, but only mildly religious or not religious at all.

All these factors play a role in influencing each other, and to a person's political socialization and ideological views. While many of these factors can combine, and one might be tempted to guess what a group's or an individual's views might be, everyone is different and can have unpredictable views. When political scientists – and often political parties looking for areas they can target to win votes – look at a district, they use all these demographic factors to predict what people are likely to believe and thus how they are likely to vote. A dense urban district on the west coast with more women than men and with a majority of African Americans will likely vote for the Democrats, as it contains all the factors which are indicators of being more on the left side of the political spectrum.

Political parties use these demographic guesses to build their campaign strategy, and policymakers use demographic information to target certain government programs in certain areas. Thus, even though demographic data cannot predict exactly what everyone might think, it can give political parties and policymakers an idea of where certain programs and campaigns are more likely to be successful. Political scientists are generally interested in trying to find correlations between political views and demographics to determine how possible future changes in population may affect the political climate.

Please, leave your Customer Review on Amazon

Chapter 3

Political Parties, Interest Groups and Mass Media

Political parties, elections, political action committees (PACs), interest groups and mass media are mechanisms that allow citizens to organize and communicate their interests and concerns. Historical evolutions of the U.S. party system, the functions, and structures of political parties and the effects they have on the political process can and have been significant. Party reforms and campaign strategies and financing in the electronic age provide important perspectives. Elections, election laws and the election systems on the national and state levels provide a framework for understanding the nature of both party and individual voting behavior. The development and role of PACs in elections and the ideological and demographic differences between both major parties, as well as third parties, are critical factors.

Political roles played by varieties of the lobby and interest groups, as well as what they do, how they do it and how this affects both the political process and public policy, can be critical to understanding the state of modern U.S. politics.

Equally important are the major influences the media has in influencing public opinion, voter perceptions, campaign strategies, electoral outcomes, agenda development and the public images and stances officials and candidates. The relationship between candidates, elected officials, and the media is often symbiotic and frequently conflicting. The goals and incentives of the media industry can influence the nature of news coverage itself. The increasing consolidation of major media outlets into fewer hands and the growing role of the Internet both carry consequences.

Notes

Political Parties and Elections

The role of political parties is not mentioned in the Constitution; they are a result of the natural evolution of the American political system. In a representative democracy, political parties were thought of as something of a necessary evil. The framers of the Constitution, especially the authors of *The Federalist Papers*, were extremely skeptical of political parties because they believed that partisan attachment to a party would cause unhealthy strife and division. While the current climate of extreme partisan division certainly demonstrates that the founders were correct, what they did not realize was that representative democracy could not function without parties.

Functions

The largest question, in a modern context, is not whether or not there should be political parties, but how many there should be. Like all other nations, America has a multi-party system with many registered parties that run candidates. However, America is unique in the continuing dominance of two specific parties over a long period. In other countries, there are more (sometimes many more) than just two major parties. In Canada and the United Kingdom, there are at least three major parties, as well as several secondary parties that have seats in the legislatures. In Brazil, there are often more than seven major parties elected.

In the American system, it is extremely hard for a third party to win elections because of numerous laws, control of public opinion by the schools and news media and how entrenched the two-party system is in the present governmental framework. Having only two parties implies that there are only two different sets of political beliefs, with voters having to choose one or the other. In reality, there are hundreds of different political views and ideologies, and having more parties would allow more choice for voters and therefore better representation. Approximately one-third of U.S. voters identify as Independent, meaning they feel no strong connection to either of the two main parties. These Independent voters are highly sought after during election campaigns in the hope they may be convinced to vote for one party or the other.

Regardless of one's opinion on political parties in general, they perform many necessary functions within the congressional and presidential branches of the political system. One of their primary functions is recruiting candidates to run for office. Because parties always want to win, they put much effort into recruiting "distinguished," high-profile people, which usually helps ensure that qualified candidates get elected.

Parties also play an important role during elections in both convincing citizens whom they should vote for, and rallying supporters to vote. When parties provide resources to help ensure their supporters go to the polling booth on Election Day, this is called "getting out the vote." Voter turnouts in the United States are relatively low compared to most other developed, democratic nations. The ability of parties to mobilize their volunteers to ensure that their supporters do vote for them is extremely important—it can be enough to decide an election.

Organization

The United States uses a system called "single-member plurality." Any candidate may run for a House or Senate seat, and the winner is simply the one who scores the largest share of the votes, even if it is less than 50% (in those elections where there are more than two candidates). Each district is decided independently. Canada and Britain are the only other countries to use this system. The rest of the free world uses some form of proportional representation, a system in which the number of candidates elected by each party is matched to the actual total level of support for the party. Ballot access laws affect when a party can field candidates. They differ from state to state, but they all originate with designations in federal law.

Political parties are categorized into three types: "major," "minor" and "new." New parties are those who are fielding candidates in an election for the first time or which have already run candidates in elections but have not obtained more than 5% of the vote. Campaign law mandates that media corporations give a minimum amount of free advertising time to political parties and provides funding subsidies for presidential campaigns, which are both greater for the major parties than for minor or new parties. Since the elected members of Congress passed this law, it was voted into law only by members of the two major parties, which it disproportionately advantages.

Logo of the Republican Party of the United States of America.
Abbreviation GOP stands for "Grand Old Party"

The official logo of the United States Democratic Party

The Green Party and the Libertarian Party are examples of parties which are still considered new and therefore eligible for significantly less free media time and federal funding allowances for their presidential campaigns than the two major parties even though they have each fielded numerous candidates for president, Congress, and other offices in many elections. Minor parties are defined as those that have obtained more than 5% in a previous election. Major parties are those who obtained over 15% of the vote in the previous election; in other words, only the Democratic and Republican Parties currently qualify as major parties and are eligible for the benefits which major parties receive under this self-serving law.

The official logos of the Libertarian party of the United States (left), and the Green Party of the
United States (right)

American political campaigns depend heavily on funding, media exposure (including advertising and debates) and mobilization of people and resources. The former two are strongly regulated by law. The process by which candidates are elected is a complicated system which is detailed very precisely in the Constitution but which, in practice, has led to many moral dilemmas. Americans have been very resistant to modifying the system which was outlined in the American Constitution and to supporting new parties, even though America had a long period of new parties in earlier years and even though all other nations routinely allow newly formed parties to win seats in their legislatures.

Development

When a group of people comes together to discuss political issues, sides will naturally form over issues, leading to alliances. This is how the party system evolved in the United States. Parties are also necessary for voters to express a choice in the direction they want the country to be governed, as opposed to merely voting for the person who is to represent them. By having political parties which set forth different visions for how the country should be governed, called a platform, voters can choose which vision they like better and thus actually have a say in how the country is governed. Without political parties, elections would be mere popularity contests, and voters would not be able to express an overall choice in the direction of the country.

Although the Democratic and Republican Parties now seem so entrenched to the point where seemingly no new party could ever achieve significant gains, the American party system has evolved. Parties first arose over the issue of federalism, or how powerful the central government should be as compared to state governments. Eventually, the split on this issue led to Federalist and anti-Federalist factions which evolved into loose alliances seen as precursors to political parties. Thomas Jefferson named his anti-Federalist party the Democratic-Republicans.

Thomas Jefferson, founder of the Democratic-Republicans

While this name may seem strange in today's political climate, the names of today's modern parties are not descriptive of their beliefs. Today's Democrats believe in republicanism; they wish to retain the existing system based on popular authority and do not wish to create a monarchy.

Meanwhile, today's Republican Party believes in democracy; they do not wish to replace elections with dictatorship. So, Jefferson's Democratic-Republican Party was a fitting description of his party's ideology and not a contradiction as it might seem. Jefferson's party eventually won wide support; until 1824, all presidents identified with the Democratic-Republicans, and there was no real opposition party.

The first real political party, in the modern sense, arose in the wake of Andrew Jackson's loss of the 1824 presidential election to John Quincy Adams. Jackson, who won the popular vote for president but lost the election in the Electoral College, created the Democratic Party to oppose the government of John Quincy Adams. After Jackson won the subsequent election, those opposed to his presidency rallied together to form an opposition party called the Whig Party.

When slavery became a major issue in 1850, both the Democratic and Whig parties split apart into pro-slavery and anti-slavery factions. Around the same time, the Republican Party coalesced from a combination of the anti-slavery wing of the Democrats in the South and the northern anti-slavery Whig faction. The Democratic Party that was left consisted mainly of pro-slavery Southerners and settlers of the western frontier. The few remaining Northern Democrats then formed their party, but this system was thoroughly disrupted with the outbreak of the Civil War.

Andrew Jackson, presidential candidate of 1824

After the Civil War, the current two-party system emerged, with the Republicans garnering support from the North and blacks in the South, while the white South supported the Democrats. Even after the abolition of slavery, the parties were still largely defined by whether they had supported or opposed slavery before the Civil War.

In the late 1800s, a new party emerged, called the People's Party, also known as the Populists. This party was supported by poor cotton farmers in the South and wheat farmers suffering from drought in the West and advocated replacing the gold standard with silver. The party was critical of the urban banking system and sought sweeping agricultural reform and a better life for farmers. In 1892, the People's Party won 8.5% of the popular vote and won five states in the Electoral College in addition to electing some members of Congress. In 1896, the prominent party member William Jennings Bryan won the Democratic nomination for president, essentially merging the Democrats and the People's Party into one party.

In the early 1900s, a new faction emerged, called the Progressives. This faction sought to regulate industrialists and bring more power to the average American. Members of both of the parties expressed support for Progressivism. In 1912, the Progressives officially became a political party after a split in the Republican Party between William Taft and Theodore Roosevelt. Roosevelt led the Progressive Party (popularly called the Bull Moose Party at the time) to a strong showing in the 1912 election but split the Republican vote in half, which allowed the Democrats to win the presidency.

Theodore Roosevelt (left) and William Howard Taft (right),26ᵗʰ and 27ᵗʰ Presidents of the United States, respectively

Progressives contested the 1914 legislative elections and won five seats. Significantly, the party ran some women candidates in this election. By 1918, however, the party had faded away as a result of a lack of electoral success. Most of those who had originally split from the Republican Party did not rejoin it after the deterioration of the Progressive Party; as a result, the remaining Republicans became much more conservative.

With the stock market crash of 1929 and the onset of the Great Depression, the Democrats shifted their political orientation with the New Deal to become more liberal. Based on the popularity of the New Deal, the Democrats of this era were able to combine their newfound support from the northern working class with their traditional support in the South. The New Deal-era Democrats also appealed to African Americans, marking the initial shift of black voters away from the Republican Party. When the New Deal Democrats under Lyndon Johnson began supporting the civil rights movement in the 1960s, white southerners switched from their traditional allegiance to the Democratic Party to support the Republicans. This party system largely remains intact today, but by looking at the history, it is clear that changes and shifts in party ideology are possible.

Since the 1960s, there have been some significant challenges by third-party candidates. In 1992, billionaire Ross Perot ran a significant presidential campaign as an Independent. He received a huge 18.9% of the popular vote, making it the most significant challenge to the two-party system since Roosevelt's Progressives. Perot did not win any states in the Electoral College, and after unsuccessfully trying to create a new party called the Reform Party, he faded from view. In 2000, Ralph Nader ran a significant third-party presidential campaign as leader of the Green Party. He won 2.7% of the vote in an election that ended as a virtual tie between the Democrats and Republicans, leading many Democrats to blame support for Nader as costing them the election. The Green Party eventually faded from prominence as well.

Ross Perot, American businessman

Effects on the Political Process

It is at the level of policy formation where political parties are the most influential. After an issue has been raised as needing action, which course of action to take can be greatly influenced by the ideology of the party in power. If unemployment becomes an issue, a pro-labor party will seek solutions that might vastly differ from a pro-big business party. While both may agree the issue demands attention, the political party's ideology will drive which sorts of policy solutions get enacted. Parties also have congressional Whips whose job is to make sure individual representatives follow the party line on an issue coming up for a vote. This makes going against one's party difficult, even if this would mean truly representing one's constituents.

When political parties bog down the policy formation and decision process, an issue becomes highly visible in the media. One party may oppose the other party's solution to appear oppositional, even if they essentially agree in principle. Small differences in procedures and implementations can get blown up into a big deal, undermining the broad agreement on the big issue. This is called *partisanship* and is often criticized as creating undue obstacles by promoting arguing over minor details.

Critics of partisanship maintain that these arguments over small details obscure the fact that Congress is not properly considering big-picture alternatives. For example, during the occupation of Iraq, partisan arguments focused on minor details like the types of equipment supplied to the military, rather than questioning big issues of strategy and whether the occupation was working. By engaging in big arguments over small details, political parties generate the perception of significant differences in their ideologies, making voters believe they have an important choice to make.

Electoral Laws and Systems

The Federal Election Commission is the official body that writes and publishes rules on the conduct and rights of parties and candidates in all elections in the United States. Its publication, *Federal Election Campaign Laws*, contains the complete list of electoral and campaign funding laws and is available on their website. Campaign funding comes in many forms and is heavily regulated by law. Direct contributions to the campaigns of individual candidates are allowed from individuals, corporations and unions, and even foreign contributors, but are held to specific limits. For example, an individual can legally donate up to $5,000 to any single campaign. However, there are ways in which these laws can be circumvented.

Presidential elections

Before discussing the processes by which one comes to be nominated to run for president, it is important to understand the criteria one must meet to be legally entitled to run for office. As stated in Article II, Section 1 of the United States Constitution: "No person except a natural born citizen, or a citizen of the United States, at the time of the adoption of this Constitution, shall be eligible to the Office of the President; neither shall any person be eligible to that Office who shall not have attained to the age of thirty-five years, and been fourteen years a resident within the United States." This creates clear criteria by which one is eligible to run for president. There are various state criteria of presidential eligibility. However, these are far too numerous to be covered in this chapter.

As discussed earlier, the United States has a two-party system on the federal electoral level. This section will discuss the processes by which one can come to be nominated by a political party to run for president at one of the two major parties' conventions. The process by which one comes to be nominated to run for the presidency for a given political party begins with registration as a candidate in the state in which one wishes to run and ends with an eventual nomination at the party convention, normally held the summer before the November general election.

1916 Democratic Party National Convention

There are two major forms of primaries in the presidential nomination process: caucuses and normal primaries. Primaries are the most prevalent means by which a candidate is chosen to run for the office of the presidency as the representative of a given party. The different parties decide the rules of the primary process, and there is some leeway given to the individual states as to how the process of selecting a nominee is undertaken.

However, the Democratic Party's rules insist that some degree of *proportional representation* must be used. To receive a proportional number of delegates, a candidate must receive at least 15% of the vote statewide. This minimum threshold is in place to prevent a candidate from receiving a disproportionate number of delegates in select districts through pandering to the interests of distinct communities living in a certain constituency. Additionally, the minimum statewide support mechanism allows the candidates who have the widest support to achieve the maximum number of delegates to prevent a fractured convention where multiple candidates have a similar number of delegates.

On the Republican side, the issue of the means by which delegates are allocated is, in keeping with the Republicans' general respect for states' rights, decided on a state-by-state basis. This has been a point of contention in that certain state electoral committees in heavily Republican states have used this ability to disenfranchise voters from minority communities.

Caucuses are the second major means by which the parties select their candidate for president. Caucuses are held only in Iowa, Texas, and Nevada. This type of electoral process is far less organized than the more formal primary voting process; as a result, small, but vocal sections of the electorate can have an outsized influence in the nominating process. An example of this is the Iowa Caucus, where many of those who actively participate in the process of caucusing are Evangelical Christians, who are unrepresentative of the nation at large. As a result, candidates that are not very prominent on the national stage (e.g., Rick Santorum in 2012) have won the Iowa Caucus even though their national support was lacking.

Presidential candidate Rick Santorum campaigning for Iowa Caucus, January 2012

Once an individual has won a state primary or caucus, that candidate is awarded a corresponding number of delegates at the respective party's national convention. These delegates, which are won through an electoral process, are called *pledged delegates*. Less important (though often crucial in gaining nomination) are a smaller number of *super-delegates*, who are allowed to cast their vote in favor of whatever candidate they favor. These delegates are often representatives of the respective party's "establishment" and will often vote as a unified block in favor of the candidate who either represents the status quo or who is thought to have the best chance of victory in the general election.

Once all state primaries and caucuses have been held, there is a party convention held the summer before the general election. There is usually a decisive winner regarding support of pledged delegates and super-delegates, which makes the convention itself merely a formality. Before the spread of mass communication technologies, conventions were an occasion for the parties and their candidate to hammer out a solid electoral "platform" of positions on issues on which the candidate would run. In the present day, this function continues as a formality and is not necessary.

Because one primary candidate usually has an outright majority of support, there is usually only the need for one ballot to name a nominee. Should this not be the case, there will be a *brokered convention* whereby all manner of political maneuvering is practiced as a means to shift delegates to one candidate. This is an infrequent occurrence because even if there is a relatively equal split in electoral support, the superdelegates often have enough power to sway the balance in favor of a single candidate.

Once the party has chosen their nominee, the candidate gives a nomination acceptance speech to the assembled convention, stirring up enthusiasm for their proposed path to victory. Also, the convention is often when the presidential nominee will announce their choice of vice-presidential nominee, creating what is known as the presidential ticket.

Once a party has chosen the candidate they wish to put forth to run for president, the respective candidates begin campaigning for the general election. The winner of the presidential general election is decided through the Electoral College.

The Electoral College is the name for the institution responsible for electing the president. It is commonly believed that the person who is elected to the Office of the Presidency is chosen through direct democracy and that the person who wins the majority of the vote is automatically declared the winner. In the United States system, this is not the case, as the Electoral College decides such matters.

The Electoral College is the number of "votes" each state is allowed to allocate for a presumptive presidential candidate. The number of Electoral College votes that each respective state is allocated is in direct proportion to the number of people residing in the state. This ranges from California's 55 electoral votes to Alaska, Delaware, Montana, North Dakota, South Dakota, Vermont, and Wyoming's three electoral votes. The means by which one wins the Electoral College votes in a given state vary, but the general rule is that the winner takes all. As a result, the candidate who receives 50%+1 vote in a given state is awarded 100% of the Electoral College votes of that state (with the exceptions of Nebraska and Maine).

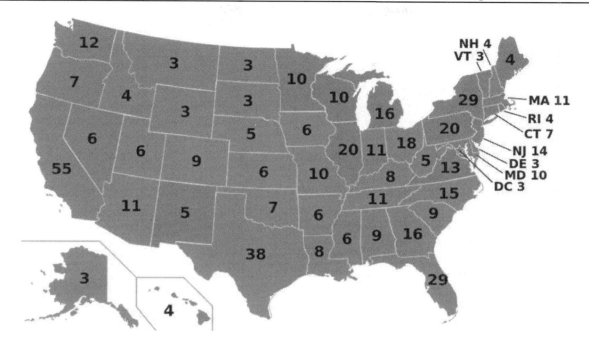

The United States Electoral College map

Many consider this to be a biased system by which a president is chosen because every vote above 50%+1 in any given state is essentially wasted because the given candidate has already been awarded the electoral votes in that state. Furthermore, all the voters who contributed to the losing candidate are not accounted for in the selection of a president, with their vote essentially wasted. Due to the Electoral College process, the person who is elected to the office of the president is often not representative of the electorate as a whole. An example of this was the 2000 General Election where Al Gore decisively beat George Bush in the popular vote (i.e., received more actual votes), but George Bush won the Electoral College and was named the 43rd President of the United States.

Al Gore, American politician, and environmentalist

The Electoral College process of electing the president is controversial in the modern era, as many feel that their voices are not heard and that the candidate who wins does not represent the majority of the country. This electoral process creates "Red States" and "Blue States," which tend to consistently elect candidates from one party or the other in presidential elections. As a result, presidential candidates tend to ignore the desires of these states in favor of a strategy intended to win "purple states," also known as "swing states" (which tend to be more politically centrist or mixed). This leads to candidates shifting their platforms to the political "center" as a means to garner the support of voters who are not loyal to one party. Many partisans on either the right wing or the left wing of American politics argue that this process waters down the potential for change and often leads to a candidate's hands being tied when trying to advocate policies for change.

Thus, there is a movement to abolish the Electoral College, but it has been unsuccessful so far. In Nebraska and Maine states, it has been neutralized by passing state laws that require that their Electoral College votes be given in proportion to each candidate's level of votes in the state rather than the winner taking all of them. However, this has had a minor effect so far because these two states have a very small share of the Electoral College.

Congressional Branch

In the United States, Congress is designed to be far more powerful than the executive or judicial branches of government as it is intended to represent the American populace at large; however, as Congress' power is more diffused, many often wrongly believe it to be the weakest branch due to the fact there are 535 representatives.

The United States Senate is the higher house of Congress with 100 members (called U.S. Senators), two senators per state regardless of population size. The longer-serving senator for a state is referred to as the "senior senator," while the more recent one is referred to as the "junior senator," irrespective of their age and political experience. The House of Representatives is the lower house but is the most populous branch of the elected portion of the federal government with 435 members (i.e., U.S. Representatives).

Senators serve staggered six-year terms in three different groups (referred to as Class I, II and III). Every two years approximately one-third of the seats are up for election. Additionally, they are staggered in such a way that only one Senate seat per state is up for reelection during an election year. Members of Congress elected to the House of Representatives serve two-year terms with all seats in the House of Representatives up for election on every even-numbered year.

Eligibility to become a senator is based on three criteria detailed in Article 1, Section 3 of the U.S. Constitution. First, the individual must be at least 30 years old. Second, the individual must have been a U.S. citizen for at least the past nine years before their election bid. Third, the individual must live in the state where they are running for office.

To be eligible for election to the House of Representatives, an individual must be a resident of the state they wish to represent, a citizen of the United States and at least twenty-five years of age. Each state is broken up into congressional districts consisting of about 700,000 residents. Each constituency elects an individual member of the House of Representatives as their representative in Congress.

The House of Representatives has a fixed number of electoral districts, but these 435 seats of the lower house are supposed to be apportioned according to each state's population, per the Constitution. Thus, every decade, according to the most recent population census, the 435 seats are redistributed as each state's share of the American population changes. This means that district boundaries are redrawn on the map. This redrawing of districts for the House of Representatives (the lower house) raises questions and criticisms because it is prone to partisan manipulation. Questions arise as to who gets to redraw the map and what criteria they use.

Political cartoon shows the newly drawn Massachusetts State Senate district of South Essex created by the legislature to favor the Democratic-Republican Party candidates of Governor Elbridge Gerry over the Federalists (1812)

In 1812 in Massachusetts, a concept called "gerrymandering" was first tried by its namesake, Governor Elbridge Gerry. Governor Gerry chose to cynically redraw district boundaries to ensure that candidates of his choosing would have a better chance of winning. In modern times, accusations have been made that gerrymandering has been used to minimize or "compress" the number of electoral districts in which blacks, Hispanics and other minorities can vote, thus lowering the number of representatives they can elect.

Senate and House elections occur on even-numbered years, on the first Tuesday after the first Monday in November (called Election Day). In election years, all House seats and one-third of Senate seats are up for contestation. In the months before Election Day, primary elections are held for each political party in different states to determine the candidates who will run in the general election for each party. Primaries are intended to give the American people a greater influence in the candidate selection process than the party leaders.

Not all primaries are structured in the same way and vary state to state. Currently, they exist in one of six variations: closed primaries, semi-closed primaries, open primaries, semi-open primaries, partisan blanket primaries, and nonpartisan blanket parties.

Closed primaries are elections in which only people who are registered members of a political party can vote in their particular party's primary election. Independents, non-partisans or unaffiliated voters, those who are not members of a political party, cannot vote.

Semi-closed primaries are similar to closed primaries in that registered party members can only vote for candidates in their political party. Independents, non-partisans or unaffiliated voters, however, can vote as well, choosing one of the party primaries to vote in either at the polling station or by registering with a party on Election Day.

Open primaries are elections in which registered voters, regardless of personal party affiliation, can vote in any party primary of their choosing. *Pick-a-party primary* is a colloquial term sometimes used because voters can choose which party to vote for on Election Day. "Party raiding" can occur during open primaries, which means that members of one party vote for another party have perceived a weaker candidate to increase their own party's chances of victory in the general election. In open primaries, no party-specific ballots are printed, and voters can select the party they want to vote for in their voting booth on a single ballot.

Semi-open primaries are contests in which registered voters do not need to declare the party primary they will be participating in before arriving at their polling station. Instead, after being identified by election officials, voters are to request a party-specific ballot. This party-specific ballot is what differentiates semi-open from open primaries.

The *blanket primary* is a system in which voters can mix the parties they vote for according to each office up for election. For example, a person might vote for a Democratic Senate candidate and could also vote for a Republican Representative candidate on the same ballot.

A *non-partisan blanket primary* (also called "top two primary") is a primary in which voters are not restricted to candidates from one particular party. All candidates run one ballot, and the top two vote-getters compete in the general election regardless of their party affiliation. These top two candidates can be from the same or different political parties.

Louisiana primary (a state which has a long history of holding nonpartisan blanket primaries) is another variation of a non-partisan blanket primary, but this election is held on the Federal Election Day. In this primary, all candidates run one ballot, and if one candidate receives the majority of the vote (50% + 1 vote), that candidate is declared a winner (which is often the case in Louisiana). If there is no majority winner, top two vote-getters (regardless of their party) will have a runoff election in December to determine the winner.

The *partisan blanket primary* is primary where all candidates run on one ballot. Then, the top vote-getter from each represented party runs in the general election. Currently, Alaska is the only state that uses this type of primary elections. Participation of each party is voluntary because, in 2000, the Supreme Court ruled that states cannot require political parties to participate in blanket primaries.

Party nominations for U.S. Senators and U.S. Representatives in some states are decided during their spring or summer political conventions, as opposed to a ballot voting system. These conventions often rely on voice votes, which either indicate continued confidence in the incumbent candidate or a lack of consensus. In the latter case, a "floor fight" can ensue where delegates vote on who will represent their party in the general election.

Interest Groups, Including Political Action Committees (PACs)

Perhaps the most powerful nonofficial element of American politics is interest groups. Interest groups are groups of people committed to a single issue, identity or cause. Interest groups generally attempt to persuade the government to take action on their issue through what is called lobbying. There can be multiple interest groups dedicated to a particular issue by taking different positions, or there can be interest groups dedicated to promoting broad causes rather than any specific issue. Any group trying to convince the government to do something a certain way can be considered an interest group.

The Range of Interests Represented

Interest groups can be organizations, informal groups of people or corporate-based lobby groups dedicated to pushing the government to act on a certain issue. Interest groups can be dedicated to virtually any issue and are therefore very diverse. Some interest groups are very powerful and corporately backed, while others rely on volunteers and sheer numbers to push for action. In relation to the policymaking process, the primary aim of any interest group is to push the government to make policy that relates to their area of interest.

While an interest group can be dedicated to virtually any imaginable issue, they can be divided into some major types. The first of these types is *economic interest groups*, who seek to lobby the government to act in a way that gives economic advantage to members of the group. These groups tend to seek private advantage for their members rather than for the overall public good and are quite controversial. The most prominent form of economic interest groups is those which are formed by a group of corporations in the same industry.

For instance, oil companies may pool together their resources to create a lobby group dedicated to convincing the government to provide tax breaks or relaxed environmental standards only to companies operating in the oil industry. Business interest groups tend to be well-funded, and thus can devote considerable resources to lobbying the government which makes them very powerful entities. Consequently, it is much easier to convince the government to act a certain way if one can pay for hundreds of experienced professional lobbyists than individuals can by writing letters, however persuasive, to their representative.

The second category of interest group is the *professional association*. These associations lobby government on issues related to a specific profession. For example, the

American Medical Association advocates for doctors, and the National Education Association promotes the interests of school teachers. Professional associations are usually not engaged in full-time lobbying like corporate interest groups but become active when they feel the government is doing something that runs against the interests of their profession.

American Medical Association headquarters building in Chicago, Illinois

Citizens groups or *advocacy groups* are those dedicated to advancing a cause or an issue that is not related to their material advantage. While economic lobby groups seek to achieve private gain, citizen groups are concerned with advancing the public good and tend to be less controversial. Given that democratic government by definition acts to advance the public good rather than enhance private gain by select groups, citizens groups are interest groups capable of achieving wide popular support. These groups, however, can have very different opinions on what the public good is, and conflicting citizens' groups' often form around a single issue, with each group believing that they are acting for the common good.

These sorts of public interest groups can cover virtually any political issue. They can dedicate themselves to one issue or advocate a broad agenda.

The Activities of Interest Groups

Lobbying and attempting to convince the government to favor one's position happens at all steps of the policy cycle. Lobbying by interest groups is aimed entirely at the president and Congress; lobbying the bureaucracy or the Supreme Court is considered "corruption," as these institutions are supposed to rely on their expertise and independent judgment.

The Effects of Interest Groups on the Political Process

The extravagance of American election spending has caused concern for many citizens. There is a strong movement to "get money out of politics." The right of corporations and unions to make campaign contributions was challenged in the Supreme Court case *Citizens United v. Federal Election Commission*. The court ruled that corporations and unions have the same right as individuals to donate to campaigns.

Justice Anthony Kennedy, author of the Supreme Court's decision
in Citizens United v. Federal Election Commission

Critics call this ruling a new avenue for wealthy individuals, unions and large corporations to spend unlimited amounts of money corruption of democracy. They point out that only people are people, and that if corporations and unions can spend unlimited money influencing politicians, this ruling has damaged the ability of citizens to have a voice in government. When elections can be influenced by such dramatic spending, this provides a huge media voice to those with much money and who can thus sway many votes.

Super PACs have also been criticized as corrupting individual members of Congress, as they may be more likely to advocate a policy position they do not agree with in the hope this will catch the attention of a Super PAC that will spend heavily in support of their reelection campaign.

So, for now, the side in favor of limiting campaign contributions has suffered a major setback, with large businesses and labor unions continuing to contribute to campaigns and PACs heavily.

The Unique Characteristics and Roles of PACs in the Political Process

PACs are interest groups which target specific members of Congress with large financial support in exchange for taking their preferred policy position. For example, an anti-abortion PAC might reward representatives who speak out against abortion with support and funding during their reelection campaigns. PACs can lobby politicians to support their causes, but often they identify politicians who already support their policy issue and then provide funding to help them get reelected and push for their agenda. Since PACs tend to be more reactive with their financial support by rewarding those politicians whose policy stances and voting records agree with their agenda, PACs tend to support incumbents overwhelmingly. This can make challenging an incumbent supported by one or more PACs very difficult, as the incumbent will have a spending advantage during the campaign. Political Action Committees are now the largest source of fundraising for candidates. Campaign funding from PACs has increased dramatically since the 1980s and continued to do so. In 1992, PACs donated $250 million to presidential campaigns.

A new category of PACs exists, formally referred to as an "independent-expenditure only committee" and nicknamed a "Super PAC." These exist solely to raise funds to support a party, as distinct from the regular PACs which raise money for a cause. Unlike the regular PACs, which donate directly to candidates and thus have to adhere to the legal limits, Super PACs spend as much as they want on advertising for their affiliated parties, doing so as organizations which are legally separate from the party. This could include running attack ads against the candidate they oppose or running "information" commercials designed to sway voters toward their side and thus get them to vote for their preferred candidate.

Since Super PACs are legally considered separate from political parties, they must not coordinate with the candidate or his or her party during the election. Despite this rule, the fact that donations to Super PACs can essentially be anonymous means that political parties could funnel money into Super PACs to skirt election financing laws. Although many states have now passed laws requiring the disclosure of Super PAC donors, these disclosures do not have to occur until after an election, opening up many avenues for corruption. In this way, Super PACs circumvent election finance laws, while having an impact on the elections. In 2014, PACs and Super PACs raised over $1.6 billion and contributed $500 million of this to candidates (primarily those of the two major parties).

Notes

The Mass Media

Given that Americans rely on the media to report what happens in government, the media is an extremely powerful political actor. Democracy requires an informed populace, and thus a free and open media is both to inform the public of what goes on in government and to hold the government accountable. The media is a tool that people can use to exercise a check on government power, whether by criticizing the government or ensuring it remains transparent. Throughout history, the media landscape has changed dramatically, with the onset of radio, television and now the Internet. Once, small or medium-sized newspapers proliferated, while today the media is concentrated in the hands of a few major corporations.

At one point in time, daily newspapers had such influence and authority that it was popularly believed that newspapers were arbiters of truth. There used to be a common expression that if something was printed in the *New York Times*, then it must be true, with the corollary that if it was not in the *Times*, then it couldn't be true. Today, many argue that daily newspapers have lost their credibility as arbiters of truth, although they once played an important role in uncovering government scandals and informing the public of political news.

The Functions and Structures of the News Media

There are many types of media, and the prominence of each has evolved. When the country was founded, print media (newspapers, newsletters, etc.) was the main means by which people received their news. While print media survived the advent of radio and television news, it has started to change dramatically in the era of the Internet. People are less inclined to subscribe to a single newspaper when they can read print media online from many different newspapers from around the world. While many newspapers lament the Internet as leading to the death of the daily newspaper, the Internet has led to a revitalization of printed media. As newspapers and newsletters used to be published by a wide range of people with different viewpoints, the ease with which someone can create a website is leading to increased diversity in print media voices.

The invention of the radio caused broadcast media to become a popular source of news. With the proliferation of television in the 1950s and 1960s, broadcast media became the dominant way most Americans got their political news. Newspapers criticized television and radio news broadcasts as lacking depth in reporting, but television news has continued to retain its popularity even into the Internet era. With the development of 24-hour news channels, beginning with CNN, it became possible to watch nothing but news on TV.

Logo for the 24-hour news channel, CNN

The need to fill 24 hours of airtime with content has led many stations to fill airtime with partisan opinions, leading to a shift from news reporting to political commentary and analysis. This is a major reason for criticism of the media as being shallow and lacking serious content. While news reporting on the radio was initially very popular, today the primary form of news radio is political talk shows. These talk shows are less about news and more about pushing opinions on listeners. They have been criticized for creating echo chambers rather than facilitating forums for legitimate debate and discussion.

As previously mentioned, the Internet has become a prominent media actor in its own right. Traditional forms of media (such as newspapers and TV stations) have had to build a web presence to stay competitive. There is much debate about whether the Internet exposes people to a wider range of news and opinion or not. However, the Internet allows the average American to easily access media from across the country and the political spectrum. Media from around the world is also now easily accessible. In the era of newspapers and television dominance, most people's media consumption was limited to whatever was locally available.

The Impacts of the News Media on Politics

Many media theorists argue that this new availability of many sources of media is leading Americans to become more informed, which should lead to a healthier democracy. If public opinion is no longer exclusively mediated through a few local news outlets, Americans should be able to see the bigger picture and do a better job of holding government accountable. The other side of this argument about the Internet is that it enables people to "live in a bubble," with other attitudes filtered out. Since it is easier to connect with and find like-minded people online, the filter bubble theorists argue that the Internet allows people to access only those media opinions with which they already agree.

In addition to the Internet being a novel form of media, it's also becoming more than just media. As a political space, people can go online to debate and argue their viewpoints just like meeting in a town hall or public square. Online avenues of popular participation in politics could work to revitalize democracy. Governments are also increasingly using the Internet to deliver services to the public. The Internet can make the bureaucracy more efficient by making it easier for people to do things like filing their taxes and renewing driver's licenses through a government website.

The News Media Industry and its Consequences

Political parties are also becoming increasingly aware of the power of the Internet to reach people directly without having to rely on the media. Political campaigns increasingly use websites, email lists, and social media to speak directly to recipients and rally potential voters. Voters used to decide whom to vote for entirely through information provided by the media; now political parties can once again speak directly to voters without media spin. This is especially important in an era where just six corporations own 90% of all media outlets in the United States. These media corporations wield a large amount of power which they can use to sway voters. In the future, it is likely that political campaigns will increasingly use the Internet to get around this corporate bias and speak directly to the voters.

While the Constitution guarantees freedom of the press, the practice is much more complicated. In addition to the fact that a handful of corporations controls most of the media, the traditional ability to use the press to speak out freely is now seriously constrained by the amount of money one has, making "freedom of speech" quite expensive to purchase. Even then, the government still regulates the media to make sure they do not act irresponsibly. The bulk of regulation has been directed toward broadcast media (radio and television) since they have traditionally been broadcast over public airwaves. Since the public owns radio and television frequency space, sending a broadcast into public space requires a license from the Federal Communications Commission (FCC).

U.S. Federal Communications Commission Inspector General badge

Another important part of the political coverage is presidential debates, aired by the major news networks. The first televised presidential debates took place in 1960. The Commission organizes these on Presidential Debates, which decides the rules of the debate and who participates in it. Public opinion polling has demonstrated that these debates have a strong impact on voting decisions. Although there are always numerous official presidential candidates in America, the only ones who are invited to participate are the candidates of the Republican and Democratic Parties. (An unusual exception to this was made for the independent candidate Ross Perot in 1992, but no other such exceptions have been made since the first televised debates were held.)

In September 2015, The Libertarian and Green Parties filed a federal suit against the Commission on Presidential Debates, for violation of the Sherman Anti-Trust Act by excluding other candidates from the debates. The plaintiffs argue that the two major parties are colluding to create a monopoly in the electoral market.

Please, leave your Customer Review on Amazon

Chapter 4

Institutions of National Government:
The Congress, the Presidency, the Bureaucracy and the Federal Courts

The United States Congress, the presidency, bureaucracy, federal courts, and other major political institutions are organized differently and possess both formal and informal powers. This arrangement of sharing power carries implications. The functions these institutions perform and do not perform, as well as the powers that they do and do not possess, are important.

These balances of power and institutional relationships to one another may evolve gradually or change dramatically as a result of crises. There exist numerous types of relationships between the various branches of the national government and political parties, interest groups, the media and state and local governments. These relationships can explain, for example, why Congress struggles to adopt a national budget.

Notes

The Major Formal and Informal Institutional Arrangements of Power

The Presidency

One of the formative ideas of the United States government rests on the premise that power should be subject to checks and balances. To accomplish this, the government is divided into three branches: the executive, the legislative and the judicial branch. The executive branch is the presidency, whose power derives from Article II of the U.S. Constitution. The president's powers outlined by the Constitution give him or her command of the Armed Forces, although Congress must approve a declaration of war. In the modern post-World War II era, however, presidents have increasingly taken their position as Commander in Chief to mean that they can initiate foreign hostilities without a declaration of war from Congress. The last formal declaration of war passed by Congress was World War II, with every military action since being initiated through the office of the Presidency. Given that Congress controls budgetary bills, these executive-initiated wars have needed to request funding from the Congress. While funding authorization is not an explicit declaration of war, presidents have increasingly interpreted Congress authorizing funds for war as tantamount to a declaration of war.

Roosevelt signs the declaration of war against Japan in 1941,

starting America's involvement in WWII

The second major power that the president holds as outlined in Article II is the ability to make treaties. The president can negotiate and sign treaties with foreign countries, subject to a two-thirds approval vote from the Senate. While Article II outlines the president's treaty-making power, it is less clear about whether the president has the power to break treaties. Former Presidents Lincoln and Carter both interpreted the ability to make treaties to mean they also had the right to break treaties.

The president has the power to appoint a Cabinet as well as ambassadors to other countries under Article II. The president's power to appoint members to the judicial branch is important as well. Since judges are appointed for life, these appointments grant the president considerable power, as the impact of judicial appointments can be felt long after the president has left his or her post. The president's authority with respect to the judicial branch also extends to his or her ability to grant pardons, allowing people to get out of jail or have their sentences changed, for example changing a sentence from the death penalty to life in prison. The president usually decides whether or not to grant pardons at the end of his or her term in office; given the nature of pardoning someone convicted of a crime, pardons tend to be extremely controversial.

Article II further outlines that the president is a legislative facilitator, meaning it is his or her job to ensure that Congress can further its work of passing legislation. In the 20th century, however, presidents increasingly took on more and more power with respect to the legislature, to the point where the president's Cabinet is often seen as where legislative policy originates, instead of the Congress. Under more recent presidents, notably George W. Bush, there was an increase in the use of executive signing statements. These statements were attached to bills passed by Congress and essentially outline the president's opinion on the bill. The American Bar Association has criticized the use of executive signing statements as undermining the separation of the legislative and executive powers, as they enable a president to essentially tell the bureaucracy how to enact legislation, often in a way inconsistent with the will of Congress.

President Ronald Reagan and Vice President George H. W. Bush,
both issued many signing statements

The president is responsible for delivering a yearly State of the Union Address. Originally, this meant that the president wrote a letter to be read in Congress that explained the general status of the country in the president's opinion. The framers of the Constitution intended the State of the Union Address as a way to keep the executive and legislative branches in conversation. With the advent of mass media, in particular, television, the State of the Union Address has evolved into a means for the president to speak directly to the American people. While congressional leaders are often given air-time to comment on the address, its intention and purpose have changed dramatically over time.

In addition to the importance of Article II of the Constitution, Article I also outlines the president's power with respect to the legislature. The president must sign, and thus authorize, bills passed by Congress for them to become law. If the president does not wish to see a bill from Congress become law, he or she can veto the bill. A veto can either kill a bill completely, send it back to Congress for modifications to be resubmitted later, or it can be over-ruled by Congress with a two-thirds majority vote. Executive signing statements, or comments included by a president on a bill he/she is signing, are controversial because they are not directly a veto, and thus Congress has no opportunity to override them.

Interpretation of Powers

Although the powers and role of the executive branch are outlined in the Constitution, these powers are open to interpretation. A general trend cited by political scientists is that in the 20th century, presidents increasingly interpreted their powers more broadly. This means that presidents today believe they have more authority than presidents in the 18th and 19th centuries. Given that the increase in executive authority has been slow, some scholars have argued that this amounts to a natural evolution of the position to meet the demands of modern politics. Conversely, other scholars have argued that the contemporary interpretation of the powers granted to the Executive Branch has become far too broad and that the framers of the Constitution intended for Congress to be the most powerful branch of government.

Many factors explain the expansion of presidential power. Against the backdrop of partisan bickering in the House of Representatives and the Senate, the president represents a singular and decisive voice on the issue(s) of the day, especially when the House and Senate are held by majorities of opposite parties, which can create a situation of deadlock that demands a single authority. In the face of disasters, the president also speaks for the government and thus is popularly viewed as the true seat of power. When the public supports the president, it is easy for him or her to expand the position's powers. The role of mass media also plays to this perception that the president essentially is the entire government. The president is by far the most visible politician, leading to an association in the public mind between the president and overall governmental authority.

President Franklin Delano Roosevelt at his fourth inaugural address

The one counterpoint to this trend of increasing presidential power has been the institution of term limits. Before the 22nd Amendment, ratified in 1951, presidents could hold office for as long as they could be re-elected. Although they historically had voluntarily limited themselves to two terms, Franklin Roosevelt won four elections and served three full terms before dying while in office early into his fourth term. After Roosevelt's unprecedented 12 years in office, term limits were set to keep the power of the executive under control.

Choosing the President

In addition to outlining the powers of the president, Article II also sets out the qualifications to be president. An important part of understanding the election of the president is to understand that he or she is not elected directly through popular vote. He or she is elected by the Electoral College, which is made up of 538 electors who are assigned on a state by state basis. For example, Texas has 38 electors in the Electoral College. These 38 votes out of 538 go to whichever presidential candidate won the most votes within Texas. Thus to get elected, a president needs to win states, and preferably ones with more Electoral College votes. When a candidate wins the most votes in a state, the media tends to label this then a "red state" if they voted Republican, or a "blue state" if they voted for a Democrat.

The Electoral College system is controversial and has been critiqued in some ways. It tends to give too much power to *swing states*, which are states that do not tend to always vote for one party over the other. Returning to the example of Texas, it tends to usually vote Republican, meaning that Presidential candidates focus less of their time there as they have a good idea of whom they will vote for before the election even happens. In Ohio, however, voters tend to swing back and forth between the Republicans and Democrats, meaning that candidates will give more of their time to this swing state because it has the potential to decide the election. As more and more states tend to solidify behind one party, the much fewer swing states become more and more important, as the Presidential election can be decided by the Electoral College votes of just a few states. This can discourage people in non-swing states from voting because they feel that their vote does not count toward deciding the election. One can imagine being a Democrat in Texas or a Republican in California feeling like one's vote does not count for much, as both those states tend to vote the same way every national election.

The Electoral College system is also problematic as it causes distortions in voting. In the 2000 Presidential election won by George W. Bush, for example, Bush won 30 states for 271 votes in the Electoral College, while his challenger Al Gore won 20 states for 266 votes.

In terms of total votes, however, Bush received 47.9%, and Gore received 48.4%. So even though more people voted for Al Gore to be president than voted for Bush, Bush was still the winner because he won more votes in the Electoral College. The Electoral College also inherently favors a two-party system, as a strong third party would have trouble gaining momentum when Electoral College votes are awarded on a winner take all basis.

In addition to needing to be selected by the Electoral College, the president has some other qualifications that he or she must meet. The President must be a natural born citizen of the United States, must be over the age of 35, and must have lived in the United States for the preceding 14 years. In 2008 presidential campaign, the natural born citizen clause has been a site of dispute. Despite President Obama providing a birth certificate proving he was born in the United States, it has been a popular cause for conspiracy theorists. However, the natural born clause is somewhat open to interpretation as well. 2008 Republican Presidential candidate John McCain was born on a U.S. Air Force base in the Panama Canal Zone, which was temporarily under American control. McCain was deemed eligible for the Presidency. More recently, potential Republican presidential candidate for the 2016 elections Ted Cruz's eligibility has been questioned because he was born in Canada. He has revoked his Canadian citizenship, but it has been a subject of debate whether this is enough to meet the natural born qualification.

2008 Republican Presidential candidate John McCain

If a president dies in office, new elections are not held, but instead, there is an order of succession. This order begins with the Vice-President, followed by the Speaker of the House, and lists a total of 18 positions in a ranked order. The goal behind having such a long succession list is to ensure that the executive office of the President will still be filled even in the event of a catastrophe killing many senior members of the government. The list of succession came into effect just after the end of World War II and at the beginning of the

Cold War. Gerald Ford has the distinction of being the only unelected President; Ford was appointed Vice President by Richard Nixon after Nixon's running mate and Vice President, Spiro Agnew, resigned. After Nixon resigned as well, Ford became President – a rare example of someone who never ran for President or Vice President assuming the top office.

U.S. President Gerald Ford

The Congress

The Congress of the United States is bicameral, meaning it is made up of two chambers: The House of Representatives and the Senate. As the legislative branch of government, Congress is vested with the power to make laws. While the House and the Senate are equal partners in the legislative process, meaning bills need to pass both chambers to become laws; the two bodies do have some unique powers set out in the Constitution. The Senate has the power to approve or deny appointments made by the President, and the House controls money-related bills. As set out in Article I of the Constitution, all revenue-raising bills must originate in the House of Representatives. The Sixteenth Amendment, passed in 1913, extended the House's taxation powers to income tax. This means that Congress, in particular, the House of Representatives, have the final say on all matters related to finance and the national budget, including tax rates, duties, and tariffs, as well as control over funding for expenditure programs such as the military or social security. With financial authority vested in the legislative branch, the President cannot simply raise or lower taxes, as such legislation must originate in the House of Representatives.

Congress has exclusive authority over matters related to national defense, including the power to declare war and the ability to determine the rules of the internal function of the military. As discussed in the previous section, many scholars have pointed out that the executive branch has increasingly begun to wield these powers, leading to a decline in Congressional authority over military matters. Before World War II, the president needed to ask Congress to declare war, which required a vote by the representatives of the people. At the time, this was considered an important check on the power of the president, but since then, presidents have initiated wars without direct approval from Congress. The Korean War, the Vietnam War, and the Iraq War were all initiated by the president without a formal declaration of war from Congress.

Congress is vested with some smaller powers which tend to be less visible. Congress has the power to issue patents and copyrights, establish post offices and to institute courts subordinate to the Supreme Court. Article IV gives Congress control over granting new states entrance into the United States. While this was once a very important Congressional power as the country grew from 13 to 50 states, this power is less practiced today; however, it is still important if, for example, Puerto Rico wished to become the 51st state – it would have to petition Congress for a decision.

Outside of the legislative powers of Congress, it plays an important role as a check on executive authority. These checks involve the ability to approve and reject presidential appointments (such as to the Supreme Court) and the ability to control the military, but also as a general investigative check on the president. Congress can wield this power by setting up committees to investigate whether the president has overstepped the bounds of executive authority and if they believe he or she has, they are given the authority to instigate impeachment proceedings. The House of Representatives can initiate impeachment against the president, vice-president or any civil officer of the United States. If the House votes in favor of impeachment, the proceedings move to the Senate where a trial takes place. The Senate then votes, based on the trial proceedings, whether the impeached official is indeed guilty of what he or she was impeached for.

Impeachment does not mean the removal of office, but merely being charged with an offense that the House deems worthy of removing someone from office over. Three presidents have been impeached. Andrew Johnson and Bill Clinton were impeached by the House but found not guilty by the Senate, and Richard Nixon resigned before his impeachment moving to trial.

U.S. Senate in session during the impeachment trial of President Bill Clinton

In addition to passing legislation, the other primary role of Congress is to represent the American people in government. District representatives are responsible for dealing with complaints from constituents and helping them navigate the bureaucracy. While President Obama has publicly argued that it is the role of the president to represent the entire American public, this has traditionally been the role of Congress. Against the backdrop of increasing partisan deadlock in the House and Senate, Obama's attempt to position the president as the singular representative of all Americans could be interpreted as either an example of the continued decrease in the power of the Congress at the hands of the Executive, or as a necessary step to get past the partisan deadlock in Congress.

Bicameral Structure

Having two chambers of Congress was envisioned by the framers of the Constitution as ensuring that legislation would be passed through a combination of popular participation (via the House of Representatives) and after consideration by those with more experience and wisdom (via the Senate). At the time the Constitution was written, there was still a real fear that allowing regular Americans (which at the time excluded women, Native Americans, African Americans and men without property) to vote for their representatives could lead to irresponsible decisions which could threaten the status quo.

To combat this fear of popular democracy, the Senate was devised as a second legislative body, which was intended to be filled with upper-class elites. Before the Seventeenth Amendment in 1913, Senators were chosen by state legislatures rather than being popularly elected as they are now.

The House of Representatives is designed to represent each person equally, while the Senate is intended to give each state equal representation regardless of how small its population is. Each state has two Senators, while bigger states have more seats in the House of Representatives. This balancing between representation by population and by the state was called the *Connecticut Compromise*. To serve as a member of the House of Representatives, one must be 25 years of age, while a Senator must be 30. While the House has elections every four years for all representatives (who are elected for two-year terms), Senators serve six-year terms, and one-third of the Senate is up for election every two years. The longer-term and lack of total turnover in the Senate were meant to insulate Senators from public opinion.

As part of a rigid two-party system, the House and Senate are always controlled by one of the two parties. The party with the most seats is called the majority party, and the party with fewer seats is called the minority party. While representatives do not officially have to vote the same way as the rest of their party, it is the job of the party Whip to rally support and ensure the party votes the same way. One of the primary ways the Whip rallies support is through dealing with caucuses.

Caucuses are non-official groups of representatives who share a common goal or concern. Some prominent caucuses include the Congressional Black Congress, the Congressional Internet Caucus and the Out of Iraq Caucus. The Whip often negotiates with caucuses by trading favors to get the members of the caucus to vote the way the Whip wants. For instance, if the majority party leadership wants to pass a bill on education, the Whip may promise that the majority party will support a bill related to the internet in exchange for the Internet Caucus voting in favor of the education bill.

Founding members of the Congressional Black Caucus

The leader of the House of Representatives is the Speaker of the House, who is elected by the majority party to control the legislative agenda of the House. The Whip assists the Speaker in ensuring that the Speaker's legislative agenda has enough support to get voted through. By contrast, the President of the Senate is the Vice President, although in practice the Vice President is not very involved with the Senate, which is de facto led by the most senior member of the majority party in the Senate. Senators are less subject to whipped votes, as they are supposed to act as independent voices of wisdom but in practice, most Senators tend to follow the party line.

Originally, the House and Senate were meant to be sites of vigorous debate on the status of the legislation being considered, but in practice, this is rarely the case. The most common way for Senators to show disapproval with a piece of legislation is through a filibuster, a process whereby a member or members of the Senate delay the passage of a piece of legislation by taking the floor and talking for as long as he or she can (which does not allow a vote to take place on the legislation in question). Filibusters can only be stopped with a 60% supermajority vote, which means even if a party does not have a majority in the Senate, as long as they can maintain 40% or more of the seats they can filibuster legislation. Senators can also attach riders to legislation, which are additional clauses to the bill. Often this is done to ensure support for a piece of legislation, but sometimes these riders have little to do with the actual bill in question. This is called pork-barreling and involves a Senator attaching a clause that supports his or her home state but had nothing to do with the original bill.

Outside of voting on bills and responding to constituents, the most important role played by individual members of Congress is their time spent serving on Committees. Committees are small groups which study bills in depth, and thus are entrusted with telling the rest of Congress whether or not they should vote for a bill. On the one hand this allows Congress to work on more bills at once, an in-depth study is divided among members, but it can lead to representatives voting on bills they have not read or even do not understand.

There are four types of congressional committees that members can be a part of. *Standing committees* are the most common and focus on reviewing specific types of legislation and deciding what levels of funding for public programs are most appropriate. *Conference committees* involve members from both the House and the Senate and are used to ensure there is an agreement in both chambers of Congress to ensure a bill gets passed. *Select committees* are created to deal with a specific event or issue and are dissolved after their work is over. *Joint committees* are like select committees but involve members from both chambers of Congress.

Logo for the U.S. Senate Select Committee on Intelligence

Committees are extremely powerful as they determine what bills are sent to the floor for voting. The majority of bills are killed in committees before the general members of Congress have a chance to vote on them. This ensures that only significant and important bills are subject to debate, as committees weed out bills that they find problematic or think will have no support in a general vote. Congress can, however, overrule the decision of a committee to kill a bill and not send it to the floor for a general vote if they feel the committee has acted inappropriately. This is done by passing a discharge petition.

The leader of each committee is chosen by the majority party, who always has a majority of members on a committee. The minority party chooses their committee leader who is called the ranking member. Given that committees do important work, leadership and membership in a committee grants a member of Congress significant power, making committee positions highly sought after. Committee members do not have to do all of their committee work by themselves, as they are assisted by staffers whom they hire directly. These staffers often engage in the nuts and bolts of committee work, including researching legislation, assisting committee members with general duties, and even writing the text of the legislation.

While the idea behind a bicameral Congress was to ensure that the Senate would act as a check on the House of the Representatives, in practice this system has produced deadlock, as bills require double approval. When different parties control the Senate and the House, this can make passing legislation extremely difficult, as rigid partisan views tend to interfere with legislative judgment. Also, if the same party controls both houses of Congress but the President is from the other party, then the President is more likely to veto bills, causing more deadlock. Many scholars have argued that the persistent deadlock in Congress in the modern era explains why the increasing power of the executive branch at the expense of the legislative branch has not upset the American people.

The Legislative Process

Passing bills through committees and then through voting and amending them in both houses of Congress can make the legislative process quite drawn out. This is by design, as the Framers of the Constitution did not want Congress to be able to hastily pass ill-conceived legislation that might limit the freedom of the American people.

There are two types of bills, *public bills* (which affect everyone), and *private bills* (which are aimed toward a single person). The process by which a bill becomes a law begins with its introduction by a member of the House of Representatives. The bill is then referred to the appropriate committee for further study and analysis. The committee can then either refer it to a subcommittee for hearings or more detailed study, kill the bill or approve it. Upon approval, the bill is sent back to the House of Representatives for debate and voting by the full body of the legislature. The debate in the House is extremely limited by the Rules Committee and voting proceeds through a roll-call where each member registers his or her vote. If the House of Representatives approves the bill, it moves to the Senate, where each Senator can speak about or propose amendments to the bill as he or she sees fit.

If the Senate and House agree to pass a piece of legislation but differ slightly in how it should be worded, the bill is then referred to a conference committee, consisting of members from both chambers of Congress, who will work together to reach agreement on the final wording of the bill. The bill is then sent to the president, who can sign it to make it law, or veto it to kill it. The veto can be over-ridden by a two-thirds vote in both the Senate and House. This is extremely hard to accomplish, so a Presidential veto almost always kills a bill for good.

The Judiciary

The Supreme Court acts as the ultimate check on the power of the legislative and executive branches. The primary role of the judiciary is to uphold the Constitution and ensure that no legislation is passed which is inconsistent with the Constitution and Bill of Rights. When an individual or group feel that a piece of legislation violates the Constitution, they can challenge this legislation in court, rather than trying to have to convince the politicians that passed it that the law violated the Constitution. For this reason, lawyers and judges play an extremely important part in the American political system.

In addition to the laws passed by Congress, it is the job of the Supreme Court to interpret the Constitution and make judgments regarding case law (which are previous court decisions). One of the most important functions of the Supreme Court is its ability to overturn precedents. Lower court judges rely on case law to rule in cases, but if situations change and individuals feel that past rulings have become unjust, they can appeal to have the precedent reviewed by the Supreme Court. For instance, in the historically important *Roe v. Wade* case, the Supreme Court ruled that the ability to have an abortion be a fundamental right covered by the Ninth and Fourteenth Amendments, overturning past court judgments and invalidating various state laws.

Normally the Supreme Court only reviews legislation, precedents, and constitutionality based on court challenges initiated by individuals and their lawyers, but it also retains the power to initiate judicial reviews of legislation passed by Congress. This power is not outlined in the Constitution but is based on precedent dating back to 1803. Since the Supreme Court does not have the power to enforce a decision against a piece of legislation unless it is a result of challenges initiated by individuals, the Supreme Court rarely uses this power of judicial review.

Supreme Court building

The federal judiciary uses a hierarchical structure of authority. At the top of this hierarchy is the Supreme Court, below it is the Courts of Appeals (i.e., Circuit Courts), and below those are the 94 federal district courts. As the highest court, the Supreme Court is the highest court of appeal, and thus it has the final say in all rulings. The Supreme Court is made up of nine justices, led by the Chief Justice and eight associates. Supreme Court justices are appointed for life but can choose to retire before they die. The president appoints the justices and approved by the Senate. Congress has the power to change the number of justices on the Supreme Court, but the current number of nine has remained unchanged since 1869.

Seal of the United States Court of Appeals for the First Circuit

While the Supreme Court receives many appeals to review cases, they do not review them all. The justices decide which cases should be reviewed on the basis of a minority vote, and generally only review cases they deem to be of significant importance. If four of the justices agree a case should be heard, then this is enough to issue a writ of certiorari, which orders a lower court to send a case to the Supreme Court for review.

When a case is reviewed in the Supreme Court, briefs are submitted by both sides of the case summarizing their position for the justices. People or organizations not directly involved in the case can also submit briefs outlining their position on the case, called *amicus curiae* briefs. After reading the briefs in detail, the justices may hear oral arguments from the parties involved, who have half an hour to present their case directly to the justices. The justices often use the oral arguments period to ask both sides of the case to clarify statements made in the written briefs. Rather than a normal court trial where lawyers present their arguments largely uninterrupted by the judge, Supreme Court justices intervene heavily in the argument phase. After reading the briefs and hearing the oral arguments, the justices then hold a judicial conference in which they discuss and debate the case with each other. These conferences are kept secret to ensure the integrity of their rulings.

Upon conclusion of the judicial conference, the justices can decide that the ruling of the lower court was adequate, and they do not wish to register a decision or opinion on the case. This is called a *per curiam* rejection and essentially means that upon reviewing the case in detail, the Supreme Court does not feel the case is worth hearing, as the lower courts did an adequate job with it. If the justices agree the case is worth ruling on, they then issue a decision and an opinion. The decision decides which side of the case wins, and the opinion provides a legal argument as to why and how the court made its decision.

There are many types of decisions the Supreme Court can make on any given case. A *majority opinion* is given when at least five justices agree with the decision and support the reasoning behind the opinion.

A *plurality opinion* occurs when a majority of the justices agree on the decision, but not the reasoning behind it. For example, seven judges may be in favor of deciding a case in favor of one side, but if they do not all agree on why it should be decided this way, a plurality opinion can be issued. If four of these justices support one set of legal reasoning and three support another, the opinion of the four is presented as a plurality opinion, since the majority does not support it.

A *concurring opinion* is issued by justices who agree with the decision, but not the opinion. In the example above, the opinion of the three justices would be a concurrent opinion, while that of the other four remains a plurality opinion.

A *dissenting opinion* is issued by the justices who disagree with what the majority ruled. In the above example, if four justices issue a plurality opinion in favor of the decision and three issue a concurring opinion in favor of the decision, then the other two justices will issue dissenting opinions against the decision.

In addition to those four major types of decisions, *memorandum opinions* can be issued. These decide a case without setting a precedent. This is done in cases where the individual circumstances of a case were exceptional, and the justices feel that their ruling should be not be used as the basis of future case law.

The Supreme Court has exercised its power to issue some landmark rulings which have fundamentally altered the political situation in America. In *Marbury v. Madison* (1803) the Supreme Court ruled that it had the power to overturn unconstitutional laws. In *Dred Scott v. Sanford* (1857) the Supreme Court forcibly returned a slave to his owner, increasing tensions and contributing to the onset of the Civil War. In *Plessy v. Ferguson* (1896) the Court upheld the legality of racial segregation, which was consequently overturned in *Brown v. Board of Education* (1954). In *Gideon v. Wainwright* (1963) the Supreme Court ruled that those who cannot afford a lawyer when charged with a crime must be provided one by the state. *Miranda v. Arizona* (1966) led to the adopting of the police being required to read "Miranda rights" to those who have been arrested. *Roe v. Wade* (1973) legalized abortion, and *Bush v. Gore* (2000) provided a ruling related to recounts in Florida which resulted in George W. Bush becoming the president. It is clear the Supreme Court's decisions have been controversial and sometimes contradictory, changing over time and demonstrating that the Court's primary role is interpretation.

Members of the Warren Court, who made the unanimous decision for Brown v. Board of Education

It is important to note that the Constitution must be interpreted and that these interpretations can change over time. This is why a Supreme Court is needed, to be the final arbitrator of these interpretations. Over time, however, the Supreme Court can change its opinions and overrule past decisions. The fact that the President appoints the justices is important to consider, as Presidents generally seek to appoint justices who agree with them politically. While the framers intended the Supreme Court to be legal experts free of partisan influence, the reality of the situation has evolved in practice over time. The ability of the judicial branch to act as a check on the executive and legislative branches is then questionable when the Supreme Court can be "stacked" with those inclined to agree with the President. This "stacking" hasn't always worked out as anticipated. For instance, the Republican President Dwight Eisenhower appointed Earl Warren as Chief Justice in 1953, expecting Warren to be politically conservative in his rulings. Warren, however, turned out to be less inclined to follow a conservative ideology, much to the dismay of Eisenhower.

Since judges are inclined to make rulings based on their political views, the president and the vetting committee in the Senate take special care to try to find Supreme Court justices whom they hope will make rulings that support the president's positions. Part of how this is done is by trying to understand the judicial philosophy of the potential justice. Some judges believe in *judicial activism*, which means that the Supreme Court should have the power to overturn bad laws that they deem unconstitutional, while those who believe in *judicial restraint* believe that the Supreme Court should only interpret existing laws. The issue of same-sex marriage legalization provides an example; a supporter of judicial activism would argue that if a law banning same-sex marriage is appealed through the court system, it is up to the court to decide whether same-sex marriage should be legal or illegal. An advocate of judicial restraint would hear such an appeal, but if they deemed the existing law to be inadequate, they would feel that it should be up to Congress to change the law rather than the Supreme Court.

Judicial philosophy can also differ in how the Constitution is interpreted, some judges, called *loose constructionists*, argue that the spirit of the Constitution should be considered when interpreting it, while *strict constructionists* argue that judges must only consider exactly what is written in the Constitution. Finally, there are those who interpret the Constitution as a living document which can be amended to meet changing circumstances, and those who argue the original document must not be contravened and original intent must always override present-day concerns. All of the different judicial philosophies, in combination with the justices' personal political views, factor into how the Supreme Court rules on the cases they accept, which have ramifications well beyond mere legal interpretation. In this sense, the judiciary is still very much a political institution.

The Constitution does not outline any specific requirements or qualifications to become a federal court judge; thus, one need not be a lawyer to be appointed to the Supreme Court. In practice, however, federal court appointees are almost always lawyers, usually with previous experience as a judge. Some political scientists argue that a degree of legal training and experience is necessary for federal judges to be able to interpret complex legal arguments, while others point out that lawyers are good at following legal precedent but lack the philosophical training and understanding to create it.

While the Supreme Court is the last resort of appeals and designed as a fundamental check to ensure that the legislative and executive branches do not pass laws which violate the Constitution, the executive, and legislative branches do have a way to check the power of the judiciary. For instance, if the Supreme Court rules that a law be unconstitutional, Congress and the president can move to amend the Constitution. At the same time, if the Supreme Court rules that a law be unconstitutional but should be replaced with better legislation, the legislative branch can simply not put forward any such new legislation. Congress can also refuse to provide funding on something, thus undermining a Supreme Court decision. For instance, after the Supreme Court ruled that abortion be a constitutional right, Congress could have worked to undermine this ruling by refusing to fund abortion clinics and organizations.

The Bureaucracy

Bureaucracy, which comes from the French word *bureau,* meaning "desk," and the ancient Greek *cracy,* which means "rule of," gives the meaning "the rule of desks." The word comes from the fact that government workers were originally seen as people who sit behind desks, carrying out the work of the legislature, though not participating in the political process. While the name suggests a somewhat negative connotation, there are many arguments for and against bureaucracy.

The German sociologist Max Weber presented one of the most thorough accounts of why bureaucracy is important in having a modern, functional government. Weber points out that without a slew of professional government employees, dealing with the government would be a nightmare of inefficiency based on personal favor (e.g., having to beg and plead with one's Congressional representative to get a driver's license). The bureaucracy plays an important role in professionalizing government to ensure that dealing with it is based on consistent rules and not a matter of the whims of politicians. Before the professionalization of the bureaucracy, a spoils system was often in place, in which the President would fire all existing government workers and replace them with his friends and supporters, resulting in an incompetent government unable to properly execute the orders of the President and Congress.

Max Weber, German sociologist

At the same time, the expansion and professionalization of the bureaucracy have created vast amounts of "red tape." Though bureaucratization was undertaken with the goal of increasing efficiency, critics have argued that dealing with bureaucratic rules and procedures is dehumanizing because government workers merely follow the rules without sympathy for an individual's plight. Critics point to a decline in personal responsibility in bureaucratic systems, as the hierarchy of the bureaucracy enables government workers to shift responsibility away from themselves. Regardless of one's opinions on the effectiveness of bureaucracy, the complex modern government requires a professional, non-partisan, workforce to act as the intermediary between citizens and government.

The fundamental job of a bureaucrat is to implement government policy. When Congress and the President decide they want something done, it is the bureaucracy who puts these laws and directives into practice. Putting government directives into practice can range from policy analysis (which takes government directives and creates rules for how this law will be applied to a specific situation) to public administration (which delivers these policies to the public). Thus, if Congress passes a piece of legislation stating that they wish to see better health care for military veterans, policy-makers in public service take this directive and write up policies and rules for how Veteran Affairs will improve health care in specific ways. Public administrators, ranging from those who run VA hospitals down to the nurses and doctors who treat patients, directly implement the policy. The bureaucracy is responsible for promoting not only government policy, but national security and policing, and various economic functions via the Federal Reserve Bank.

The bureaucracy is also responsible for regulation, in addition to policy-making and implementation. Regulation involves making sure that existing rules and standards are followed. Regulatory bureaucracies include the Environmental Protection Agency, which assures that regulations on pollution and environmental protection are upheld, and the Securities and Exchange Commission, which ensures that the stock market is regulated.

The federal bureaucracy employs approximately 2.6 million people and is largely directed by the executive branch of government. Since the President appoints Cabinet secretaries, who run the various branches of the bureaucracy, the bureaucracy is primarily an instrument of presidential power. 97% of government employees are members of the federal civil service and 10% work in Washington D.C. Congress and the judiciary have their bureaucracies, but these are much smaller and less powerful. For example, Congress' most powerful bureaucratic branches are the Library of Congress and the Congressional Research Service, which pale in comparison to federal bureaucracies such as the FBI or Homeland Security. Congress does, however, act as a check on the power of the bureaucracy, as it has oversight power enabling it to monitor the bureaucracy to make sure that it is acting properly.

For much of American history, the bureaucracy was relatively small. In part, this was simply because the population was much smaller and society was less complex. Part of the growth in the size of government bureaucracy, however, was a result of a change in philosophy. President Roosevelt's New Deal and President Johnson's Great Society policies actively sought to increase the size of the bureaucracy to expand the capacity of the government to meets the needs of the average American. There has been a shift since the 1980s toward the acceptance of "big government" in the form of a large bureaucracy, especially in the wake of the September 11th, 2001 terrorist attacks. In 2002, there was a second major expansion of the bureaucracy as new departments related to national security were created, most notably the Department of Homeland Security.

President Lyndon B. Johnson at the University of Michigan commencement in 1964, where he made his first public reference to his Great Society policies

The Cabinet

The most important positions in the bureaucracy are the Cabinet. These are leaders (officially called Secretaries, but sometimes informally called "czars" in the media) of major government departments. The President appoints the Cabinet and the Senate must approve each Cabinet member. The Cabinet is important not just because they are the heads of the major executive departments and are in charge of the bureaucracy, but because they also are part of the order of succession should the President and the Vice President be unable to continue in office.

The main branches of the bureaucracy and their functions are outlined here in order of importance. The Secretary of State heads the U.S. Department of State, which deals with issues related to foreign affairs. The Department of the Treasury is in charge of financial and monetary policy. The Department of Defense handles the military. The Attorney General is the country's top lawyer and is in charge of the Justice Department, which handles criminal matters and policy. The Department of the Interior concerns itself with geographical issues, land management, and national parks. The Secretary of Agriculture is followed by the Secretary of Commerce, both with self-explanatory roles. The Department of Labor enforces workplace regulations and manages laws related to unions. Next in the succession order are the Departments of Health, Housing and Urban Development, Transportation, Energy, Education, Veterans Affairs and finally Homeland Security.

These major departments of the bureaucracy form the bulk of government employees and provide the services that citizens rely on. In addition to the heads of each bureaucratic department, the Cabinet also includes the White House Chief of Staff, who is the president's primary assistant, the Director of the Office of Management and Budget, the Administrator of the Environmental Protection Agency, the U.S. Trade Representative, the Ambassador to the United Nations, the Chairman of the Council of Economic Advisors and finally the Administrator of the Small Business Association. As evidence, the president has many people at his disposal whose job it is to give him or her advice and carry out his or her orders to ensure that government operates efficiently.

Appointees and the Civil Service

The president appoints cabinet secretaries, but the bulk of the bureaucracy is part of what is referred to as the civil service. At the discretion of the president, approximately 2,000 positions, called presidential appointments, are filled as part of the bureaucracy. When the president rewards loyal allies or fundraisers with a bureaucratic appointment, it is called patronage. Before the professionalization of the bureaucracy, the president's influence in appointing the bureaucracy was much greater. The spoils system, in which the president could hand out jobs and rewards to supporters, was generally seen as corrupt. The spoils system was officially no longer used after the assassination of James Garfield by one of his supporters, angered that Garfield did not give him a desired bureaucratic appointment.

The assassination of President James Garfield

After Garfield's assassination, the United States moved toward a professional bureaucracy consisting of specialized experts, rather than presidential appointees. By 1900, the majority of the civil service was no longer subject to the spoils system, greatly increasing efficiency and reducing executive authority and the potential for corruption. At the state and city level, however, spoils systems lasted well into the 20th century. Civil servants were to be selected based on competence and knowledge instead of political loyalty beginning with the 1883 Pendleton Act, or Civil Service Reform Act. The Pendleton Act, which was progressively expanded in the 1978 Civil Service Reform Act, was meant to ensure that the civil service was free of political interference.

To become a civil servant, one must pass an entrance exam to try to ensure that job appointments are based on merit. The goal is to hire civil servants who are the most qualified to increase bureaucratic efficiency. Civil servants have strong protections against political interference which give them very high job security. While this can prevent the president firing civil servants he or she disagrees with, it also makes it very difficult to fire incompetent civil servants. Unlike elected politicians, the civil service does a better job of representing the demographic diversity of America.

Given that bureaucrats have the power to write policy, which determines how laws and directives passed by Congress and the president will be administered, many scholars question the role of the bureaucracy in relation to the system of checks and balances. While citizens can vote out bad presidents and members of Congress, civil servants are not fired based on public opinion, and this raises issues of democratic accountability. Some departments, such as the CIA, have very little transparency and for reasons of security, the public is not allowed to know what civil servants in the CIA are doing.

Seal of the C.I.A.

These realities raise concerns that the bureaucracy has expanded its power in such a way as to be detrimental to democracy. When high-ranking officials of the CIA refuse to answer questions in Congressional committee hearings, it can seem that such secret agencies are more powerful than Congress. This is a problem, as Congress is supposed to provide oversight on the bureaucracy. In extreme cases, Congress has the power to deny funds to a department of the bureaucracy. However, this would likely instigate a conflict with the president, who could retaliate by vetoing laws passed by Congress. The president's main check is the ability to appoint the heads of each department, but the president has the power to reorganize the bureaucracy and create new departments as well. The judiciary acts as less of a direct check; as it is mainly concerned with ensuring bureaucrats have not engaged in illegal activity.

In response to the fear of an undemocratic overgrowth of the bureaucracy's power, there have been increasing attempts since the 1970s to reform or reign in its power. The Sunshine Act of 1976 was meant to force many departments of the bureaucracy to open themselves up to public inspection by forcing them to hold public meetings and proceedings, with the intent of shining light onto their activities. This act was both meant to make the bureaucracy more transparent and increase public confidence in the bureaucracy by allowing a glimpse into their inner workings. Congress can also place sunset provisions onto government programs, which require the program to meet certain standards for it to be renewed. The goal of such provisions is to maintain congressional oversight and reel in the power of the bureaucracy. Congress and presidents have also tried to tie financial incentives to exemplary job performance, providing bonuses when bureaucrats increase efficiency.

Further measures have been added to try to protect whistleblowers, which are civil servants who report the misdeeds of their superiors. The results of such whistleblower protections have been mixed, as often the government does not like what the whistleblower has to say. Reporting illegal activity, corruption or inefficiency as a whistleblower is still a risky and dangerous activity. Some civil service whistleblowers are hailed as heroes, while others are demonized as traitors.

Another approach to reforming the bureaucracy began in the 1980s when President Ronald Reagan adopted an economic ideology known as neoliberal economics. Neoliberal economics argues that government is inherently inefficient because there is no profit motive or competition to drive it. Following these principles, presidents since Reagan have sought to privatize some aspects of the bureaucracy, in the belief that private corporations competing with each other can do a better job of delivering public services.

In reality, government services do not lend themselves to privatization because they tend to be unprofitable by nature – these services are often referred to as "public goods." As a result, privatized bureaucratic functions tend to create monopolies in which one company receives all government contracts without competition. This opens the door to corruption and spoils, as governments often give these contracts to companies operated by their political supporters.

President Ronald Reagan

For example, privatized prisons cannot compete in a free market with other prisons, as no one wants to go to prison. Such an example of privatization can be viewed as reintroduction of the spoilage system through the back door. Other problematic examples of privatization relate to the military, especially with the use of "no-bid" contracts in the Iraq War of 2003, where politically connected organizations were able to receive contracts from the federal government without even having to bid for the contract (e.g., Halliburton for logistics, Blackwater for private security).

Relationships Among These Four Institutions and Varying Balances of Power

The four institutions of national government have different powers but are constantly interacting with one another. The idea behind dividing the government into different branches is the principle of the separation of powers. The idea of separating governmental powers into different branches was developed by the French political theorist Montesquieu, whose work greatly influenced the constitutional framers. By separating the government into executive, legislative and judicial branches, the idea was that each branch would act as a check on the power of the other two. The goal of separating the powers is to ensure that no one branch accrues too much power. Montesquieu was particularly worried about unchecked executive power becoming despotic or tyrannical, and thus the legislative and judicial branches needed to have the power to keep the executive in line.

Montesquieu, French political theorist

By balancing these three powers equally, the goal was to ensure that no one branch could abuse its power and get away with it. In the United States, this system of separating powers is called checks and balances. The downside of such a system is that it tends to make it difficult to get anything done, as there are many ways another branch can block progress, leading to deadlock

The president, as the executive power, is elected independently of Congress, which is part of the separation of powers. It is much easier for the president to advance his or her agenda if the majority party in both houses of Congress is the same one the president belongs to. This is a major difference from the Westminster system used in Canada and the United Kingdom; in these governments, the executive power is simply the leader of the largest party of the legislature and is not elected independently. In the American system, the separation of the executive and legislative branches both diminishes and enhances the power of the executive. Compared to the Canadian or British systems, the president has less power than a Prime Minister given that the executive does not directly control the legislature in the United States as it is in Canada or the UK. In the United States, Congress can vote in a way contrary to the wishes of the president and Congress can even be controlled by a different party than the president. This checks the president's power and makes the position less powerful than a Prime Minister.

Conversely, the President of the United States' separation from the legislature makes the president more powerful in that he or she is not beholden to the wishes of their political party. If the Democratic Party in Congress, for example, were to turn against President Obama, Obama would remain president and be able to continue to exercise presidential authority. In a parliamentary system, if the Prime Minister loses the confidence of his or her party, the party can remove the Prime Minister from power without the need for an election. This happened recently in Australia, where the governing party decided they did not like the current Prime Minister, and replaced him with another member of their party, all without an election. This is impossible in the United States and is an example of how the president can be more powerful than a Prime Minister.

Each branch has a set of powers which they can exercise to check the power of other branches and maintain a balance between the three. The executive branch's primary check on the legislative branch is the presidential veto, which can prevent any law from passing. The president has the power to direct the course of a war, meaning that even though Congress is supposed to have the power to declare war, once the war is declared, it is up to the president to decide how that war will be fought. The president has the power to make decrees and declarations that override usual procedure, for example declaring a state of emergency in the event of a natural disaster or a terrorist attack. The president has the power to influence the agenda of the other branches through the State of the Union address, which outlines his or her agenda for the government directly to the American people. The president's ability to appoint judges and bureaucratic leaders is an important check on the judiciary and the bureaucracy, as they continue to serve at the discretion of the president. Finally, the president can check the power of the judiciary by granting pardons to anyone convicted of a crime by the court system. This check can be used if the president feels the court system has acted unfairly or has convicted an innocent person.

Unlike the other branches, Congress has an internal check and balance as it is divided into two houses. In a wider system of checks and balances, it is peculiar that the legislative branch should have an extra check and balance built into it. As discussed earlier, part of this stemmed from a distrust of popular democracy in the House of Representatives, but part of this design simply involved copying the United Kingdom. Without a clear separation of powers, the two-chamber legislature in the United Kingdom served as an example of a form of checks and balances, albeit not as sophisticated as what was established in the United States.

Since the UK had no separation of executive power, the two houses of Parliament in the legislative branch were meant to provide something of a check. Agreeing with this general rationale of checks and balances, a two-house, or bicameral legislature, was adopted in the U.S. Such a system has drawn criticism for creating a partisan deadlock and being unnecessary in the wider context of checks and balances. Many countries use unicameral systems, where the legislature is only one directly elected house, and there is no equivalent of a Senate.

The legislative branch in the United States balances the power of the president and judiciary by being able to write laws and control the budget. Congress is supposed to have the exclusive power to declare war, although this power has been ceded significantly to the executive branch in the post-World War II era. Congress can check the power of the President, the Supreme Court or the bureaucracy by initiating investigative committees which have the legal authority to compel truthful testimony from all witnesses. These investigative committees have played an important role in ensuring the president's power is kept under control.

For example, Congress initiated investigations into the Watergate scandal which revealed that President Richard Nixon had tried to bug the offices of political opponents and that he had attempted to cover up a break-in committed in an attempt to steal information from the opposition. This investigative committee eventually led to the resignation of President Nixon, before what appeared to be inevitable removal from office.

President Richard Nixon

The Senate has the power to check the President by being able to reject any presidential appointment, such as a Supreme Court judge or bureaucratic official. In 2005, President George W. Bush's nominee for the Supreme Court was criticized by the Senate, and it was expected that the Senate would have voted not to approve the nominee. To avoid the embarrassment of being rebuffed by the Senate, President Bush withdrew his nominee. The Senate also has the power to ratify or reject treaties with other countries, which is a check on the power of both the executive and the bureaucracy. The House of Representatives can impeach, and the Senate can remove members of the executive and judicial branches. This power is exercised rarely but is critical to balancing and checking power. Also, Congress has the power to change the number of Supreme Court justices and can overturn presidential vetoes with a supermajority vote.

The judicial branch's separation from Congress and the president is meant to ensure that they do not do anything that contravenes the Constitution. While the framers of the Constitution sought to create a judiciary branch that would be completely free of political influence, this separation of powers has diminished over time. Given that the president appoints members to the Supreme Court not on their legal merits but based on the president's belief that the justice will make rulings he or she agrees with, the Supreme Court's power is often conditional on the power of the President. In other countries, such as Canada, the Supreme Court members are appointed based on judicial merit, and it would create a contentious public debate were the Prime Minister to appoint a justice by his or her political views. In this sense, the judiciary in countries with a parliamentary system is often more independent of the political system, and more independent of the executive and legislative branches. Though the American system is based on the idea of separate powers, often this is not the reality.

The main checks that the judiciary, primarily in the form of the Supreme Court, can use to balance the power of the executive and legislative branches are numerous. Primarily, the Supreme Court can invalidate a law by determining it to be unconstitutional. This is an important power and checks on Congress, as it enables the judiciary to protect the rights of the minority against majority votes in Congress. This means that Congress cannot pass a law that violates an individual's rights as outlined in the Bill of Rights, even if the majority votes to violate these rights. This makes the judiciary an important check on the possible formation of a "tyranny of the majority," which can happen when the majority of a population votes in favor of taking away rights from a minority.

The Supreme Court also has the power of interpretation of laws, which means they can determine where and when any given law passed by Congress applies. This is an important power because often Congress passes laws that are vague and allow the potential for injustice, or when old laws need to be reinterpreted to make sense in the modern era. The judiciary is also responsible for policing its members, which means that if a judge or lawyer acts inappropriately, the court system should be the first ones to seek to punish them. Strict standards are applied to lawyers and judges to maintain the integrity of the justice system. If Congress has to intervene to remove a judge, this is considered a rather large failing of the justice system because it is supposed to police itself.

The appointed Cabinet, who are the heads of the departments of the bureaucracy is not only appointed by the president but also considered his or her senior advisors. This means that the Cabinet has something of a check on some aspects of the president's power as its members are supposed to advise the president on issues relating to their Cabinet department. Since the president is not an expert in everything, he or she often defers heavily to the experience and expertise of appointed Cabinet secretaries, giving them a great deal of power.

In parliamentary systems, Cabinet leaders, called ministers, are chosen by the Prime Minister from those elected to the legislature. The advantage of the American system is that the president can appoint experts in their field to lead government departments, without having to worry about whether they can get elected or not. The disadvantage is that the people can not democratically remove these Cabinet secretaries if they do a poor job.

Abraham Lincoln with his cabinet

Relative Powers

While the idea is that each branch should be equal in power to act as a sufficient check against the others, most political scientists agree this is not the case in reality. As has been discussed above, the power of the executive branch has been expanded in the modern era, at the expense of the legislative branch. Most experts agree that the judicial branch is by far the weakest. The primary check on power exercised by the Supreme Court, namely its ability to rule laws unconstitutional, was not granted in the Constitution but was a result of a court decision.

Even the Constitution sets the judiciary branch as having significantly less power than the other two. While the Supreme Court does have this power now, major rulings which render laws unconstitutional are relatively few and far between, demonstrating that Congress is significantly more powerful than the judiciary. By contrast, the Supreme Court of Canada struck down as unconstitutional at least one major law per year that was passed by the government of Prime Minister Stephen Harper from 2006 to 2015. Whether this was because the Canadian Supreme Court was more powerful than the American Supreme Court, or simply because the Canadian government under Harper tended to try to pass more overreaching laws than the U.S. Congress does, is open to debate.

U.S. President Barack Obama with Canadian Prime Minister Stephen Harper

The balance of power between the branches has seen major shifts throughout its history. As outlined above, the Supreme Court started very weak but carved out the power of judicial review for itself in an attempt to strengthen its power. Immediately after the Civil War, Congress passed some acts to make the president subordinate to Congress, including the Tenure of Office Act, and passed legislation to diminish the power of the presidential veto. With the onset of World War II, power shifted back to the President as he needed broad authority to conduct a major war.

Presidential powers continued to expand, especially under President Nixon who invoked national security as an excuse for greater presidential secrecy and power. Despite Nixon's fall from grace, his attempts to increase the power of the presidency in the name of national security set a precedent which has generally been followed by all presidents since.

Notes

Linkages Between Institutions and the Following:

While the three branches of government and the bureaucracy have a system of checks and balances to ensure no single branch can abuse its power, the institutions of American government are also influenced and checked by other political actors. The government does not operate in isolation, and there are some linkages between institutional, governmental authority and other aspects of society.

Public Opinion and Voters

As a democracy, the primary responsibility of the United States' government is to carry out the wishes of the American people. American citizens hold the ultimate check on the power of the president through their ability to elect the executive. If the voters feel that the president has not been doing a good job, they can exercise their power to elect someone else in the next election. While the president's constitutional role is not explicitly to represent the American people, if he or she ignores public opinion, their chances of re-election will be significantly diminished.

When the president has public opinion on his or her side, it becomes easier to advance the executive's agenda, especially if Congress is attempting to prevent the president's actions. However, in the president's second term in office, when he or she cannot be re-elected, public opinion becomes less of an influence as the president does not have to worry about being re-elected. Conversely, towards the end of their second term, many presidents start to consider how they will be remembered in history and continue to seek popular approval for their acts in the hope that they will be favorably remembered in the history books.

Since public opinion is so important, polling organizations play an important role by trying to convey what people think about an issue. Polling firms will contact a small number of people and ask what their opinion is on an issue, or if they approve or disapprove of the performance of the President or Congress. People often complain that polls are inaccurate, but using statistical sampling, polls can present a somewhat accurate assessment of the general popular opinion with an acceptable margin of error. These polls are extremely important because they discover the opinion of the people on any given issue, which helps the President and Congress decide where to give their support. Government is also interested in public opinion polls to successfully change its public messaging in an attempt to make people agree with government actions. In this sense, public opinion is a two-way street. The people's opinions can push the government, while the government itself continually tries to shape and manipulate public opinion.

Logo for the Gallup Corporation, one of the main polling firms of the U.S.

Congress, and especially the House of Representatives, is constitutionally expected to represent public opinion directly. Members of the House of Representatives are constantly concerned with being re-elected, as they have no term limits and their terms last only two years. Representatives usually pay close attention to public opinion in their home districts. This can often lead to clashes between a member of the House and their party if the member's district is opposed to a policy that their party favors at the national level. In situations such as this, the Whip will need to try to convince this member to vote with the party rather than with the district. Situations like this pose a dilemma for a member of the House, as voting against the wishes of those in the home district could mean not being re-elected. At the same time, voting against the wishes of one's political party could mean that the party will choose someone else to run in that district next election, making being re-elected impossible.

While Senators are subject to re-election, their longer six-year terms are meant to insulate them somewhat from the demands of public opinion. Senators were originally meant to be unelected to ensure that only wise and experienced people could become senators; their job is supposed to require them to consider issues outside the demands of public opinion. Being elected, however, makes them subject to the same need to appeal to voters in their home state as members of the House of Representatives, thus undermining the intent of the framers of the Constitution of making the Senate a bastion of experienced wisdom capable of acting as a buffer against public opinion.

Public opinion and voting play no role in the bureaucracy or federal judiciary, although lower court justices at the state and local level are often elected. Judges are to consider the law and Constitution, regardless of popular opinion. The bureaucracy, largely getting jobs through experience and expertise, are not subject to popular approval, even if the public may have opinions on the job they are doing.

Interest Groups

Taking part in a public interest group requires dedication to a cause apart from the desire for personal gain. If a cause is successful, it is theoretically beneficial to everyone, even those who did not take part in lobbying the government. Political scientists call this the "free rider" effect, and it demonstrates how people uninterested in political activity can benefit from the hard work of others.

To advance their cause, lobby groups engage in a variety of tactics. Primarily, they want access to a government representative, so that they can directly tell a member of Congress or the President about their cause. Given how many lobby groups there are relative to the number of politicians, gaining access can be very difficult. One of the primary ways that lobby groups gain access to politicians is through large campaign donations. A wealthy interest group will donate a large sum of money to a politician trying to get elected, and if that politician wins, he or she will feel a debt of gratitude for the large donation and offer more access to the donors. This is a controversial aspect of lobbying, as it greatly favors corporations and the wealthy, who can essentially buy access to politicians. Another effective method is to recruit a high-profile celebrity to the cause. Celebrities command much public attention, and if a politician should refuse to meet with a celebrity promoting a popular cause, this can hurt the politician's reputation. As such, many interest groups actively seek out celebrities to endorse their campaign as a way of winning political access.

If interest groups cannot win direct access, they will attempt to influence politicians via public opinion campaigns. This is usually accomplished by running high profile media campaigns about an issue, to get the public talking and asking questions. If a group can raise public awareness of an issue to a high enough level, it can become impossible for politicians to ignore it. Such campaigns often rely on celebrities and require large sums of money for advertising, again favoring wealthier and corporate interest groups. If both of these methods fail, then lobby groups can turn to the judicial system and attempt to instigate change through litigation. For example, the National Association for the Advancement of Colored People (NAACP) used lawsuits in the 1940s and 1950s to overturn racial segregation laws.

President John F. Kennedy meets with representatives from the NAACP:

Dr. E. Franklin Jackson (left) and Bishop Stephen G. Spottswood (right)

If all three of these methods fail to bring change or the attention of politicians, then interest groups can engage in protests and civil disobedience to force politicians, the media, the legal system, and public opinion to pay attention to their cause. Having been ignored by all of the forms of government, Martin Luther King Jr. led the civil rights movement in non-violent protests and civil disobedience to finally bring the cause of racial equality to the attention of the government. While such disruption techniques tend to be a last resort of frustrated interest groups, if the government refuses to pay attention to important issues, protests and civil disobedience can be a very effective means of political action.

Other successful outcomes of civil disobedience and protest campaigns included the eight- hour workday (reduced from the previously allowed 12-hour workday), the women's suffrage movement, which culminated in women winning the right to vote and, more recently, the gay rights movement which has effected legislative change in regard to the rights of gay, lesbian and transsexual Americans and led to more knowledge and acceptance of the LGBTQ community. Such protest-based lobbying tends to be favored by those who lack the money to buy access to politicians.

Interest groups also serve to hold members of the bureaucracy accountable. They report violations of policy to the media and lawmakers and challenge them in court. They sometimes demand the removal of offending government workers who are obstinate. In America, many members of the bureaucracy are directly elected by the public. This can include district attorneys, chiefs of police, county clerks and more. Interest groups can influence these elections.

A good example is from the civil rights era in Alabama. When Congress passed the Voting Rights Act, Selma's black population turned out at the next election and defeated the racist chief of police. Members of interest groups may also be members of the bureaucracy.

Interest groups interact with the courts as well. They are usually the first to bring court cases against civil servants who violate the law and sometimes even the government if there is a case to be made that Congress may have violated the constitution. A current case of how interest groups use the court system is the lawsuit which was filed in November 2015, by the Libertarian Party and the Green Party of America as joint plaintiffs, against the Federal Debate Commission. They complain that the Commission refuses to allow any presidential candidates other than the Republican and Democrat party candidates to participate in the election debates, which the plaintiffs see as a violation of the Sherman Anti-Trust Act.

Political Parties

Political parties play an important role in the legislative branch, as the leader of the majority party in the House and the Senate control the legislative agenda. When different parties control the executive, the House of Representatives and the Senate, however, obstruction and deadlock can occur. The system of checks and balances which is meant to prevent abuse can be used to prevent legislation altogether due to partisanship. This tendency to engage in partisan-based obstruction and blocking leads to political parties developing poor reputations and generally low public support for Congress. The system of checks and balances designed by the framers of the Constitution was meant for a situation without political parties, and thus they could not have foreseen how introducing parties into this system of checks and balances could lead to government shutdowns and unnecessary legislative and executive obstacles.

As with Congress, the president is a member of a political party. For a short time at the beginning of the Republic, the president and vice-president were of different parties. The winner of a presidential election would become the president and the second-place candidate – the president's political opponent – would become the vice-president. This was changed in the early nineteenth century. Presently, the president and vice-president are elected in separate votes, but the candidates always have running-mates from the same party, and there has not been a case of a president being elected without his running mate. Once in office, a president may be facing members of another party in the upper bureaucracy, and federal courts and opponents may hold the majority in either or both houses of Congress. This demands that a president be a strong negotiator. Where a president has more partisan power is with the executive; an incoming president appoints all members of the executive he or she will be working with – the Secretaries of defense, justice, education, etc. – and these are usually appointed on a partisan basis. Sometimes, however, presidents have appointed executive members from a different party, as long as they share some vision in common with the president. The important thing to note is that the president has the power to appoint executives of his party and do so immediately on being sworn in, whereas judges can only be appointed if and when a vacancy occurs, and the president can not select members of Congress.

The process of appointing many bureaucrats who are members of one's party is called the "spoils system." In exchange for support during elections, party members expect to be rewarded with government appointments and often are, while vocational merit is a second-place consideration. This is the way appointments to the bureaucracy are made in America and has been since the beginning of multi-party democracy in the early nineteenth century. Partisanship in the bureaucracy often affects the way policies are implemented – in extreme cases, even to the extent of blatant violations of the law.

Although government workers are expected to uphold the law with impartiality in theory, in reality, they are opinionated human beings and voters as much as any politician is. They can be held accountable for egregious breaches of the public trust, but there are many ways that an unsympathetic bureaucracy can retard the implementation of a policy. For example, they can interpret the wording of a policy in extreme ways to obstruct, or they can take excessive amounts of time to do what is required of them. Adding on qualifications which are not expressly omitted in the law is one of the most frequently used strategies. The most publicized recent example of this is the finding, in 2014, that the I.R.S. made partisan decisions in applying a political funding law. I.R.S. employees were accused of deliberately failing to apply a tax exemption to a disproportionate number of political activist groups which supported conservative causes and candidates. The I.R.S. employees are overwhelmingly Democrats. The Department of Justice closed the case in 2015 with no convictions, but for many, this only raised the question of whether or not the Department of Justice is partisan.

Internal Revenue Service Building on Constitution Avenue in Washington, D.C.

The federal court system includes the Supreme Court, 94 federal courts, 13 courts of appeal and two special courts. Nine judges sit on the Supreme Court and rule as a committee. Judges on all of these levels are appointed by the President and need to be approved by the Senate. Appointments are usually partisan. This matters because, while it might seem like a judge cannot choose the outcome of a trial based on his or her personal opinion, the reality is that compelling legal arguments can be made to support any point of view in a complex disagreement. Only those disagreements which are the most difficult to resolve get to the Supreme Court, since its very purpose is to rule on such extreme cases. Thus, partisanship matters very much. Presidents tend to appoint federal judges who are sympathetic to the beliefs held by the president and his or her party. At times when the President and the majority in the Senate are from different parties, it can be difficult for the president to make appointments since an unsympathetic Senate can block them. Presidents get around this problem by negotiation. Presidents can agree to things the majority party wants to get some support for an appointment. When a Senate is unsympathetic, the president does not need the support of the entire opposing party; all that the president needs to do is sway the minimum number of Senators needed to win the vote. Alternatively, a president can choose a moderate candidate who is likelier not to be rejected by the other party.

As with appointments, the outcomes of Supreme Court decisions often hinge on swaying at least one judge who is of an opposing point of view. For example, in 2015 there were five Republican appointees and four Democratic appointees among the judges.

However, many "liberal" rulings were made because at least one of the conservative judges was convinced to rule with the more liberal ones. Such rulings are the upholding of the Health Care Act and gay marriage rights. In *Obergefell v. Hodges* (June 26th, 2015) the Supreme Court ruled that all States must license gay marriages. This was a landmark decision which puts all legal contention over the legitimacy of gay marriage in the United States to rest. There were four dissenting judges, but the ruling passed with the support of one sympathetic conservative judge. A similar voting pattern in an earlier case upheld the Health Care Act when it was challenged in the Supreme Court.

The Media

The news media and social media are two of the most vital tools the public has as an indirect check on government abuse of power. Members of the public can expose incidents of corruption and violations of the law by politicians and bureaucrats, either to the news agencies or personally, on social media. However, these tools are not infallible. Political parties demonstrated their willingness and ability to co-opt the news media, beginning shortly after the development of "muckraking journalism" in the 1890s. News articles are now used to shape public opinion, not only to report facts in clinical and non-partisan ways. Thus, social media has an additional use as a public check on the news media. The news media can be a tool for exposing incidents of corruption and violations of the law by civil servants and politicians. However, to the extent that the targets are members of the party that the media staff are sympathetic too, the media can use strategies such as defending the accused or squelching coverage of the story. Social media keeps the formal news media honest as well because any member of the public can publish something which is not being covered in the news or expose irresponsible journalism. A weakness of social media is that it is unfiltered: Inaccurate information can be posted with no professional editing.

The Bureaucracy regulates the media. The Federal Communications Commission acts as a kind of "media police," and its primary job is to ensure that broadcasters obey public decency standards. If a TV station continually violates these standards, the FCC can cancel its license, and the station will be shut down. Usually, the FCC imposes fines based on individual incidents. For example, the FCC handed out significant fines to radio talk show host Howard Stern for his use of profanity on the air, and to CBS for violating public decency over the 2004 Super Bowl halftime show in which singer Janet Jackson had her infamous "wardrobe malfunction." Many have argued that the FCC's public decency rules amount to censorship and that the American people are mature enough to decide for themselves what to watch and what not to watch. While the FCC is controversial in this respect, it generally does not censor political matters and works to promote fairness during political campaigns.

Logo of the Federal Communications Commission

Congress and the president have a two-directional power relationship. The government has created the goals which the F.C.C. enforces as well as laws which it must follow in its operations. The FCC sets out the rules for how political campaigns during an election are allowed to use the broadcast media. The FCC enforces the *equal time rule*, ensuring that every broadcaster must give equal time to all candidates who request it. For example, if a local news station allows a candidate to run a one-minute advertisement in prime time, the opposing candidates can demand to also receive a one-minute advertisement in the same time slot. The goal of this rule is to prevent a media outlet from favoring one candidate over another. It is vital to note, however, that although America is a multi-party democracy with many registered alternative parties who run candidates, the equal time rule mentioned above largely only applies to the Republican and Democratic parties. Parties in America are categorized by law into "Major," "Minor" and "New" parties, with different allowances of media time and campaign funding.

The second major FCC rule for political campaigns is the *right to rebuttal*. This means that a broadcast outlet must offer a chance for a candidate to respond if another candidate criticizes or attacks them on air. This rule is meant to prevent the media from allowing one candidate to attack the others without the others being able to respond publicly to those attacks.

The Fairness Doctrine was the third FCC political rule. It has not been enforced since the mid-1980s and was subsequently removed as a rule in 2011. This rule required broadcasters to balance out viewpoints in the media and required them always to present multiple sides of a controversial issue. Many political scientists believe that the decline in enforcement and the eventual overturning of this rule has contributed to partisan polarization, as news outlets no longer have to present opposing viewpoints to the public.

It is important to remember that the FCC can only regulate broadcasts over the air, which means that cable television and the internet are exempt. The FCC has sought to expand its reach to regulate all media, finding some supporters in Congress and some opposed to this evolution.

State and Local Governments

The United States is a federal system, meaning that there are layers of governmental authority. The national government is the top layer of government, with state governments and local governments below it regarding overall power. Article VI of the Constitution sets out the supremacy clause, which declares that the national government has power over the state governments and that state governments cannot pass laws that contravene the Constitution or laws passed by Congress at the national level. State governments, as such, do have the power to pass their laws, which makes them relatively powerful units of government.

The national government has some exclusive powers which state governments do not. Its enumerated powers involve the ability to declare war, manage the currency system and regulate commerce. This means that, for example, Alaska could not declare war on Canada, nor could it make its currency. The national government has implied powers, meaning it deals with issues that are of national concern, such as building interstate highways or regulating the public airwaves. The inherent powers of the federal government mean that it has the responsibility to protect its citizens. This means that if Canada decided to attack Alaska, it would be the job of the national government to intervene and defend Alaska as the federal government cannot simply leave a state to fend for itself in the event of an attack. The Constitution also outlines powers that the national government is not allowed to exercise, called prohibited powers. This means that Congress cannot tax the exports of an individual state and cannot tell a state how to choose electors in the Electoral College.

Each state government also uses a three-branch structure and has its judiciary, but the balance of power and number of checks is often different in each state; the Governor may hold the most power in some states, while in others the legislative branch is the most powerful entity. The amount of relative power of states has been an issue throughout American history, beginning with the arguments in the Federalist Papers (which led to Jefferson's anti-federalist political party), and during the Civil War, where the rights of states to set their laws relating to slavery were challenged. In the modern era after World War II, most scholars agree that the federal government has become much more powerful than individual states.

Painting of Thomas Jefferson (leader of the anti-federalists) and Alexander Hamilton (author of The Federalist Papers) with George Washington in the Capitol building

More recently, however, state governments have been driving the national agenda on social issues. Individual states, such as Vermont, allowed same-sex marriage and had pushed the federal government to decide the issue nationally. Some states, notably Colorado, have legalized marijuana despite it being illegal at the federal level. States passing legislation which forces the federal government to act on ignored or controversial issues have been viewed by some political scientists as a resurgence of state power.

The Constitution does not mention any specific powers for local governments. Courts have interpreted this to mean that local governments have no independent authority and are purely under the power of the state. Individual states can then create or abolish municipal governments as they see fit. After the financial crisis of 2008, many cities faced serious budget issues. Many state governments intervened by either providing funds or taking control of the city services themselves. Such acts were controversial because they directly undermined the authority of local government, but the states were well within their constitutional rights to intervene. In 1995, the state government of Illinois was upset at the poor condition of schools in Chicago. In an attempt to fix this issue, they completely re-arranged the structure of the Chicago government, taking away almost all authority over the school system from the local board of education and giving this power to the mayor.

To create a local government, the state creates a charter outlining what powers the local government will have. These charters usually grant some degree of autonomy to local decisions, but the localities have to pay for programs without financial help from the state. Most states have different types of charters which grant different levels of power depending on the size of the population. Most states differentiate between a town, a village, a township, a county, and a city, granting each a different charter with a different set of powers and responsibilities. For example, a large city charter may allow a city to have its police force, while a village charter may leave policing in the hands of the state government. Most local governments consist of an elected mayor and elected city council. Some smaller towns use town hall meetings to make decisions. The structure of local governments is completely up to the state, and thus the state can decide what sort of structure these governments should have.

One notable exception to state control of local government is reservations. These are pockets of land which are managed by Native Americans under the authority of the U.S. Bureau of Indian Affairs, rather than the state government. The structure of government on reservations usually takes the form of an elected council. Since these territories are outside of the control of state governments, reservations can pass laws which differ from the state they are contained within. For example, while gambling is illegal in New York State, reservations within New York can pass laws to make casinos legal. While the reservation council is supposed to have sovereignty over the land, making it the highest authority (over the state or federal government) the reality of the situation has been much more complex, resulting in various conflicts.

Seal of the U.S. Bureau of Indian Affairs

Please, leave your Customer Review on Amazon

Chapter 5

Public Policy

Public policy is the result of interactions and dynamics among actors, interests, institutions, and processes. The formation of policy agendas, the enactment of public policies by Congress and the president and the implementation and interpretation of policies by the bureaucracy and the courts are all stages in the policy process. Policy and issue networks in the domestic and foreign policy areas, affected by federalism, interest groups, parties and elections on policy processes and policymaking in the federal context, can also exact a significant influence.

Notes

Policymaking in a Federal System

The *policy* is the set of procedures and rules to be followed to achieve a set of specific outcomes. When the government decides on an issue, the policy is created to enact that decision and guide administrators. Policy is different from legislation because legislation creates laws which are meant to compel or prohibit certain behaviors; policy is meant to provide guidelines toward the achievement of certain goals. Policymaking, in its most basic form, is choosing how to enact a decision. For example, if the government decides it wants to reduce poverty, it will then make policies which are designed to achieve the outcome of reducing poverty.

The policymaking process is complex. Even though policy is meant to achieve a specific outcome, the policymaking process often results in unintended consequences of decisions (e.g., the Iraq War leading to ISIS). It is especially difficult to ensure that policymaking leads to the desired outcome in a large, complex federal system, such as the United States government. With many possible actors and branches of government involved, the policymaking process requires a large number of government employees working on these issues. The complexity of the policymaking process is one of the primary reasons a large bureaucracy becomes necessary in modern societies.

Policy can be made by all branches of the government, including the bureaucracy. State and local governments can make their policy, but they cannot make policy that directly contravenes federal policy without instigating lawsuits and involvement from the judicial branch. In the modern era of American government (post World War II), the overall policy agenda is largely driven by the president. In particular, the Executive Office of the president, created in 1939 by President Roosevelt, is essential in the policymaking process.

Official logo of the Executive Office of the President of the United States

When the president wants to achieve a certain outcome, he or she will consult with the White House Chief of Staff who will bring together leaders of important advisory offices. The president rarely makes decisions alone, but usually consults with heads of the various bureaucratic offices and Cabinet members. Once the president makes a decision, much of the policymaking specifics are handed over to experts from the bureaucracy. For example, if the president wants to enact a policy to make the internet more accessible in schools, he or she would consult with the Office of Science and Technology Policy and the Secretary of Education. Bureaucrats would then implement the policy in those offices.

Official logos of some U.S. Federal agencies

The role of Cabinet members in the policy process has evolved. Cabinet members originally had a great deal of autonomous influence. The president typically appointed advisors who were experts in their fields and, as such, could initiate policy themselves. Most political scientists observe that the independence of the Cabinet has been on the decline since the Kennedy administration, with his trusted advisors, who were often allowed to exercise the roles of their offices with executive-like authority. Increasingly, policy originating from the executive branch has been exclusively initiated by the president.

Cabinet members have shifted to the roles of advisors and administrators who carry out the president's orders, rather than people who come to the president with their ideas and policy agendas. In the modern era, the White House staff tends to control the policymaking agenda, whereas under Franklin Roosevelt for example, policymaking authority was more distributed to the various Cabinet members and departments of the bureaucracy. The decline in the influence of Cabinet members correlates to the general increase in Executive power in the modern era.

An example of the control the White House now exerts over the policy agenda can be seen in President Obama's intervention in the work of the Attorney General in regards to prisoners in Guantanamo Bay. The Attorney General had decided that, as part of Obama's decision to try to close the Guantanamo Bay prison holding terrorism suspects, that some of these suspects should be tried in a criminal court in New York City. The Attorney General initiated this policy himself, but after public outrage, President Obama stepped in and decided these trials would not happen. Further policymaking on the Guantanamo Bay issue was then shifted away from the Attorney General's office and has since come from inside the White House.

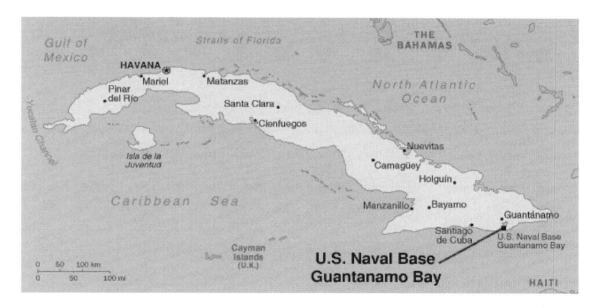

Guantanamo Bay map

Policymaking in the legislative branch usually stems from the work of committees and sub-committees who specialize in specific areas. The judicial branch can make policy through its interpretation of the law. By a ruling that creates a new interpretation, policy changes to implement it. The bureaucracy is often tasked with fine-tuning policy details and thus has some room to maneuver in the crafting of policy. While the bureaucracy cannot make decisions or act independently of the executive branch, if the policy that comes from the president is vague, the bureaucracy must transform it into specific actionable steps for administrators to take. The president might decide he or she wants to increase energy efficiency and that this should be done by promoting energy efficient housing. In this case, the bureaucracy would develop specific policy incentives, such as tax rebates for buying green homes that would lead to the outcome the president wants.

The Policy Cycle

The policymaking process generally goes through steps which political scientists use to analyze how policy is made. The first step is *agenda-setting* which involves the government identifying that a problem exists and needs to be acted upon. Problems can come to the attention of the government through a variety of means. Interest groups can lobby the government, activists can engage in protests, and the media can bring issues to the attention of the government. Next, the policy formation process step involves considering a variety of options and methods to deal with the established problem. This may involve the president consulting with advisors, or hearings and discussions within a legislative committee. The goal of this step is, generally, to discuss and formulate options that could be used to solve the problem.

The next step is *decision-making*, where all of the previously considered options are discussed, and a choice is made as to which best addresses the issue at hand. This decision could be to enact some policy to address the problem, to pass the issue to the legislature to create a law to deal with it, to ignore the problem, or to dismiss it as not a problem.

After a decision is made, the next step is *policy implementation*, where the actors involved figure out how to translate their intended policy into action. Implementation is usually done at the bureaucratic level, as government agencies create guidelines, detail procedures and allocate funding to put the decision into practice.

The final step is *policy evaluation*, which assesses how effective the policy implementation step was at turning the decision into action to solve the problem. In this step, those inside and outside the government evaluate the policy and try to determine if it successfully solved the problem or not. If the policy failed to solve the problem, the policy cycle could start over at any step.

Types of Policy

Policies can be broken up into different types depending on how they are implemented and what sorts of goals they seek to accomplish. The type of policy a government may seek to implement depends on the problem being addressed, as well as the general ideological orientation of the government. For example, whether a government seeks to implement a redistributive policy to solve an issue tends to be driven more by ideological beliefs than whether this is the most suitable way to address a problem. The major policy types are distributive, redistributive, regulatory and constituent.

Distributive policies are those who seek to distribute government goods to the population. Examples would include funding schools, building highways and promoting public safety. *Redistributive policies*, by contrast, seek to reallocate government goods from one sector of the population to another. For example, if the government is seeking to increase economic equality, it may make wealthier people pay more taxes to allow poorer people to pay fewer taxes. This would be an example of redistributive policy. *Regulative policies* attempt to compel the behavior of individuals or organizations by putting in place limitations. These sorts of policies work best to control excessive behaviors. Examples would include speed limits, limits on pollution for industry and limitations on the types of stock trading that are possible. The *constituent policy* creates an authoritative body to deal with a problem. For example, after the 9/11 terrorist attacks, President Bush created the Department of Homeland Security to solve the problem of keeping Americans safe from terrorist attacks.

President Bush signs the Homeland Security Appropriations Act of 2004

Due to the system of checks and balances between the three branches of the federal government, the policy process in the United States is somewhat drawn out. Policy proposals must filter through various branches of government and are subject to interest group lobbying throughout. When Congress is studying an issue, they will often hear compelling arguments from interest groups who are against or in favor of an issue or believe an entirely different approach should be taken toward the issue. Government tends not to act quickly on an emerging issue of public concern, and the policy change process is often referred to as *incrementalism*, meaning change comes slowly, bit by bit.

The process of legalizing same-sex marriage is an example of policy incrementalism on the federal level. The issue first received public awareness in the 1970s when LGBTQ activists attempted to marry and were denied. Continued activism eventually led to court challenges and rulings throughout the 1990s, which led Congress to pass (with the support of President Clinton) the 1996 Defense of Marriage Act, specifically banning same-sex marriage on a Federal level. In the early 2000s, courts began to rule that same-sex marriage should be legal, which spurred state legislatures to consider making policy on the issue, with some states moving to legalize. Most changes came at the state level, but meanwhile, the federal government was continually being lobbied by both sides of the issue. Eventually, some states adopted same-sex civil union clauses as an incremental compromise. By 2011, the government no longer actively enforced the Defense of Marriage Act, but would not overturn it either.

U.S. President Bill Clinton signs the Defense of Marriage Act in 1996

The executive branch led policy while Congress was still deeply split on the issue. Since Congress alone has lawmaking powers, the Executive could not overturn the law, decide not to enforce it. As more and more state courts and legislatures passed rulings on the legality of same-sex marriage, eventually a case was brought to the Supreme Court in 2015. The Supreme Court ruled that all bans on same-sex marriage be unconstitutional and effectively legalized it across the country. Many same-sex marriage advocates often complained about the slow pace of policy change coming from the president and Congress. The fact that this change ended up coming from the judicial branch demonstrates the slow and incremental nature of policy change in the American federal system.

Notes

THE FORMATION OF POLICY AGENDAS

Policy agenda formation refers to the process by which certain issues are raised to the status of demanding government action. This is the first, and generally the most important step in the policy cycle. Just getting the government to pay attention to a certain issue can often be a huge accomplishment, even if no policy changes are made. The formation of policy agendas is very important, being the primary mechanism through which citizens, corporations and interest groups can try to get the government to act on issues they care about.

There are a variety of ways an issue can be raised to a matter of national concern, placing it on the government agenda for action. In many cases, issues get placed on the policy agenda because they arise as part of a new trend or changing circumstances. For example, as the internet became more prevalent in daily life through the late 1990s and into the 2000s, it became an issue that government felt it must make policy on to keep up with changing technological trends. Often this trend-based policymaking is reactive in nature; governments see overall changes in society and generally act after the fact. They can see these changes as a good thing, and try to encourage the trend, or they can see them as negative and enact policy to try to reverse the change.

Major events can also be strong drivers of forming new policy agendas. The media gives major events coverage, pushing issues to the forefront of citizens' and politicians' minds, which often leads to policy change. When something exceptional happens, it becomes front and center in both the minds of the public and government officials. Given the prominence of major events in the media, such events are often strong drivers of policy change. After the 9/11 terrorist attacks, the government quickly brought about policy changes to try to prevent future attacks and increase national security.

In certain circumstances, government policy is dramatically sped up for more immediate results. The speedy policy has been criticized by the advocates of incrementalism. They see fast government action in the wake of a major event as leading to poorly thought out policy that can have negative consequences down the line. An example was President Bush's Patriot Act, which was quickly passed in the wake of 9/11, but was widely criticized as curtailing civil liberties. Incrementalists argued that such dramatic changes should have been carefully considered, like other issues, and the urgency to act led the government to create and pass bad legislation.

President Bush signs the Patriot Act

Interest groups, social movements, and advocacy from individual citizens can provide a strong impetus to put an issue on the national agenda for policy action. Interest groups lobby the government, often spending large amounts of money to hire professional lobbyists who spend all their time directing government attention to a group's issue. Lobby groups can also donate large sums of money to the campaigns of political candidates, which may buy them direct access to members of Congress to advocate for issues they want to push to the national policy agenda. Often this is practiced through promising well-paid jobs to members of the bureaucracy and/or politicians when they leave office, known as the "revolving door" between government office and the sector of the private industry they are tasked with regulating.

Social movements rely on the large numbers of people participating rather than large sums of money to get the government to pay attention to their issue. When the numbers of people involved in these movements (for example the Civil Rights movement in the 1960s) becomes large enough, eventually the government is forced to address the issues they raise. This may take time, but social movements tend to have a snowball effect. They start small and with little attention, but once a social movement reaches a critical mass of supporters and participants, media coverage increases, and this usually forces the government to address the issue. In some cases, individual citizens can push an issue onto the policy agenda. This is rare, but occasionally a citizen meeting or exchanging letters with a politician can convince the politician of the need to act on an issue. This can be done by meeting with one's local representative or writing letters to politicians.

Leaders of the Civil Rights March on Washington (1963)

Politicians themselves sometimes drive the policy agenda. Someone who is passionately interested in a specific issue may run for Congress and win, allowing him or her to use his or her influence as a politician to advocate for a certain issue. Sometimes politicians become convinced of the worthiness of a cause after they are in office and decide to dedicate their time to push for that issue. Al Gore, for example, became an advocate for dealing with climate change after he first became a politician. Once he realized the severity of the issue, he began to attempt to put the issue on the national agenda.

Once issues are raised to a national agenda, policy-makers need to decide which ones to act upon. Deciding which issues to move forward on involves a variety of considerations. To choose, they must consider if there are any constitutional issues involved and if this issue might be better dealt with through the court system. Returning to the example of same-sex marriage, President Obama decided not to use executive power to push this issue onto the national policy agenda because he believed it was a constitutional issue that was better dealt with by the judiciary. The second consideration for policy-makers is whether or not the issue under consideration is a new problem or not. Since the policy process is slow, and Congress does not want to waste its time passing redundant legislation, politicians must carefully consider whether an issue might be dealt with under existing legislation or could be tacked onto another issue's policy agenda.

The final and perhaps most important consideration is what would happen if the government does not act on this issue. Congress and the Executive want to be actively doing things in response to the demands of the people. This means that if the government ignores an issue that has been brought to their attention by many people, there could be major consequences. Consequences include not being re-elected if an opposing party promises action on the issue. Such issues that one party may deem unimportant, but the other party sees as extremely important, are often called *wedge issues*. The party that believes the issue is important will use it aggressively to rally voters to their side.

Wedge issues are often things that one group of people care passionately about, but the majority of the population are not interested in. Supporting action on wedge issues can win many votes and is unlikely to cost votes because those who are against action on the issue think it irrelevant. The other major consequences for inaction on a publicly-raised issue are potential long-term consequences. If scientists tell the government that they need to reduce greenhouse gas emissions; the government needs to decide if the long-term consequences of inaction are worth it or not.

Often the government will not act on an issue because they believe that in a few months the issue will be forgotten about. Politics is inherently risky because the outcomes of policy action can never be known in advance. Governments must continually weigh the risks of not acting against the risks of acting. While sometimes issues do blow over (as they are not that important and were over-hyped), often when the government misjudges the importance of an issue and does not act strongly enough or over-reacts in a way that becomes widely resented.

There are many ways that issues can become included in the policy agenda; which of these methods is most powerful and most effective at driving the policy agenda? Political scientists have developed three competing theories to explain who has the real power to make the policy agenda.

Pluralists believe that issues become part of the policy agenda by different groups and individuals pushing the government to act. They believe that the government is constantly bombarded by demands to act on various issues from people and groups with a range of views. According to *pluralism theory*, this bottom-up bombardment with demands drives the policy agenda in a democracy and gives the people the real power.

In contrast to the bottom-up idea of pluralist theory, the *elitist theory* argues that policy is top down. This means that the issues that make it onto the national policy agenda are those that are personally important to the president. Elitist theory acknowledges that corporations with lots of money can exert considerable influence over what issues are acted on and that policymaking is driven by the interests of the wealthy, rather than the average American. The elitist theory claims that issues raised by the people, the media, interest groups, and social movements are generally ignored, and that power over the policy agenda comes from the top. There is a growing body of political scholarship supporting this position, the most well-known of which is a study published by Princeton University in 2014, which showed that over the last 30 years, public opinion had had zero correlation with the policies implemented by the government.

The third theory is *institutional theory,* which argues that the bureaucracy sets the policy agenda based on issues that are important to those institutions. For example, the Department of Homeland Security pushes terrorism as a major issue because it is in their interest to keep this issue relevant to maintain their institutional and bureaucratic power. Institutional theorists argue that policy agenda-setting power is neither exerted top-down by the president and large corporations, nor bottom up by the people, but is almost exclusively in the hands of the bureaucracy, who seek to strengthen institutional power at the expense of both big money and the wider population.

Counter Terrorist Unit seal for the Department of Homeland Security

Economic Policy

The types of policy agendas can be divided into foreign and defense policy, economic policy and social welfare and domestic policy. Economic policy is driven by the concerns of political economy. *Political economy* is the interaction between government and markets. When governments enact policies meant to shape the economic situation, they engage in political economy. One of the major issues in political economy is the balance between government regulation and capitalist markets.

There are many different theories within political economy dedicated to arguing what the exact amount of government regulation of markets should be. Some theorists argue that the government should heavily regulate all of the economies, some argue that regulation is only needed in certain industries and sectors and others argue that government regulation should be kept to a minimum. As with all contentious issues in politics, there is not a single, correct theory and as such, elections play an important part in allowing the people to indicate what direction economic policy should take by voting for a party whose economic policy platform they agree with.

However, there have been broad, global economic trends which have tended to dictate the direction of American economic policy. Before the stock market crash of 1929 and the Great Depression, it was believed that governments should generally refrain from regulating domestic markets and should instead regulate external markets. These policies worsened the economy during the Great Depression, however, and it became necessary for the government to intervene in the domestic economy to correct market failures, a policy which has now become commonplace. Beginning in the 1980s, there was another shift, this time toward deregulation and the opening of borders to transnational corporations.

The role of the United States has been extremely important in setting global economic trends. President Roosevelt's New Deal to end the Great Depression became a model for countries around the world, as did President Reagan's embrace of deregulation and government non-intervention. President Obama's stimulus plan to get out of the 2008 financial crisis was also viewed as a model by the rest of the world. American economic policy not only influences the domestic economy but can also dramatically influence the economic policy of other countries.

President Roosevelt signs the Tennessee Authority Act, part of the New Deal

The primary economic policy tool is the *annual budget*. Depending on the economic theory that the government adheres to, the budget can be used for a variety of purposes. By changing tax rates, the government can seek to promote economic equality, or it can give tax breaks to the wealthy. The overall amount of spending in the budget is also a policy tool. Unlike when a business or individual manages their finances, the government spending more money than it brings in can be economically beneficial. If this happens, the government is said to be running a deficit.

Deficit spending can help stimulate the private economy, as the government pumps more money into the economy making up for the slack produced by a decline in private economic activity. Conversely, when the government brings in more money (primarily through taxation) than it spends, this is called a budget surplus. While some theories of political economists argue that running budget surpluses and deficits can be an important tool to stimulate sluggish economies and slow down bubble economies, other theories argue that this form of fiscal policy is ineffective.

The second major form of government economic policy is called *monetary policy*. Unlike fiscal policy, monetary policy is controlled entirely by the bureaucracy in the form of the Federal Reserve Bank. The Federal Reserve Bank determines what the interest rate should be, and can, therefore, stimulate the economy by making it cheaper to borrow money by lowering the interest rate, or it can slow down the economy by making loans more expensive by raising the interest rate. Monetary policy and fiscal policy work best in combination, but since different branches of government control them, cooperation and collaboration do not always occur. The Federal Reserve Bank may see the economy as sluggish and want to lower interest rates, while Congress may claim the economy is doing well and seek to run a budget stimulus, thus slowing down the economy. When these two forms of economy policy work in opposition to each other, they can cancel each other out, causing the government's economic policy agenda to fail.

The Federal Reserve headquarters in Washington, D.C.

Some important issues directly affect the economic policymaking process. The ideological approach to these issues determines what sorts of economic policy will be implemented. Four major economic factors come into play when configuring the direction of economic policy. The first is *inflation*, which is the overall average increase in the price of goods and services across the country. The bureaucracy monitors inflation by choosing a "basket of goods," which are common items that people often buy, and tracking the changes in price over time. So long as the economy is growing, prices will go up; this is called inflation. Inflation can become a problem if it gets too high, often called hyperinflation, as it makes money less valuable. What could be bought this week for $5 might cost $10 next week in a situation of hyperinflation. Since wages usually do not grow at the same rate as prices during a period of hyperinflation, it is very bad for the economy and makes everyone poorer. Generally, economic policy-makers want small amounts of limited and controlled inflation.

The inverse of inflation is *deflation*, which has much worse consequences than hyperinflation. Even a little bit of deflation is bad since it means the economy is shrinking, and everything is getting cheaper. On the surface this might sound good, what cost $5 today might cost $3 next week, making money one has today more valuable. However, if prices keep going down, it reduces the incentive for people to spend money, knowing that the price will be lower the longer they wait. This causes a deflationary spiral, as it slows down the economy even more since no one is buying anything. Controlling inflation became one of the primary objectives of economic policy from the 1970s to the 1990s, and in the wake of the 2008 financial crisis, deflation and disinflation have become much bigger threats to deal with. Inflation and deflation can be manipulated through fiscal policy and monetary policy, as increasing the interest rate encourages saving which can be deflationary and lowering it encourages spending, which leads to inflation.

Unemployment is the second major consideration for economic policy. Depending on which economic theory one follows, there are different approaches to dealing with unemployment. Some theories see unemployment as a positive, as it helps keep wages low and thus increases profitability. Other theories see unemployment as a problem because it leads to less consumer spending in the economy and more poverty, which means more government spending on social assistance.

Economic policy is also concerned with the *balance of trade*, which is the number of imports compared to exports. If imports vastly outnumber exports, it can affect the value of the American dollar relative to other countries, while more exports mean that the economy is doing so well its production is more than what is needed domestically. While the trade balance is generally important, it is less of an issue for the United States, which has the world's largest economy. The U.S. dollar is considered the world's reserve currency, which means that governments and corporations around the world perceive the U.S. dollar as safe and tend to exchange their local currency for U.S. dollars if the local currency's value is fluctuating. The status as reserve currency keeps the U.S. dollar's relative value fairly steady.

The fourth economic issue is the *environment*. Many industries are inherently harmful to the environment because of pollution or emission of greenhouse gasses. A careful economic policy should seek to balance economic growth with environmental concern, though this has not always been the case. Environmental considerations when making economic policy have not been as prominent due to the vast influence of corporate lobbying. The Kyoto Protocol (1992), which was an international agreement to regulate economies to reduce greenhouse gasses, was not signed by the United States, demonstrating that environmental concern continues to have a lower priority than economic issues.

Often the environment and the economy are seen as opposites, though many industries are environmentally friendly or do not produce carbon dioxide emissions. These industries tend to be less prominent in lobbying the government than "dirty industries," such as oil and coal, which make bigger profits and therefore have the "deep pockets" to influence the political process.

Foreign Policy

The second major policy type is *foreign and military policy*. Policymaking power about military and foreign policy is almost exclusively the prerogative of the executive branch. As the Commander in Chief of the military, presidents since World War II have carved out the power to determine military policy exclusively; presidents now send the military into other countries without approval from Congress, despite congressional authorization being required in the Constitution. Senior Cabinet members are also very important for setting foreign and military policy, which makes the Secretary of State and Secretary of Defense powerful positions for setting the policy agenda. In negotiations with other countries, the president has the power to meet with other world leaders and come up with policy and resolutions that are not subject to congressional oversight. Trade policies can be negotiated by the president but must be approved by the Senate.

The most important drivers of the foreign policy agenda are the National Security Council and the Central Intelligence Agency (CIA). The National Security Council consists of the president, vice president, Secretary of State, Secretary of Defense and any other leaders the president wishes to hear from, such as the Joint Chiefs of Staff, who are senior members of the various branches of the military. When developing a foreign policy agenda, the president will consult the National Security Council and use intelligence gathered by the CIA to make decisions. Foreign policy can cover virtually anything related to the United States' interaction with other countries. Examples range from negotiating climate change treaties to condemning the actions of other countries. The American approach to foreign policy has changed dramatically in the modern era.

President Barack Obama and Vice President Joe Biden meet with members of the National Security Council in 2014

Before the early to mid-20th century, American foreign policy was premised on the idea of isolationism. This was largely based on the Monroe Doctrine: President Monroe had declared that the United States would only be involved in the intervention in the Western Hemisphere. American leaders saw the United States as removed from the old conflicts in Europe and its colonial possessions and generally did not wish to entangle itself in the foreign wars of the European powers. The priority during this period was developing policy on internal issues while leaving Europe and the rest of the world alone.

This policy changed with World War II and in particular the Japanese attack on Pearl Harbor. Before this attack, the United States did not see itself as a world power or a major player in world politics. This attack forced the United States to realize its emerging position in the world as a superpower and ended the policy of isolationism. After World War II, the U.S. adopted a policy of aggressive interventionism in the rest of the world. During the Cold War, the U.S. sanctioned covert actions, support for governments fighting Communism and even military invasions. With the decline of the Soviet Union in 1991, the U.S. was left as the world's only superpower, and many inside the government's foreign policy circle came to see the role of the United States as a policing the world.

The USS Arizona burning after the Japanese attack on Pearl Harbor on December 7, 1941

There are two main theoretical approaches to foreign policy within the modern interventionist era: realism and idealism. *Idealism* saw the horror of World War I and argued that a global body needed to be created to ensure international cooperation which would serve to prevent a future world war. The League of Nations and later the United Nations were heavily supported by idealists as mechanisms to promote international cooperation. Idealists generally wanted American foreign policy to support democracy, human rights and the peaceful resolution of conflicts.

Realism argued that international cooperation is impossible and that every state had to look out for its interests. This does not mean that states cannot cooperate; rather it means that cooperation should only be undertaken for pragmatic, self-interest reasons. During the Cold War, realists in American foreign policy supported anti-communist dictatorships which tortured and murdered their people, arguing that it was better to have allies against the Soviets than to worry about human rights and democracy.

During the Cold War, idealism was generally promoted by liberals and realism by conservatives. There was a reversal in this alignment beginning with the Presidency of George W Bush. The Bush Doctrine, often called *neoconservatism*, was a form of conservative idealism. President Bush argued that with the end of the Cold War, it was now the job of the United States to promote democracy and human rights around the world through forceful military intervention. This policy was evident in the invasion of Iraq in 2003. At the same time, realism became the preferred stance of liberals, who argued that invading Iraq, criticizing Iran and supporting Israel was working against American interests in the global war on terror. Liberal realists were now arguing that America should be willing to support dictators like Saddam Hussein, who were potential allies against al-Qaeda.

Saddam Hussein, Iraqi dictator and terrorist shortly after his capture (2003)

In the wake of the failure of the invasion and occupation of Iraq, there have even been some calls for the U.S. to return to its pre-World War II policy of isolationism, arguing not only that foreign intervention tends to lead to larger issues in the future, but that America should focus on helping Americans before the rest of the world.

The military policy comes from the president, but more heavily involves the Secretary of Defense and the Joint Chiefs of Staff. Military policy is most obvious when there is a decision to attack another country, such as in the 2003 invasion of Iraq, but has many other less obvious aspects. The military actions of other countries are closely monitored by the Department of Defense and the military, and the president is constantly briefed on these evolving situations. The president must decide if such matters are worthy of American involvement and to what degree.

The Joint Chiefs of Staff photographed in the Joint Chiefs of Staff Gold Room, more commonly known as The Tank, in the Pentagon on December 14, 2001.

From left to right are: U.S. Air Force Chief of Staff Gen. John P. Jumper, U.S. Marine Corps Commandant Gen. James L. Jones Jr., Vice Chairman of the Joint Chiefs of Staff Gen. Peter Pace, U.S. Marine Corps, Chairman of the Joint Chiefs of Staff Gen. Richard B. Myers, U.S. Air Force, U.S. Army Chief of Staff Gen. Eric K. Shinseki, U.S. Navy Chief of Naval Operations Adm. Vern E. Clark.

While wars and invasions are the most extreme outcomes, the president can also issue warnings to countries, such as when President Obama warned Russian President Vladimir Putin to move troops from the Ukraine border. The president can also use the CIA to engage in intelligence monitoring or covert actions. In some cases, the president may order a small-scale use of the military, such as a drone strike, or sending in a small team of elite military forces, such as when President Obama sent Seal Team 6 to kill Osama Bin Laden.

Domestic Policy

To study how issues become part of a policy agenda, there are five broad categories of domestic policies that have driven the policy agenda in the modern era: welfare, crime and law enforcement, the environment, social security, and education. While not all issues fit under these categories, these issues have achieved the greatest attention in the post-WWII era. *Welfare policies* are designed to help those in need and are redistributive in nature. This means that helping those in need is paid for by those who are wealthy.

Welfare and public assistant programs first became prominent drivers of the policy agenda in the 1960s when President Lyndon B. Johnson declared war on poverty in the

United States. Johnson saw income inequality as inherently harmful to the national fabric of America and sought to instigate policy programs to help the poor. Some examples of programs that were driven by welfare policy are the food stamps program (which gives low-income Americans vouchers that they can exchange for food), the creation of public housing (which subsidizes housing costs for low-income people in order to try to prevent homelessness), and Medicaid programs (which provide assistance to low-income people for paying medical bills).

President Lyndon B. Johnson signs the Economic Opportunity Act of 1964

More recently, especially in the wake of the 2008 financial crisis, the government has engaged in welfare programs for large corporations. In 2008, the US government bailed out banks and automotive companies, leading some to call this "corporate welfare." Critics of such bailouts complained that the government was helping corporations, while the average Americans received no governmental support. While this policy gained attention with the bailout of the banks and the auto industry, corporate welfare has been in place for decades. For example, many profitable companies (e.g., General Electric) pay a negative effective tax rate after accounting for deductions and subsidies. However, special tax benefits and loopholes are available to many qualifying companies, while bailouts for mismanaged corporations are discretionary acts.

Crime is another major driver of the policy agenda. In the 1970s, violent crime began to increase, and politicians were quick to place crackdowns on criminals at the top of the policy agenda. Cracking down on crime is generally a popular policy since no one other than criminals is in favor of there being more crime, and thus this issue tends to get acted on more quickly than others. Since the 1990s, crime rates across the country have been in decline, but politicians often still push crime and law and order issues to the top of the policy agenda, though earlier efforts in the 1970s have worked to reduce crime. More recently, issues around gun control and the war on drugs have dominated the policy agenda, demonstrating how crime and law issues tend to get elevated to the policy agenda quickly.

The *environment* became an important policy issue in the 1960s. An oil spill in 1969 led to the first legislation meant to protect the environment, and legislation passed the next year was intended to reduce the amount of air pollution. Issues related to clean water, pesticide use and toxic waste dominated the 1970s and were led by the Environmental Protection Agency (EPA), created in the early 1970s by President Nixon. For the past four decades the issue of climate change has been an important issue, but the government today has become much slower to act on environmental issues than they were in the 1970s and 1980s.

Official logo of the Environmental Protection Agency

The *social security* pension has continued to be an important issue since its creation in 1935 by President Roosevelt as part of the New Deal. By having every working American pay a small portion of their salary into one giant fund, the government attempts to ensure that senior citizens do not live in poverty. Preventing the elderly from dying in poverty was the original intent of the program, and what pushed the issue onto the policy agenda. Today, the issue is significant also because the largest cohort of the population, known as the baby boomers, is about to retire. Many people are worried that there will not be enough money being paid into the social security system since soon the number of retired people will grow to its largest proportion in American history. An *entitlement* is a program, such as Social Security and Medicare, which provides benefits to any person meeting a set qualification.

Finally, *education* has always been a major driver of the policy agenda. Education is a complicated issue because it affects all Americans but tends to be controlled by state governments. The federal government provided no funding for education until 1965 when the Higher Education Act and the Elementary and Secondary Education Act were passed. The federal government became even more involved in education policy in 1979, with the creation of the federal Department of Education as a prominent bureaucratic department with a Cabinet secretary. In 2001, the federal government got involved in regulating the quality of schools, with the No Child Left Behind Act. This act proved to be extremely controversial, as it promoted standardized testing and punished schools whose students had low scores, rather than helping them. More recently, the issue of student debt from attending college, which is currently the number one source of personal debt in the US and cannot be written off even with the death of the debtor, is becoming more urgent and could drive future policy agendas.

President George W. Bush signs the No Child Left Behind Act

Notes

The Role of Institutions in the Enactment of Policy

Each of the institutions of the American government has a role to play in enacting and implementing policy. The bulk of the power in enacting public policy rests in the executive branch of government and the bureaucracy, which for public policy purposes is considered an extension of the executive branch. As the most public figure of the government, the president tends to be the focus of public opinion. The president pushes the public policy agenda in such a way so that he or she can maintain popular approval by pointing to programs, policies, and projects which effect positive change. The president is often motivated by a desire to get re-elected in his or her first term in office, while the second term is often driven by the need to "leave a legacy." Presidents want to be remembered in history for having completed great accomplishments. For example, everyone remembers Franklin Roosevelt for the New Deal, considered his lasting legacy to the American people.

The president's staff in the White House is usually very active in monitoring public opinion. They help the president find issues that he or she can enact policy on and that will lead to re-election or a lasting legacy. A good example is President Obama's Affordable Healthcare Act. Obama decided that health care was too expensive for the average person and found that many citizens supported making health care more affordable. Obama saw this as a chance to win votes to help him get re-elected and to leave a lasting, positive legacy.

After consulting with various interest groups who had been lobbying for reform, Obama put health care reform on his policy agenda. The issue was then discussed in Congress, and a bill was created to push the policy agenda forward. Congress approved the bill, and Obama signed it into law in 2010. At this point, policymaking authority is passed to the bureaucracy, who follow the directions of both the president and the legislation to develop a series of procedures to get the results the president intended. The policy procedures crafted by the bureaucracy are then acted upon by front-line administrators who interact with the public to provide health services.

Congress' role in the implementation of policy comes largely through its legislative powers. In most cases, Congress tends to take policy direction from the president, but it still has the power to craft legislation how it pleases. Congress can also influence the policy agenda, as the House of Representatives is supposed to present issues relevant to the public for consideration. While this can sometimes be the case, especially if an issue becomes so big it threatens the re-election chances of a representative, the reality of the situation is that individual representatives have very little power to push the policy agenda on their own.

Barack Obama signing the Patient Protection and Affordable Care Act at the White House

The president and the leadership of the political parties have most of the power to set the policy agenda and decide what issues are acted upon. Through committees and sub-committees, Congress decides which legislation to focus on, based on discussion and consideration of issues. When members of these committees have connections to like-minded people in interest groups and the bureaucracy, an issue network is formed which can help push policy forward. Congress is in control of money bills and can influence the enactment of policy by providing more or less money. For example, if the president wants to advance a health care spending agenda and Congress disagrees, Congress can vote to provide very little money to the project, therefore crippling the policy implementation process.

Legislation differs from policy directives in that legislation is meant to fix a policy issue through the law permanently. Given that most policy issues are complex and cannot be fixed simply by legislation, the legislative powers of Congress are not as strong compared to that of the president and the bureaucracy when it comes to implementing policy. If Congress passes legislation to address an issue and they do not like how the bureaucrats are implementing it, there is little they can do. If the president does not like how the bureaucracy is implementing policy, the president can get directly involved by firing Cabinet members and replacing heads of bureaucratic departments.

The Role of the Bureaucracy and the Courts in Policy Implementation and Interpretation

The judiciary is not involved in forming policy directly but can indirectly cause the other branches of government to act by issuing rulings and judgments. One of the main powers of the judicial branch is to rule on whether or not an existing policy is legal or constitutional or not. If the Supreme Court finds that an existing policy contravenes the Constitution, the Supreme Court will strike it down, nullifying the policy. An example of this was the recent Supreme Court ruling overturning bans on same-sex marriage.

By striking down the policy and legislation created by governments, the Supreme Court is essentially establishing a new policy framework. As a result of the same-sex marriage decision, bureaucracies have had to craft new policies related to handling local authorities who, for example, disobey the new law and refuse to issue marriage licenses to same-sex couples. At the same time, the Supreme Court can also rule that policy created by Congress or the president is and should be upheld. While this does not "create" policy, it upholds it in a way that can embolden further action. For example, if the Supreme Court has already ruled in his or her favor on an issue, the president may become less cautious in pursuing a certain policy agenda.

When the Supreme Court rules that policy is unconstitutional and overturns existing law, this is often called "legislating from the bench." Such rulings do not create new laws; they are invalidating old laws and are in turn creating a new policy situation. After the Supreme Court struck down laws against abortion in *Roe v. Wade*, no new laws were created, but an entirely new policy regime had to be created to provide access to and regulate abortions. With issues like this, where something that was previously banned became legal (more specifically no longer illegal), the bureaucracy must spring into action to create a new policy framework to deal with issues that may arise from the new legal framework.

Pro-Life March for Life in Washington D.C. in 2008, protesting Roe v. Wade

The policy enactment process is carried out through the bureaucracy, while the president and, to a lesser extent, Congress, set the overall policy agenda. Since the bureaucracy is staffed with trained experts, they can better figure out how to implement a policy than politicians. Technically speaking, the bureaucracy has no power to create policy and exists to implement what the government decides. However, there is some leeway for the bureaucracy to interpret what government policy means when they undertake implementation of it. Depending on which theory of public policy formation one believes is most accurate, the policy power of the bureaucracy varies. Elitist and pluralist theorists see the bureaucracy as simply carrying out the orders of government, while institutional theorists believe that bureaucratic policy implementation is where the true power lies.

While the president and Congress drive policy, implementation is largely up to the bureaucracy, which makes controlling how policy is implemented difficult. The sheer size of the bureaucracy means so many people are working on implementing policy that the president cannot keep tabs on everything that is happening. This gives room for bureaucrats to interpret policy and implement it according to their idea of what the policy means.

In most cases, the bureaucracy is filled with experts who know a great deal more about the issues than do the politicians; this means that bureaucrats are once again given space to use their policy expertise to implement policy in a way they see fit. Bureaucrats are also largely immune from being fired, making it difficult for the president to fix a poorly implemented policy. For these reasons, many presidents have expressed frustration with the bureaucracy for not implementing policy in a way that they originally envisioned. The president must work with the bureaucracy to persuade them to implement policy according to his or her vision for that policy

The procedures and rules that are created to govern how a policy is implemented and thus administrated by public-facing civil servants give the bureaucracy some legal authority as well. When the bureaucracy decides how a program will function, these rules become *de facto* laws and must be followed by everyone involved. Once the bureaucracy decides on the rules of implementation of a policy, it must wait 60 days before enforcing those rules, regulations or administrative guidelines. During this time, Congress can review the rules and make suggestions for changes if it sees fit; policy rules, especially regulations, can be contested.

In what is called *administrative adjudication*, the federal departments can function like courts to determine what exactly a regulation entails. In the case of regulations, an individual or a company may present a case which they believe is special and not properly covered by existing regulations. Administrative adjudicators will then review the case and make a ruling which can establish precedent for how the bureaucratic rules will be applied to other cases. While this function of the bureaucracy usually involves enforcing regulations, the general trend in policymaking since the 1980s has been towards deregulation. The bureaucracy then has to figure out how to remove regulations a way that is consistent and promotes self-regulation by those affected.

Notes

Linkages Between Policy Processes

In addition to public policy being influenced by the various institutions of government, the direction of public policymaking is influenced by numerous other factors. The relation between the federal and state governments is important for policy. Political parties can have a large impact on what policies are pursued. Interest groups and lobbying are hugely important within the policymaking process. Public opinion can drive the president and others to act on certain issues and neglect others. Elections can determine which policy agenda is acted on and in what manner. Finally, policy networks are essential to advancing agendas. Each of these items will be discussed in more depth below.

Political Institutions and Federalism

The role of federalism in the policymaking process has always been important. In the Federalist Papers, James Madison argued that the biggest problem facing the new country was the existence of factions. Madison was worried that one faction, or interest group, might be able to control the government and thus pursue policy that was against the wishes of the majority or the well-being of the minority. Madison's federalism was meant to foster the system of checks and balances at the national level, and also provide leeway to state governments to enact their policy agendas. Through these various branches and levels of government, Madison's goal was to diminish the influence of interest groups over the government severely. Given how prominent interest groups have become, it seems that Madison's fears of factions having too much influence in the policymaking process have become a reality. Conversely, factions and interest groups often represent the wishes of the people better than elected representatives and can get the government to pay attention to important issues.

President James Madison, co-author of The Federalist Papers

In a federal system, there is often overlap between states and the national government. While the national policy agenda is always of prime authority, state governments have their policy agendas on issues that are under their authority. On issues that overlap with other states or with the national government, another step in the policy process is often introduced at the policy formation level. This is called *multilevel consultations*.

An example of a multilevel consultation would be if Arkansas or Mississippi wanted to dump waste into the Mississippi River, with Louisiana being greatly affected since it is downstream; the upstream states would have to consult with Louisiana, and since environmental protection is federally regulated, they would have to consult with the national government. Because the waste would drain into the Gulf of Mexico, Mexico and Cuba may be affected as well. This would mean that the federal government, specifically the State Department, would also be involved. Multilevel negotiations tend to be very difficult and often dramatically slow down the policy process. They are, however, necessary because if Arkansas were to unilaterally decide to dump waste into the river without consulting anyone else, there might be a severe backlash.

While it is generally a good idea for states to engage in multilevel engagement on issues that overlap with other states, the federal government or even other countries, they sometimes simply set their policy agendas and purposely defy the federal government. The most obvious example of this was the issue of slavery, which led to the Civil War. Southern states believed that slavery was an issue that should be left to state discretion and was not a concern for the national government. The national government saw this not only as a human rights issue but as a means of keeping the country united under the federal government. While this conflict between states' rights and federal rights led to a war, there are often policy clashes between states and the federal government without such dramatic escalation.

Before the recent Supreme Court ruling, which decreed same-sex marriage to be legal across the country, this issue was set by national government policy. The Defense of Marriage Act (DOMA) outlawed same-sex marriage nationally, but many state governments developed policies allowing same-sex marriage, in opposition to the policy of the federal government. Eventually, the federal government changed its position, following the policy initiatives of individual states. Sometimes the federal government will give in and change to accommodate the needs of states, but sometimes the federal government will crack down and restrict the policy agenda of state governments.

A same-sex couple celebrating overturning of DOMA in San Francisco in 2013

Political Parties

In a democracy, policy formation begins in two places: the public, or in government. The public might inform the political parties of their wishes on a certain issue or advance a new issue which has never been debated in the legislature before. New agendas can also be created by the government, in the political party caucuses.

The goal of political parties is to get public policy to match their beliefs. Political parties want to be seen as galvanizing action on the policies that they campaign on and which their supporters believe in. This means that political parties are especially influential in the policy formation process. Given that political parties run campaigns on a certain set of issues and ask voters to choose them because of their proposed solutions, policy is extremely important to how voters see political parties. If a political party runs on a platform but is unable to implement any of the policy, voters will be skeptical of future promises made by the party in question. As a result, political parties are especially motivated to move the policy process along on issues that they ran on during the election.

Political parties have a complex interaction with the first policy step of agenda formation. Since political parties run campaigns on a set of existing issues, it can seem like these are the only issues that a party cares about. The president or Congress may not want to deal with new issues that have arisen until they have moved along the issues that they campaigned on. Thus, political parties can impede the policy agenda process by pushing politicians to disregard more important issues that were not part of their campaign. At the same time, since political parties are a group of like-minded people all in government, they can get rapid policy action on the issues they ran on. Political parties can both impede the policy agenda and help push it along, depending on whether or not the issue was part of their election campaign.

The strategies which a party will use to get a new policy enacted depend on how strong the opposition to it is and how high a priority it is for the party. New legislation is proposed, debated and then voted on. Before it comes to a vote, the party which wants it to pass may revise it according to the suggestions of those who oppose it. If that is not acceptable, they might engage in a process called "log rolling." This means that parties make a trade: The party which is opposed to a new policy may agree to vote for it in exchange for the favor being returned in a vote on a favored bill of theirs. Note that a major consideration in this sort of negotiation is the other party's "preference intensity," in other words, how strongly each party opposes each of the policies involved. A modern tactic in Congress is called a "rider clause" – if the policy does not pass a vote on its own, the party may attach it to a totally unrelated bill which is favored by the opponents, so that in order to have their favored legislation passed, they also have to accept the unfavored policy as part of the same bill.

An important element of the way Congress changes government policy is called "incrementalism." This was described as a theory by Charles Lindblom. Incrementalism states that when there is too much opposition to a policy to get it enacted at once, the agenda can be advanced in small bites over a long period – incrementally. This has worked either because the public's attitude about an issue change over time and the loyalties of politicians along with it, or because smaller parts of a larger agenda are acceptable to the opponents while others are not. Incrementalism is particularly suited to the American system because it is already designed to ensure that changes to government policy happen slowly.

Political parties do not only play a positive role in policy. Parties which oppose a new policy can obstruct it at all of the stages. Political parties can obstruct the formation of new policies aggressively, by strategies such as challenging them in political campaigns or threatening to support the other party on other issues as well. They can do so more passively and constructively, however, by proposing alternative legislation which addresses some of the other party's concerns while also neutralizing the more controversial parts of the proposed policy. Political parties can obstruct the enactment of a new policy in many ways, the most obvious of which is voting against it. They can also stall it by foot-dragging in Congressional committees.

Political parties become involved in the policy implementation stage only indirectly. Since this stage is largely directed by the bureaucracy, which is not aligned to one party or the other, political parties can use their control of Congress to adjust funding levels. If they do not like how the bureaucracy is implementing a program, the majority party in the House may move to cut its funding. Political parties can also make public critiques in the media of policy implementation in the media in an attempt to sway public opinion. The same is true for policy evaluation, which may be conducted internally by political parties to determine if their support of a certain policy has popular support.

Political parties can obstruct implementation through the courts if their members file legal challenges. For example, the Health Care Act was challenged in the Supreme Court, using the argument that one clause within it represented a new tax, which was not passed the legitimate way. (The Supreme Court ruled in favor of the defendants and the Health Care Act remained.)

President Obama discusses health care reform in a speech to Congress

Policy can be obstructed in the bureaucracy some ways when the specific bureaucratic department responsible for implementing the new policy is staffed with people who oppose it: Two of the many possible strategies they can use are delaying and diversion. They can delay a policy by taking extreme amounts of time to process claims or do other tasks that are pivotal to implementing the policy. They can divert the policy's objectives by reinterpreting the language to mean something other than what it intended. An instance of obstruction by a bureaucrat recently is the case of Kim Davis, a government clerk in Kentucky who refused to issue marriage licenses to gay couples, in breach of the current law.

She claimed religious reasons for doing so and was held in contempt of court for refusing a judge's order to begin issuing marriage licenses.

Political parties often convene focus groups to ask people about their views about a certain policy program. Political parties will use this information to evaluate what policies they should support in the future and what sort of issues they should include in their next campaign. If political parties find that the public is not supportive of the policies they favor, then they may commence a public relations campaign to try to move public opinion. Representatives from the party may go on political talk shows, try to get news shows to interview them or try to get invited to lighter talk shows that normally interview celebrities. In this way, political parties can try to change the public's perception of the effectiveness of a policy program.

First Lady Michelle Obama on the Ellen DeGeneres show

Interest Groups

Domestic issues are the major focus of interest groups. When the government engages with interest groups and brings them into the public policymaking process, they are called stakeholders.

Lobbying the government, which means attempting to make them enact policy a certain way, is usually a multi-step process. For many interest groups, their primary form of lobbying is through raising awareness. These groups feel the government is completely ignoring their issue – or approaching the issue incorrectly – and they are trying to garner interest in their cause. Attempting to raise awareness relates to the first step in the policy cycle and involves trying to get an issue onto the radar of policy-makers. This is the most important step for many interest groups. If the government is simply unaware of their issue, then obviously no policy relating to it will be enacted,

The second aspect of lobbying in the policy process is attempting to get the government to make policy in a certain way, once the issue has been raised and is on the policy agenda. Interest groups may provide specialized information to policy-makers, or lobby them to push policy in a certain direction.

In the example of environmental protection, raising awareness and getting the government to pay attention to the issue may be driven entirely by just one or two organizations dedicated to environmental protection. However, once the issue gets on the policy agenda, new interest groups will emerge. One interest group may have successfully lobbied the government to pay attention to their issue; however, this does not mean that the government will listen to that interest group when making policy. For example, the government's awareness of environmental issues may have been raised by an interest group such as Greenpeace, but they could make environmental policy (or refrain from doing so) as a result of lobbying from oil industry groups.

Once policy is made, interest groups will shift their focus to lobbying Congress to try to change the amount of funding a policy agenda gets. Returning to the example of environment protection, if policy that favors the Greenpeace point of view is made, the oil industry may then begin lobbying Congress and try to get them to provide very little funding for the environmental policy initiative and thus undermine it from a financial standpoint. Even if the presidential and congressional leadership are strongly in favor of acting on a policy agenda, those opposed to it can undermine it by reducing its funding in Congress. Since individual members of Congress are more susceptible to being swayed with large financial donations or other offers of re-election help, the policy is often undermined at the funding stages. It is here that *Public Action Committees* (PACs) often play a prominent role. PACs target sympathetic members of Congress with large financial support in exchange for taking their preferred policy position.

More recently, with the Supreme Court's *Citizens United* ruling, Super PACs have become prominent. A *Super PAC* is an interest group, often with large corporate donations, that can spend an unlimited amount of money helping their preferred candidates get re-elected. While there are legal restrictions on traditional PACs regarding how much money they can spend, where they get their funding and rules related to revealing where this funding comes from, Super PACs are not subject to these rules.

Unlike a regular PAC, Super PACs cannot directly contribute to a candidate's re-election campaign. They are, however, allowed to spend unlimited amounts to help the candidate indirectly. This could include running attack ads against the candidate they oppose or running "information" commercials designed to sway voters toward their side and thus vote for their preferred candidate. Since Super PACs are legally considered separate from political parties, they must not coordinate with the candidate or his or her party during the election. Despite this rule, the fact that donations to Super PACs can essentially be anonymous means that political parties could funnel money into Super PACs to skirt election financing laws. Although many states have now passed laws requiring disclosure of Super PAC donors, these disclosures do not have to occur until after an election, opening up many avenues for corruption.

Critics call this capacity of wealthy individuals, unions and large corporations to spend unlimited amounts of money corruption of democracy. When elections can be influenced by such dramatic spending, this provides a huge media voice to those with much money and thus can sway many votes. Super PACs have also been criticized as corrupting individual members of Congress, as they may be more likely to advocate for a policy position they do not agree with in the hope this will catch the attention of a Super PAC that might spend heavily in support of their re-election campaign.

Interest groups are also at the center of direct democracy campaigns. Many states have ballot initiatives or referenda. A ballot initiative is when the citizens write and propose legislation, without the involvement of the legislature. If a minimum number of citizens endorse it, the initiative is put on the ballot at the next election, for the public to pass or reject. A long campaign ensues in which those for and those against the initiative try to persuade the public to vote with them. Although the federal government has no direct democracy, the passage of a law in a state puts direct pressure on the federal government in many ways. It might put the federal law in direct opposition to state law, which forces one side or the other to change their legislation. It can embarrass Congress by making them look ineffective.

Interest groups can play a prominent role in policy evaluation. Continuing with the environmental policy example, both Greenpeace and the oil industry lobby might write evaluations of the policy. This can be for internal and external use. Internal evaluations will look at how the policy affected their specific interest on the issue. Greenpeace would evaluate how effective the policy was at protecting the environment, and the oil lobby group would evaluate if the policy cost their member corporations any loss in profit. These organizations may write external facing evaluations, which tend to be less honest and more biased, in an attempt to sway the opinion of the government's policy analysts. So even if the policy did not cost the oil industry much money, they may release an external evaluation claiming that the environmental policy was very costly to their industry, simply as a technique to try to prevent further environmental regulations.

Interest groups have less of a role with implementation, but a strong one nonetheless. As an interested party which has worked hard to see their agenda get passed and which benefits from the policy directly, they are a natural watchdog to make sure that implementation is not obstructed in any way. Taking the example of Kim Davis once again, Gay rights activists made sure that Davis was challenged at every step and that her supporters were not the only voice in the media. Interest groups provide legal funding for their side should a policy confrontation come to court. They may also become the employees who are responsible for implementation, as was often the case for Southern blacks when voting rights legislation was enacted in the 1960s.

Public Opinion

In a democracy, public opinion preferences are supposed to be the only factor which determines public policy. The reality is that there are many different competing interests, factions and actors at work in the policy process that can overshadow public opinion. The role of public opinion on the policy process also depends on how one views democracy. The most general theory of representative democracy is that politicians are elected by the people to represent their interests in the national government. Thus, a representative is supposed to represent public opinion once in office, not simply do what he or she feels is the best course of action. Conversely, the theory of representative democracy known as *competitive elitism*, argues that public opinion only matters for electing representatives. Once they are elected, representatives are free to ignore public opinion and do what they feel is the best course of action.

Both of these understandings of representative democracy have advantages and disadvantages when interpreting their effect on the policymaking process. In the first theory, politicians act democratically by putting the interests of public opinion ahead of their personal views. This means that the government, in theory, is always making public policy in response to what the public wants. The problem is that public opinion is not always obvious or easily discernible. Even with modern polling methods, which uses statistical sampling to provide an accurate picture of public opinion, there are questions about how well the sample represents the populace as a whole.

On certain complex issues, if the public has not had a chance to deliberate and discuss this issue, to educate themselves and truly understand it, their opinion can be ignorant or prejudiced. Should politicians listen to public opinion when it is uninformed? At the same time, what about opinions that are in the minority? If the job of the elected representative is only to pursue policy supported by the majority, it leaves the minority unrepresented completely, which goes against the spirit of representative democracy.

In response to these problems, the competitive elitism theory of representative democracy arose. It argues that people get their say on Election Day, but once in government, representatives should not pay attention to public opinion. While this corrects the problems mentioned above, it also makes government quite undemocratic. This theory is simply elected dictatorship, as once in power politicians are expected to do whatever they wish regardless of what the people want. This opens up all sorts of possible abuses and corruption, as it promotes lying to get elected, and policy that may harm the public interest.

President Barack Obama votes on the 2012 Presidential Election Day

Shifts in public opinion can be motivated by a variety of factors, but one of the things politicians and political parties monitor to try to predict future changes in public opinion are demographics. *Demographics* is the study and collection of the residents of a given space, in this instance the United States. By monitoring shifts in population in certain areas, public opinion shifts may be predicted. For example, if the population of cities is increasing while rural area population is decreasing, this may indicate certain future shifts in public opinion. Demographics also involve monitoring the political engagement of certain groups of people.

Recently, political parties have started to realize that Hispanic Americans are a major group that is becoming more and more politically involved. By using demographic information, political parties can identify how this might impact certain issues, such as immigration from Mexico and Central America. Another important demographic consideration for public opinion is age; older people tend to be more conservative, and thus a shift in the distribution in age can indicate a shift in support for certain policies over others.

Regarding the policy cycle, the policy agenda is where public opinion should have the most effect. The president and Congress want to be seen as responding to issues people care about, even if their actions do not match their words. Public opinion can be conveyed to policymakers to help them set the policy agenda through a variety of outlets. In addition to public opinion polls, the media plays a major role in both forming and reporting public opinion. If the media plays up an issue day after day, then people will care more about it and demand policy action.

While the president may be able to ignore public opinion on some issues, once the media sides with public opinion it becomes very hard to ignore the issue. In the media, there is also a linkage between policy-makers, public opinion, and interest groups. If interest groups do not have direct access to politicians to directly influence them, they will rely on influencing public opinion instead. Interest groups will often focus their lobbying on major news networks in an attempt to gain access to airtime and to get reporters to cover their story. By raising awareness in the media, interest groups hope they can shape public opinion that will then force the government to address the issue by placing it on its policy agenda.

Public opinion can also be consulted in the second step of the policy process, which involves determining options. When it comes to determining the public's opinion on an issue with multiple sides, it can be difficult for politicians to follow public opinion since there is not a single majority. If an issue has four possible solutions and public opinion is split between the four options, no matter what option the policy-makers decide to choose, it will be going against the wishes of the other three-quarters of the population. Thus, making decisions based on public opinion tends to be rare, unless public opinion is overwhelmingly in favor of one option.

The policy implementation process is subject to public opinion as well. Even if the public brought an issue to policy awareness and supported the government's decision on what to do about it if the policy program is poorly implemented then public opinion can turn against it. An example was the invasion of Vietnam, which was at the time supported by a slim majority. As the war continued without a significant advance in achieving the stated goals of the intervention in Southeast Asia, public opinion began to change in favor of opposing the war due to its implementation, rather than against the underlying reasons for intervention.

Even when the public may agree with a certain policy in principle, if it is implemented poorly, then the public can turn against it and force the government to cancel it. This step also relates to policy evaluation. While public opinion is generally ill-equipped to determine the effectiveness of policy, interest groups can advertise and use the media to shape public opinion about an outcome of a policy. In many cases, interest groups have been able to convince Americans that policy was ineffective, even when it was a success. A modern example of this is the opposition to the Affordable Care Act (which became known as "Obamacare"), which was widely characterized as a failure by right-wing interest groups. Public opinion is always linked to all aspects of the political system and can be rallied in the name of democracy and public interest or manipulated to undermine democracy. This speaks to the notion that the only way to have a healthy democracy is to ensure that people are well-informed and not prone to the influences of biased political propaganda.

President Obama receives an update on the Affordable Care Act

Elections

Elections are important to the policy cycle as they enable voters to choose which parties will control the various organs of local and federal government. Voting is a means for citizens to express a choice in the future public policy direction of the country and the locality they inhabit. By having political parties with different approaches to what should be on the policy agenda and how to do deal with that issue, the election is when voters get a say in the public policy process. Since parties are elected on a platform of policy issues, these issues become the most important issues on the policy agenda. These issues are the most important because they are what matter to the political party, but also by winning the election, the government has a mandate from the people to pursue these issues.

While parties generally set the policy agenda and the people choose which agenda they prefer by voting in an election, sometimes the election campaign itself can drive the policy agenda. If a major event happens during an election campaign, voters will want to know how each party will deal with the issues that arise from it. Such unexpected events are often the most important policy issues for deciding an election, as these are issues that require immediate responses. Parties have not had time to run focus groups and poll public opinion, and thus their response to such events is often the best measure of what a candidate or a party believes. In this manner, the electorate can drive the policy agenda and reward parties and candidates that can respond to changing circumstances by electing them into government.

While elections give the people the opportunity to choose between different policy options, in the modern era elections have increasingly become more about personality than issues. With the Democrats and Republicans converging into a consensus on most big-picture issues (hidden by bitter disagreements on minor issues), the parties have increasingly promoted the qualities of their leaders over using the election campaign to present a policy agenda to the voters to decide on. Many political scientists lament the decline of issue-based elections as an erosion of democracy. If people are voting based on the personality of the leader, rather than their policy agenda, then elections no longer give citizens the ability to make a choice on which policy agenda should be followed. This diminishes democracy as the people are not able to choose what issues are important and how policy should be enacted.

Above is an example of how the two major theories of representative democracy can clash. The first theory would argue that the current system undermines representation and democracy itself, as politicians are supposed to represent the wishes of the people as determined by the people voting in an election. However, if people do not vote based on issues, then politicians can no longer represent the majority. The theory of competitive elitism would argue that the present situation of candidates running on personality rather than issues is what representative democracy should be, as people should be electing the most qualified people to make decisions for them.

Once a government is elected, it is considered to have a mandate from the people, and thus, in theory, its policy agenda represents the wishes of the majority. Some states have recall mechanisms which make it possible for the electorate to remove the governor from office if he or she is not focusing on the issues of their election platform. *Recall mechanisms* give the citizens an ability to intervene in the policy decision and implementation stages by removing a politician who is poorly implementing policy.

Seattle recall petitions in 1910

At the national level, however, there are no recall mechanisms, and therefore the president and Congress are free to pursue any policy they wish, even if it was the opposite of what they promised during an election. The fact that once voters set the policy agenda through an election but have no other means of input until the next election, is seen by many as evidence that representative democracy is not very representative at all. Political scientists have argued that politicians who do not implement the policy agenda they were elected on undermine confidence in the political system and are one of the major reasons why voter turnout has dropped to just over half the population in the 1990s and 2000s. When citizens do not trust politicians to enact their policy promises, faith in the entire political system is undermined.

While the electorate is left out of the policy formulation, decision-making, and implementation stages, they come back into play in the evaluation stage. Citizens can study the implementation of policies they are interested in and develop their evaluations of how effective the previous government's solutions were. Then in the next election, citizens can render judgment on an incumbent government. If a citizen feels that an important policy issue was handled well by an incumbent, the citizen can reward him or her with re-election. If the incumbent made a mess of implementing the policy, the citizen, mindful of their policy failure, will vote for someone else. It is crucial for citizens to have some knowledge of politics to be able to evaluate past government performance and thus make an informed choice on Election Day.

Policy Networks

Policy implementation is often described either in terms of an Iron Triangle or through issue networks. *The Iron Triangle theory* has Congress, the bureaucracy and interest groups as the three points of a triangle which all interact with each other to implement policy. Alliances are formed between prominent members of issue-related committees in Congress, members of interest groups wanting a specific implementation on a policy issue, and prominent appointees in positions at the top of the bureaucratic hierarchy. The direction of policy implementation is then driven by these informal alliances in the three different sectors, who can control the policy implementation process and get the results they are after. Many people see iron triangles as a corruption of the bureaucracy since instead of letting experts in the bureaucracy use their skills to make the best policy implementations, power networks control how policy is shaped.

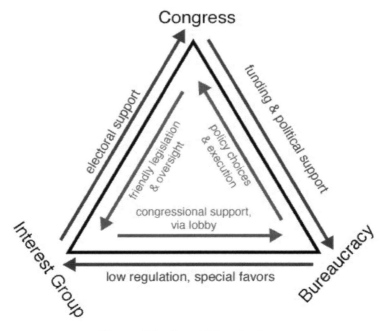

Chart of the Iron Triangle theory

Issue networks, in which iron triangles may form, can also explain the policy implementation process within the bureaucracy. A group of people dedicated to implementing an issue will form and rally members of the government, media, bureaucracy, and regular citizens to support certain policy implementations. Issue networks are more open and broad than iron triangles, as they are not necessarily dominated by political insiders but are open to action by those outside the government and bureaucracy. If the president's advisors, senior members of Congress, the media, the public, and prominent bureaucrats are all part of the same issue network, then policy implementation tends to move faster.

The main difference between an issue network and an Iron Triangle is that issue networks tend to promote the public good, while iron triangles tend to be more focused on advancing private interest. In cases where public good and private interest conflict, issue networks, and iron triangles can come into conflict. For example, environmental issues are a public good and are promoted by issue networks. Oil industry lobbyists seek a private advantage for their industry and form into an Iron Triangle with like-minded supporters seeking personal gain within the bureaucracy and Congress. In such a situation, an environmental issue network might come into direct conflict with an oil industry iron triangle. While issue networks tend to be looser collections of groups and individuals, and thus have lest vested power as an iron triangle, the fact that an issue network can rally public opinion and appeal to the common good can make them indirectly powerful.

Chapter 6

Civil Rights
and Civil Liberties

The development of individuals rights and liberties has had a meaningful impact on citizens and United States politics. Intrinsically tied to this topic are the workings of the United States Supreme Court and its most significant decisions.

The judicial interpretations of various civil rights and liberties, such as freedom of speech, assembly and expression, the rights of the accused and the rights of minority groups and women, offer critical insight into the evolution of United States politics.

The Fourteenth Amendment and the doctrine of selective incorporation have been used to extend the protection of rights and liberties, and the Supreme Court decisions have been tools for social change.

Notes

The Development of Civil Liberties and Civil Rights by Judicial Interpretation

The theory behind the idea of civil rights or civil liberties is that people have basic rights which cannot be violated, especially by the government. Through the codification of these rights in the Constitution through the Bill of Rights, people have the right to seek redress through the Supreme Court if Congress should pass a law which violates the rights and liberties of an individual. Critics of democracy often caricature it as two wolves and a sheep voting on what to eat for lunch, but with a set of constitutional rights, the minority is protected from this kind of abuse by the majority. While the Bill of Rights sought to outline what was considered basic and universal rights at the time, as times have changed, it has become clear that these rights have not always been applied fairly or equally to all segments of the population.

Since the unequal application of rights usually affects only minorities, Congress has traditionally been very slow to act, leaving them to the courts and popular movements on such issues. The issue of the applicability of rights first arose to prominence over the problem of slavery, which had divided American society from the establishment of the Republic. While slavery was legal and practiced throughout the thirteen colonies, the American Revolution sparked the idea of equality and freedom which led to five northern states abolishing slavery by 1789, just a few years after the formation of the United States. Despite the Constitution setting out rights for all, it was conspicuously silent on the issue of slavery, which would lead to problems down the road.

The Constitution indirectly dealt with the issue of slavery by stating in Article I, Section 9 that Congress will not change laws related to the migration or importation of people until the year 1808. At the end of 1807, Congress promptly passed a law that took effect on January 1, 1808, which banned the importation of slaves and thus put an end to the slave trade. Owning slaves was still legal but importing people to make them slaves was now banned.

Slavery was banned in most of the North but legal in the South, which was pursuing a divergent path of economic development, into the mid-1800s. Due to the lack of need for slave labor in the industrializing northern states, the institution of slavery was seen as unnecessary and without any value in the economic process. The southern states were reliant on labor-intensive cash crops, which would remain profitable even if looked after by paid laborers; however, the revenues would be drastically reduced. These economic differences, underscored by the status of being "free" states or slave states, led to important cultural and political differences between the North and the South.

Slave auction in America

Slavery became a major issue when considering which new states would be admitted to the Union. In 1820, Missouri applied to be admitted into the United States as a slave state. This caused a crisis because admitting Missouri as a slave state would mean that slave states would have held a majority in the Senate. Northern states were strongly opposed to admitting Missouri, but the federal government was adamant that its territory continues to expand to the west. As a result of this controversy, the Missouri Compromise was created, in which Missouri would be admitted as a slave state, but Massachusetts would be divided to create a new free state (Maine). The issue of the balance of power between slave states and "free" states would continue to be controversial and eventually lead to the outbreak of the Civil War.

In addition to the role of slavery on a state level within the Union, the more liberal political climate in the North led to the first Civil Rights Movement, led by the abolitionists, who publicly advocated for ending slavery. Abolitionists engaged in a variety of tactics to undermine slavery. Before the outlawing of the transatlantic slave trade, abolitionists would buy people who had been captured and sent to America to be slaves and then pay to ship them back to Africa. In the 1820s, former American slaves formed the independent state of Liberia in Western Africa and joined with the American abolitionists to send freed slaves to live in this new country. This was an extremely expensive proposed solution, and the abolitionists soon ran out of money. It was also controversial because by this time many American slaves were second or third generation and had little to no ties to Liberia or Africa in general.

The tone of the abolitionist movement shifted under the leadership of William Lloyd Garrison. Garrison called for immediate emancipation rather than trying to resettle former slaves in Liberia. At this time, the abolitionist movement was also being led by many free African-Americans such as Frederick Douglass, Robert Purvis, and James Fortin. These African-American leaders not only wrote important philosophical works condemning the injustice of slavery but were also responsible for leading various organizations in the abolitionist movement.

Many whites saw the collaboration of black and white Americans working together to abolish slavery at the time as scandalous. The major northern universities—Yale, Harvard, and Princeton—opposed the abolitionists on these grounds, leading to the establishment of more liberal colleges that admitted black students. New religious denominations, such as the Free Methodists, also came into being. Abolitionists started their newspapers, including Frederick Douglass' *North Star*, to promote the cause of abolition.

William Lloyd Garrison, leader of the abolitionist movement

In the 1850s, the abolitionist movement had a major split over the constitutionality of slavery. One side, led by William Lloyd Garrison, saw the Constitution as pro-slavery and called for a new constitution that explicitly outlawed it. The other side, led by Lysander Spooner and supported by Frederick Douglass, argued that the Constitution already outlawed slavery in practice, and just simply needed to be properly applied. Around this time the movement also split along class lines. Many wealthy northern industrialists began to support abolitionism in part because they saw slavery as providing an unfair economic advantage for the South, while the working class opposed this argument and insisted that equality be the most important principle.

In addition to internal efforts at reform, abolitionists played a prominent role in the development of the Underground Railroad, a network of safe houses set up by Abolitionists to allow escaped slaves to travel to the North and eventually on to Canada. Led by prominent activists such as Harriet Tubman, the network was able to transport approximately 30,000 people to freedom; most of them settled in Canada because of their illegal status in the United States under the Fugitive Slave Law of 1850. In some cases, abolitionists took more direct action to free captured escaped slaves. In 1858, abolitionists were able to free an escaped slave who was captured by the U.S. Marshal in Ohio, allowing him to escape to Canada. This became known as the Oberlin-Wellington Rescue, and the abolitionists who took part were put on federal trial, allowing them a national stage to argue the case for emancipation.

Another prominent abolitionist was John Brown, who advocated armed insurrection to overthrow slavery. Brown attempted to spark a national slave revolt through seizing arms at a U.S. military arsenal in Harper's Ferry, Virginia. Brown gathered twenty men and attempted to seize control of the arsenal but was defeated by a detachment of U.S. Marines led by Colonel Robert E. Lee. Although the raid was considered too risky by most abolitionists, including Douglass and Tubman, with Garrison calling it "misguided, wild, and insane," the trial turned John Brown into a hero in the North. His supporters included prominent philosophers such as Henry David Thoreau and Ralph Waldo Emmerson, and after the state of Virginia executed Brown, abolitionism became more prominent in the North where Brown was seen as a martyr. In the South, Brown was seen as a petty criminal trying to take away people's property, again revealing the major cultural and political differences in the North and the South that would culminate in the Civil War. Abolitionists strongly supported the Union and the Republican Party during the onset of the Civil War, which eventually led to Lincoln's Emancipation Proclamation that ended slavery.

U.S. Colonel Robert E. Lee

With the Union victory in the Civil War and the end of slavery, many abolitionists such as Garrison considered the movement a success and sought to disband the organizations he had founded. The Reconstruction Amendments were passed which outlawed discrimination against former slaves and black Americans, but some states passed legislation which skirted the intent of these amendments. Southern states passed the Black Codes immediately after the Civil War which dramatically restricted the freedom of African-Americans by preventing them from serving on a jury, voting, owning guns, and even gathering in public in a group for any purpose, including education or religious service.

Although slavery was no longer legal, blacks were still not free in the South. In an attempt to remedy these injustices, Congress passed the Civil Rights Act of 1866 which was intended to overrule the Black Codes. President Andrew Johnson used his presidential veto on the Civil Rights Act, but Congress, in an unprecedented move, used its ability to override a presidential veto, ensuring the law would take effect.

In the wake of the defeat of the Black Codes, southern states initiated Jim Crow laws which mandated racial segregation in all public facilities, affirming that blacks and whites were equal but should remain separate. Public schools, public spaces, public transportation, restrooms, restaurants, drinking fountains, and even the U.S. military were all segregated, meaning blacks and whites had to use separate facilities. By 1883, the Supreme Court ruled on some cases related to Jim Crow called the Civil Rights Cases. The court ruled that Congress can prohibit government discrimination based on race but had no jurisdiction to enforce civil rights in areas not directly related to the federal government.

In the 1896 *Plessy v. Ferguson* ruling, the court once again held up the legality of segregation by declaring that the separate but equal reasoning was valid. The challenge was initiated after a man who was seven-eighths white and one-eighth black had been denied a seat in the "whites only" section of a train. Since the 15th Amendment outlawed discriminating against people based on race for voting, southern states used other means to prevent blacks from voting. Many states adopted clauses that said one's grandfather must have been able to vote in order for one to vote legally. They also adopted property requirements and poll taxes which were only applied when African-Americans would try to register to vote, and some places even instituted biased tests which they could use to disenfranchise black Americans arbitrarily.

The Jim Crow laws and racial segregation remained in effect until a new Civil Rights Movement began to challenge these laws in the 1950s once again. In the landmark *Brown v. Board of Education* Supreme Court case, racially segregated schools were ruled unconstitutional, which was a major advance against segregation spurring renewed activism. The Supreme Court ruled that racial segregation in schools must be dismantled with "all deliberate speed" and federal court judges were put in charge of overseeing desegregation. In 1957, Arkansas governor Orval Faubus announced he would deploy the National Guard to forcefully prevent desegregation in the schools of Little Rock. This provoked a crisis with fears of another Civil War but was resolved when President Eisenhower sent federal troops to escort black students into a newly integrated high school. Desegregation in schools continued to be a controversial issue, especially with schoolchildren becoming pawns in the political posturing.

During this time in the 1950s, the Civil Rights Movement, emboldened by the *Brown v. Board of Education* ruling, began to increasingly challenge segregation in all aspects of society. In 1955, Rosa Parks made civil rights for black Americans a globally recognized issue after she refused to give up her seat on a bus to a white passenger. After Parks was arrested, the Montgomery Bus Boycott began, pushing for desegregation of public transport, a goal which was achieved the next year. Dr. Martin Luther King Jr. led the bus boycott among others, and the Civil Rights Movement went into high gear.

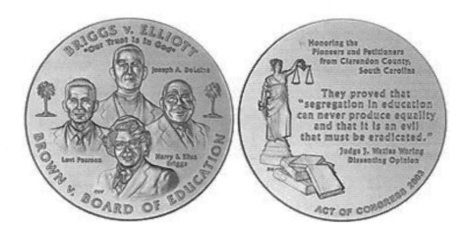

Medals that commemorate the leaders of the desegregation of public schools that led directly to Brown v. the Board of Education

Led by Dr. King, the Civil Rights Movement engaged in sit-ins, boycotts, and marches to draw attention to the injustice of the Jim Crow laws. The campaign spread and was supported by people of all skin colors, leading to the Freedom Riders. The Freedom Riders were a mix of black and white students who booked bus trips across the United States, purposely choosing mixed-race seating to force desegregation of intercity bus trips. These civil rights activists were met with violent resistance from local authorities. Eventually, the national and global media began to cover the violence by local police against the civil rights demonstrators and American public opinion began to favor Dr. King and the Civil Rights Movement overwhelmingly.

By 1963, President Kennedy asked Congress to pass a law banning racial segregation in public places. King believed the law was inadequate and wanted a ban on all forms of racial segregation. King organized a march of over 250,000 people in Washington D.C., culminating in his famous "I Have a Dream" speech. Meanwhile, President Kennedy was assassinated, leaving his successor, President Lyndon Johnson, to push for the bill in Congress, which was filibustered by senators from southern states. The law eventually passed, becoming the Civil Rights Act of 1964, which outlawed segregation on interstate transportation, allowed the federal government to withhold funding from institutions or groups engaged in racial discrimination, and specifically enshrined protection against discrimination by race, color, religion, sex or national origin into law.

The Civil Rights Movement in the South led by King saw this law as progress, though they believed it to be largely inadequate in addressing the central race-related issues of the day. Meanwhile, blacks in northern states faced economic issues, and a new movement led by Malcolm X emerged calling for more direct forms of protest and action against racial and economic discrimination. Originally, Malcolm X advocated for Black Nationalism and argued that blacks needed to make their own country in America because living equally with whites was impossible. Eventually, he came to see these views (influenced by the Nation of Islam movement) as racist and came to support King's Civil Rights Movement, although he favored more aggressive protest tactics and argued that the movement should focus on linking the plight of blacks in America to human rights issues around the world.

The issue of voting rights continued to be an issue after the passage of the Civil Rights Act of 1964. To protest discrimination against potential black voters, a march from Selma to Montgomery in March 1965 was formed. The march was attacked by vigilantes and state troopers, with local organizer Amelia Boynton being beaten unconscious. A second march was planned for two days later, to be led by Martin Luther King Jr. despite various threats on his life. King led the march to the bridge where the demonstrators were attacked two days later, and after a standoff, the police and vigilantes stepped aside. King decided to lead the marchers back into Selma to wait for possible federal protection. That night activist James Reeb, a white minister from Boston who had come to support King, was beaten to death by vigilantes.

James Reeb's murder catalyzed public opinion once again in favor of the marchers, and President Johnson asked for Congress to immediately put forward a voter protection act and offered federal troops to protect the marchers. After leading the push for equal rights in housing, the movement spurred Congress into considering a new Civil Rights Act in 1968 in the wake of King's assassination and a renewed push for protests. This act was passed despite another filibuster attempt from southern senators and outlawed discrimination on housing issues.

Women's Rights and the Suffragette Movement

As with the issue of slavery, the status of women was left to individual states. Shortly after independence, the status of women was somewhat unclear, and women with property were allowed to vote in states such as New Jersey. As states adopted their legal frameworks, however, women's political rights were quickly outlawed, and the women who could vote in certain states had lost that right by 1807. As the abolitionist movement picked up steam in the 1830s and 1840s, many of the participants started to question the second-class status of women as well as slaves. In 1848, prominent abolitionist Elizabeth Cady Stanton organized the Seneca Falls Convention, which was the first gathering of women's rights activists and the birth of the suffragette movement in the United States. Suffragettes were women who advocated for universal suffrage, meaning that anyone should be able to vote, whether man or woman. This convention set the stage for the women's rights agenda, advocating for changes in various social and legal codes to grant women more of a voice, however, the issue of voting rights for women was controversial even within the women's rights movement.

Suffragettes Elizabeth Cady Stanton (left) and Susan B. Anthony (right)

Elizabeth Cady Stanton, Susan B. Anthony and Lucy Stone began to organize women after the Civil War to promote voting rights. In 1867, they addressed state governments in New York and Kansas and started to form more explicit links with African-American groups who were facing similar issues in the sphere of disenfranchisement. Around this time, the passing of the 14th Amendment also divided the women's movement. While most suffragettes were also abolitionists, the 14th Amendment specified representation for male citizens, which suffragettes pointed out was discriminatory language. The 15th Amendment was also problematic; it outlawed discrimination based on race, color or previous condition of servitude for voting but made no mention of sex as a possible basis of discrimination.

The women's movement felt that the Reconstruction Amendments were a lost chance to remedy the injustice of their lower position in American society, as they felt that women's issues could have been linked to the injustices suffered by slaves. After initially opposing the 14th Amendment, the suffragettes changed their strategy and decided that it could be the legal basis for the right to vote for women. In 1871, Victoria Woodhull spoke at the House of Representatives and argued that the 14th Amendment should grant women the right to vote, but the House disagreed with her. In 1872, Susan B. Anthony took matters into her own hands and registered to vote in Rochester, N.Y., citing the 14th Amendment, which led to her arrest and ultimately jail time.

Feminist and suffragette Victoria Woodhull

During this time, the United States was expanding west, and many of the new western states were granting women the right to vote, creating inconsistent rights (much like slavery) across the United States. Victories for the right to vote in the West emboldened the suffragette movement in the East as they continued to push Congress to legislate voting rights for women. Throughout the 1880s, many states revoked women's voting rights while other states, including Rhode Island in the East, granted women the right to vote. This frustrating flip-flop of rights continued into the early 1900s when American suffragettes joined with suffragettes in ten other countries to form an international movement. By 1910, the suffragette movement had grown and was now holding mass demonstrations, with over 3,000 women marching in demonstrations in New York City.

In the 1910s, the movement continued to pick up steam as more western states adopted universal suffrage, and in 1912 Theodore Roosevelt's Progressive Party included women's voting rights as part of its election platform. After intensive lobbying by women's groups, in 1916 Woodrow Wilson promised that women's suffrage would be part of the Democratic Party's platform in the next election. In the same year, Jeannette Rankin of Montana was elected to the House of Representatives, becoming the first female member of Congress at a time when many states still not allowing women to vote.

Spurred by a wave of protests and more western states granting women's suffrage, in 1918 the 19th Amendment was passed in the House of Commons after Rankin opened the debate. The 19th Amendment was originally proposed in 1872 by a Senator who had become friends with Susan B. Anthony. The Amendment was identical to the 15th Amendment except it outlawed voting discrimination based on sex. After the amendment passed in the House in 1918, it failed to pass in the Senate by just two votes. The failure in the Senate caused President Wilson to get involved and directly support the cause of suffrage, which eventually led to the amendment being ratified in 1920, granting full suffrage to women across the country.

Having won this victory in 1920, the women's rights movement was quiet until the 1950s and early 1960s. Women participating in the Civil Rights Movement again began to see parallels between the lack of proper rights for themselves and African Americans. In 1961, women were not allowed to serve on juries in many states, including Florida. In the famous *Hoyt v. Florida* case, a woman who was convicted by an all-male jury of killing her abusive husband, filed a Supreme Court appeal, with her lawyers arguing that she was insane, and the male jury had refused to consider this; therefore, women should be allowed to serve on juries to balance potential bias. However, the Supreme Court upheld the ability to discriminate against women by preventing them from serving on juries, a ruling which angered women across the country and spurred a new push for women's rights. The *Hoyt v. Florida* ruling was not overturned until 1975.

The 1960s also saw two major legal advances. The first was the Presidential Commission on the Status of Women (PCSW) initiated by President Kennedy in 1961 and revealed its findings in 1963. The PCSW garnered a great deal of public attention as it criticized the unequal status of American women in what was supposedly free society. This work culminated in the 1963 Equal Pay Act which prohibited employers from purposefully paying women less than men for doing the same job. The second major advancement was the inclusion of a ban on sex discrimination in the Civil Rights Act of 1964.

Eleanor Roosevelt (left) and Esther Peterson (right)
of the Presidential Commission on the Status of Women

The ban on sex discrimination was added onto the act by a southern Democrat, Senator Howard Smith of Virginia, who thought by adding women's rights to the act, he would make the act fail to pass Congress. He erroneously believed that even if civil rights were widely supported, rights for women were not. He was embarrassed when the act passed, and then publicly argued that he was actually a strong supporter of women's rights and was not simply trying to make the act fail to pass Congress. Many historians are skeptical of his later claims, and believe his true motivation was trying to sink the bill. By having women's issues included in the Civil Rights Act, the women's rights movement was emboldened and became more active now that it had a legal basis to challenge discrimination.

In 1973, the women's movement had begun to focus on issues related to reproductive freedom. The landmark 1973 *Roe v. Wade* case was a huge victory for women's rights. The Supreme Court ruled that women had a constitutional right to privacy, and thus the decision to terminate an abortion was no one's business but that of the individual woman. State laws criminalizing abortion were struck down as a violation of women's right to privacy and ability to make their own choices.

In 1971, the *Reed v. Reed* Supreme Court ruling interpreted the 14th Amendment as covering sex discrimination and thus throughout the 1970s and into the 1980s, the Supreme Court began to interpret the 14th Amendment as protecting women's rights and increasingly ruled in favor of women's rights, using this ruling as a legal basis.

Continuing Rights Issues

While the civil rights and women's movements were the two biggest movements for basic rights, other groups who have been denied rights or equal treatment have been active in fighting for their causes more recently. Hispanic Americans began pushing to end discrimination in the late 1960s and early 1970s. In particular, the Mexican American Legal Defense and Education Fund (MALDEF) has played a prominent role. Recently MALDEF has pushed to end discrimination against migrant workers and has fought to ensure that redistricting does not lead to deliberate attempts to disenfranchise Hispanic voters. In May 2006, they organized a massive one-day march to oppose new restrictions on immigration and oppose proposals to build a militarized wall along the Mexican border.

Native Americans have also had to fight to end discrimination and have their rights recognized. While indigenous peoples have had the right to vote since 1924, they began to organize as a collective force against discrimination in the 1960s. In 1968, the American Indian Movement (AIM) was formed to promote civil rights for Native Americans, ensure treaty rights were recognized and advocate for the economic well-being of indigenous people. AIM was one of the main targets of the FBI's highly secret COINTELPRO program, which used covert and often illegal tactics to infiltrate and discredit activist groups from the 1950s to the 1970s. COINTELPRO also infiltrated and attempted to spread malicious disinformation and internal dissension in the Civil Rights Movement, targeting Martin Luther King Jr. and Malcolm X in particular.

While COINTELPRO was originally designed to spy on suspected communists in the 1950s, it quickly morphed into a mechanism through which the FBI attempted to disrupt the growing activists of the 1960s who were trying to end discrimination and assert their basic rights. The program was finally exposed by the Senate's Church Committee (named after Senator Frank Church) who led an investigation into the program and had it shut down.

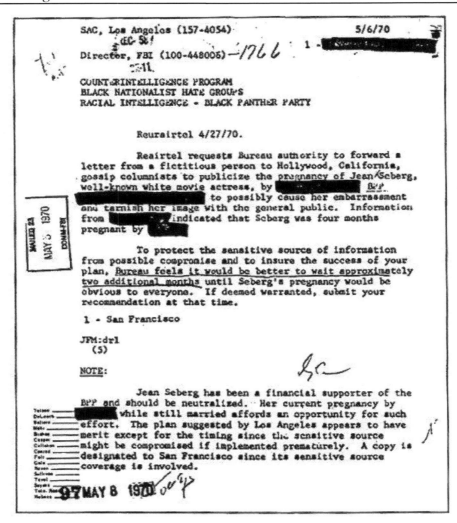

A COINTELPRO document outlining the FBI's plans
to 'neutralize' activist Jean Seberg for her support of the Black Panther Party

Amid FBI infiltration and internal division, AIM's most famous action was the occupation of the town of Wounded Knee, South Dakota, in 1973. AIM was trying to draw national attention to the mistreatment of Native Americans from local authorities, but the FBI sent in U.S. Marshals who escalated the situation into a siege. One AIM activist was killed, an FBI agent was shot and left paralyzed, and a dozen activists were wounded during the seventy-one-day siege. Eventually, the FBI arrested 1,200 members of AIM, but all charges were dismissed at trial due to the overreaching and heavy-handed actions of the government. The situation has since improved, with many Native American groups winning land sovereignty which allows them a form of self-government within the larger American context. More recently, Native American groups have been turning to the official political process and trying to organize people to elect Native Americans to the House of Representatives to give their issues official representation.

One quirk of the sovereign land situation is that the Constitution does not apply to legally recognized sovereign tribes. This became an issue in 2015 with the Supreme Court legalizing same-sex marriage. While virtually all tribal laws either defer this issue to federal or state legislation, the Navajo nation explicitly forbids same-sex marriage, and the Supreme Court ruling cannot override this. As a result, lesbian and gay activists within the Navajo community are now engaged in fighting for the recognition of their rights at the local level of government.

In 2015, lesbian activist Cleo Pablo launched a challenge of the Navajo ban on same-sex marriage, arguing that it violates the Navajo constitution which guarantees equal rights for all. This case presents an interesting collision between two sets of rights, as what is considered beneficial for one group is considered problematic for another. Thus, while sovereignty rights ended discrimination against Native Americans as a group, individuals within the group can still feel that their rights are not properly recognized as they become targets of discrimination for being a minority within a minority.

The issue of colliding rights claims is also becoming increasingly prominent about the First Amendment's separation of church and state. As many Christian groups have begun to undermine this separation backed by changing legal interpretations, minority religious groups such as the Church of Satan have taken the opportunity to cite these public displays of religion by Christians to allow them to demonstrate in favor of Satanism openly.

While the Church of Satan is somewhat ironic in that they do not believe in Satan, the public displays of their religion are often enough to make Christian groups rethink whether they want to open the public realm up to religion. After a Christian group's installation of a monument depicting the Ten Commandments outside a courthouse in Oklahoma was ruled constitutional, the Church of Satan installed a monument beside it depicting a goat-headed Satan. Under the Equal Protection Clause of the 14th Amendment, the Church of Satan argued that if Christian symbols can be displayed on government property, then their Satanic imagery must be legally protected as well.

People with disabilities faced discrimination in the past as well. Often led by veterans who had been wounded in war, the disabled Americans movement culminated in 1990 with the passage of the Americans with Disabilities Act, which banned discrimination on account of physical or mental disability. This legislation required that public facilities be accessible to people in wheelchairs, alternate services are provided to hearing-impaired people, and that employers had to be flexible in accommodating people with disabilities. This act has been subject to various pieces of litigation and Supreme Court rulings, which have decided that the ADA protect pregnant women from discrimination as well as people living with AIDS.

President George H. W. Bush signs the Americans with Disabilities Act of 1990

In 2004, the *Tennessee v. Lane* case was an important ruling on the ADA, as it set a precedent enabling the federal government to enforce it. The plaintiffs argued that a Tennessee courthouse was in violation of the ADA after a man in a wheelchair had to crawl upstairs to meet a court appointment to avoid being jailed and that this amounted to discrimination. Tennessee argued that the ADA did not have jurisdiction in a state courthouse, but the Supreme Court ruled that it did.

One of the enduring controversies today is the issue of affirmative action. In general, affirmative action is based on the principles of restorative justice and is meant to help people from groups which have been historically discriminated against. Critics of affirmative action argue that it is a form of discrimination itself. The Supreme Court first ruled on the issue of affirmative action in 1978 in the *Bakke v. Regents of the University of California* case. Bakke argued that U.C. Davis discriminated against him because they had two separate admission criteria, one for black students and one for white students. The court ruled that this amounted to discrimination and ordered U.C. Davis not to use racial quotas in its admissions.

Affirmative action programs were still legal but only if they did not have strict quotas and there was clear evidence of past historical discrimination. In 1986, after President Regan's Supreme Court appointee William Rehnquist became Chief Justice, the court increasingly began to rule against the constitutionality of affirmative action programs. This prompted the Democrat-controlled Congress to pass the 1991 Civil Rights Act which affirmed the legality of affirmative action, so long as quotas were not used. Throughout the 1990s, the Supreme Court continued to rule against affirmative action, including major rulings in Texas and California.

U.S. Supreme Court Justice William Rehnquist

In 2003 the landmark *Grutter v. Bollinger* case upheld the legality of the University of Michigan Law School's affirmative action plan, arguing that it was in the public interest to ensure that diversity was represented in the legal profession. The ruling meant that considerations such as race or economic class could be a factor in college admission, but that every individual needed to be considered based on their merit, and it once again upheld that any sort of quota system which might bar someone from being admitted to college on the basis of race would be illegal. This case was important because it reframed affirmative action to be about ensuring that student populations would be representative of the diversity of American society.

While previously affirmative action was argued as a means to overcome past injustice, the court was now interpreting it to maintain current diversity. A further ruling based on the precedent set in the 2003 case came in 2007 with the *Parents Involved in Community Schools v. Seattle School District No. 1* case. In this case, schools were using racial classifications to assign children to school districts to ensure that individuals were not "racially isolated." The court upheld that diversity was in the public interest but ultimately ruled that these programs should be stopped because they were not being implemented properly.

Gay Rights

One of the most recent groups to win legal protection against discrimination has been the LGBT community. The bulk of the progress on gay rights has come through activism and Supreme Court decisions, with Congress often lagging behind popular opinion. Laws against homosexual activity date back to the founding of America. Originally punishable by death, by the late 1700s, the most common punishment for engaging in homosexual activity was life in prison. The issue remained largely taboo until the 1940s and 1950s when the scientific study of sexuality (known as *The Kinsey Report*) provided a counter-narrative to the Christian-dominated sexual mores of the previous era.

Some Supreme Court rulings which advanced the cause of ending discrimination against gays and lesbians. The first of these rulings came when the gay liberation movement was in its infancy. In 1958, the Supreme Court ruled that a gay-themed magazine could not be banned as this was a violation of the 1st Amendment. This ruling was a landmark case as it was the first to deal with the issue of homosexuality.

Amid the sexual revolution of the late 1960s and the general upheaval in the context of the civil rights and women's movements, the Gay Liberation Movement was formed in the late 1960s. A major turning point in the movement came in June 1969 when police in New York City raided a popular gay, and transgender bar called the Stonewall Inn. While police had regularly conducted raids on gay bars, jailing those they caught inside for various crimes, the raid on Stonewall was different because the patrons inside the bar actively resisted the police and fought back against arrest.

Stonewall was a significant event because it demonstrated to gays and lesbians that they did not have to accept persecution and police brutality but could fight back and assert their rights. Various activist groups were formed in the 1970s with the intent of liberalizing laws against homosexual activity. Many of these groups explicitly linked gay rights to human rights and positioned themselves as part of the wider movement to push governments to not discriminate against groups of people for any reason whatsoever.

In the early 1970s, there was a trend toward gay migration, in which gays and lesbians would seek to move to cities which were deemed less hostile. In particular, San Francisco attracted many people in the 1970s, especially with the election of openly gay city councilor Harvey Milk. Milk played a prominent role in the Gay Rights Movement, being perhaps the first openly gay prominent politician in American history, but like so many other civil rights leaders of the time, he was assassinated in 1978. After Milk's assassin was convicted of voluntary manslaughter (the lightest possible sentence) for killing both Milk and the mayor of San Francisco, riots erupted in the streets as people were outraged by the light sentence for a political assassin. Later that year, the first gay rights march took place in Washington D.C., attended by 100,000 people.

Politician and activist Harvey Milk

The next wave of the Gay Liberation Movement began in the early 1980s when the AIDS epidemic swept through the gay community. This era was focused on sexual education and ending stigmas against gay men and AIDS sufferers. After the invention of AIDS drugs which dramatically increased the life expectancy of people with the disease in the late 1990s, the movement shifted again to ending hate crimes and promoting same-sex marriage rights.

In 1972 a teacher in Tacoma, Washington was fired for being gay; the Supreme Court refused to hear his appeal. The lower court argued that being gay was inherently immoral and thus having immoral people as teachers would corrupt the students. In 2014, the school board finally issued an apology to the teacher after 42 years. This case was important because it was one of the first times an issue related to gay rights was reported on by the nightly television news. Thus an estimated 60 million Americans learned about this case of discrimination on an issue that had been previously taboo to speak about publicly.

The issue of gay teachers came back to the Supreme Court in 1984 with the *National Gay Task Force v. Board of Education* case. The Supreme Court was divided which led to the lower court's order striking down the ability to fire gay teachers to stand. This case was argued in terms of the 1st and 14th Amendments. This was the first time that the non-discrimination clauses of the 14th Amendment were applied to the issue of discrimination against sexual orientation, thus setting an important precedent. In the same year, however, the Supreme Court refused to hear an appeal by a gay student association at Texas A&M that had been banned by the university.

In a major defeat for gay rights, the 1986 *Bowers v. Hardwick* Supreme Court ruled that gays and lesbians do not have the right to privacy afforded by the 14th Amendment, and thus Georgia laws banning homosexual acts in private among consenting adults were upheld as constitutional. This ruling was later overturned in 2003 with *Lawrence v. Texas* which decided that laws against homosexual acts be unconstitutional under the 14th Amendment's due process clause.

In the 2000 case *Boy Scouts of America v. Dale*, the Supreme Court ruled that the Boy Scouts have a right to exclude gay Scout leaders under the 1st Amendment. It was not until the 2003 *Lawrence v. Texas* case that the Supreme Court finally started to treat sexual orientation as a serious form of discrimination. Before this 2003 ruling, same-sex sexual activity was illegal in 14 states. This case is seen as a landmark ruling as it finally and fully asserted the legal right of gays and lesbians against discrimination and ensured that same-sex acts were legal.

Although gays and lesbians recently won full legal rights in 2003, the Supreme Court has acted fairly swiftly since then. In 2013, just ten years after *Lawrence v. Texas*, the Supreme Court ruled that President Clinton's Defense of Marriage Act was partly unconstitutional and that the federal government could not outlaw marriage between two people of the same sex because this violated due process. In 2015, the landmark *Obergefell v. Hodges* case struck down all state bans on same-sex marriage, making it legal nationwide. The due process and equal protection clauses of the 14th Amendment once again formed the basis for this ruling. The court cited the *Loving v. Virginia* case of 1967 which removed bans on interracial marriage as precedent. Thus, once again, the Civil Rights Movement continues to have ramifications in protecting the rights of all Americans.

Knowledge of Substantive Rights and Liberties

The legal basis of the rights of American citizens is derived from the Bill of Rights and the later amendments that dealt with rights issues. The Bill of Rights was the first Ten Amendments to the Constitution and were proposed to ease the fears of the Anti-Federalists who believed that the new American government would have too much power. The authors of *The Federalist Papers*, including Alexander Hamilton and James Madison, were originally leery of including a set of rights in the Constitution because they were worried that it would be assumed that any rights not specifically mentioned would be assumed not to exist. As a result, a bill of rights was not included in the original Constitution. Prominent Anti-Federalists such as Patrick Henry and Samuel Adams argued that the new Constitution provided no protection for individual rights against the government, and thus inverted the fears of Hamilton by pointing out that if rights are not spelled out in the Constitution, it will be assumed no rights exist at all.

Ratifying the original Constitution without a Bill of Rights was controversial, especially in Massachusetts, where the state convention on ratification turned ugly. When Anti-Federalist Elbridge Gerry was not allowed to speak to the assembly, a fist fight broke out between him and Federalist delegate Francis Dana. The melee was stopped only after Samuel Adams and John Hancock got involved and agreed on a compromise which said that Massachusetts would ratify the existing Constitution on the condition that Amendments would be proposed outlining a set of rights for citizens. These proposals would go on to become the 5th and 10th Amendments.

Elbridge Gerry, American politician, and Anti-Federalist

After the success of the Anti-Federalists in Massachusetts of adding conditions to ratification, similar conditions were put in place in Virginia and New York. Over the course of these disputes over ratification, James Madison came to see the necessity of a Bill of Rights after his initial opposition and began to craft a first draft of the Bill of Rights for consideration by Congress.

Federalists in the House of Representatives were initially strongly opposed, as they saw amending the Constitution so soon after its ratification as something that might shake the public's faith in the stability of the new government. Eventually, the House passed seventeen of Madison's proposed twenty amendments onto the Senate. The Senate reworded many of these amendments and chopped them down to just twelve. A joint committee between the House and Senate eventually got the language of the amendments agreed upon and in 1789 passed the proposed twelve amendments onto the states for ratification. Articles III to XII was ratified in 1792 and became the first ten amendments, which make up the Bill of Rights.

After the Bill of Rights was ratified, it essentially lay legally dormant for 150 years. The Supreme Court made no important rulings based on these rights, and they were rarely invoked in the context of legal arguments. For example, the Supreme Court did not make a ruling on a free speech issue until 1931. Part of the reason for this lies in the fact that these rights were thought of as only between citizens and the federal government, allowing state governments to pass their laws that essentially contravened the Bill of Rights. Once again, it was not until the 14th Amendment declared that these rights would trump any law passed by a state government.

First Amendment

The 1st Amendment states "Congress shall make no law respecting an establishment of religion or prohibiting the free exercise thereof; or abridging the freedom of speech, or of the press, or the right of the people peaceably to assemble, and to petition the Government for a redress of grievances." This amendment is perhaps the most complex, as it includes some different and even unrelated basic political rights. The basis for this amendment stems from similar statements in nine of the state government constitutions. This amendment was strongly supported by Anti-Federalists who argued that civil liberties needed to be explicitly protected in the Constitution.

The first part of the amendment relates to freedom of religion and is based on Thomas Jefferson's argument that there needed to be a "wall of separation between church and state."

Jefferson argued that religion was a matter between "man and his god" and thus the government should have no business legislating on religious matters. Jefferson also saw this right as protecting the beliefs of minority religions from persecution and protecting the right to hold any opinion one wished. For Jefferson, religion happened in the church, politics happened in government, and any overlap between the two would infringe on the freedom of both. In an early Supreme Court ruling on this issue (*Reynolds v. United States*, 1878), the court ruled that freedom of religion apply to belief and opinion, but not to action. This meant that one could not break the law and claim freedom of religion as a justification; freedom of religion meant freedom of belief, not of action.

In the Cold War period, the wall of separation Jefferson had wanted, and which was guaranteed by the 1st Amendment began to unravel somewhat. Religious language was added to money and the pledge of allegiance, and court rulings began to interpret the 1st Amendment differently to allow public money for religious schools. The staunch secularism of the constitutional framers has given way somewhat to new interpretations allowing what would have seemed like egregious breaches of the 1st Amendment in Jefferson's day to persist. Displaying religious symbols is now permitted in courthouses in many states, and this is increasingly being interpreted as compatible with the 1st Amendment.

Free speech is the second aspect of this amendment and is mainly designed to prevent prosecution of people who are openly critical of the government. The Supreme Court was silent on this issue until the 20th Century, but under the second president, John Quincy Adams, a law was passed banning anyone from advocating overthrowing the U.S. government. Jefferson and Madison argued that this was a flagrant violation of the 1st Amendment, but the court did not rule on it. Adams' anti-free speech laws were publicly very unpopular, leading Jefferson to become president and quickly eliminate those laws. During World War I and in the wake of the Communist Revolution in Russia, Congress passed the Espionage Act of 1917, which placed restrictions on what American citizens could say about the U.S. military; in particular, any attempts to promote insubordination were punishable with twenty years in prison.

After a Socialist Party member was convicted for handing out pamphlets advocating for Americans to resist the draft, he challenged the conviction as a violation of his 1st Amendment rights to freedom of speech. The Supreme Court ruled against him, and his conviction was upheld. In 1918, the famous political activist Eugene Debs gave a speech criticizing prosecutions under the Espionage Act as violating the freedom of speech of Americans, leading him to be arrested under the act as well. He challenged the case, but once again the Supreme Court upheld his conviction, claiming that his words presented a clear and present danger to America. As can be seen from these cases, the Supreme Court has not always upheld the basic rights outlined in the Bill of Rights, as the political context of mass hysteria about Communism led to rulings which later legal scholars have argued were erroneous.

Eugene Debs, political activist

Throughout the 1920s, the Supreme Court issued some rulings that continued the trend of ruling against freedom of speech. Finally, in 1937, after an African-American Communist leader was charged with insurrection under a Reconstruction Era law in Georgia meant to outlaw rebellions by former slaves, the Supreme Court ruled that this law be an unconstitutional violation of freedom of speech, marking the first significant court victory to uphold the right to free speech.

In 1940, Congress passed the Smith Act, which was used to jail Communist leaders. The Supreme Court upheld this law in 1951, but in 1957 the Supreme Court ruled that the act could not be applied to those who simply believed in Communism, but only to those who explicitly acted to overthrow the government, which was a significant victory for freedom of speech and the 1st Amendment. By the late 1960s and early 1970s, the court shifted and began to accept that freedom of speech included the right to openly criticize the government in major rulings, upholding the 1st Amendment rights of those opposed to the Vietnam War.

The third aspect of this amendment is the right to freedom of the press, which means that the government cannot control what is published. While the language refers to printing presses and thus newspapers, it has been interpreted to refer to any form of public media, including radio, television and even video games. The first major test of freedom of the press did not come until 1931 when Minnesota passed a law which enabled the state to shut down any newspaper it deemed to be publishing malicious or scandalous writing. The Supreme Court ruled that this law be an unconstitutional violation of the 1st amendment, and quoted James Madison's argument that a courageous and vigilant press was necessary to prevent democracy from being impaired.

James Madison, fourth President of the United States

The court once again upheld freedom of the press in 1971 when President Nixon tried to prevent the *New York Times* from publishing leaked documents. The documents, called the Pentagon Papers, proved that the United States had secretly begun carrying out bombing campaigns and deploying ground forces to Laos and Cambodia without the consent of the Congress. Nixon attempted to argue that the publication of these documents would threaten national safety by giving away troop movements, but the court ruled that these were documents describing events that had already happened, rather than plans.

The fourth and fifth clauses of the 1st Amendment guarantee the right for citizens to petition the government and to assemble peacefully. The right to petition means that citizens have the right to contact government officials and politicians, engage in lobbying and file grievances with the court system on political issues. The petition clause was first challenged in 1830 when Congress banned petitions from abolitionists, but they overturned this law a few years later before the court could rule.

In the early 1920s, those signing petitions in favor of repealing the anti-freedom of speech Espionage Act were thrown in jail, but again the Supreme Court did not rule on this violation of the 1st Amendment. Freedom of assembly means that any group of people can get together for political purposes, including petitioning the government, such as in a public protest. Non-violent protests broken up by police intervention, such as during the Vietnam

War, are often cited as a violation of the right to freedom of assembly. In protests against the Iraq War, police often established small "free speech zones," which were set aside for protesters; the implication was that freedom of speech and assembly were not permitted elsewhere. Many activists sought to challenge these tactics under the 1st Amendment, but no case was ever heard by the court.

Second Amendment

The 2nd Amendment states "A well regulated militia being necessary to the security of a free state, the right of the people to keep and bear arms shall not be infringed." This has proven to be by far the most controversial amendment and also the one open to the widest range of interpretation. The context of this amendment comes out of the early Revolutionary period in American history, in which American rebels against British authority relied on their ownership of personal firearms to start an insurrection against British rule. There was a strong thrust of intent behind this amendment which invoked the pre-independence period and also implied that citizens have the right to violently overthrow the government should they deem it to be tyrannical.

The 2nd Amendment was also a means to get the Anti-Federalists on board, as it preserved state militias and provided reassurances against the central authority of the federal government. In today's context, these concerns seem completely irrelevant and even alien, as owning a gun to overthrow the government should it become tyrannical is liable to get one thrown in jail as a terrorist.

In the first few decades after the amendment was ratified, the focus was on the issue of militias. Many Americans were extremely opposed to the idea of having a standing federal military and instead argued that the 2nd Amendment outlawed such a professional military in favor of citizen militias. This interpretation focused on the right to form a militia, rather than gun ownership. Such early militias were considered a matter of civic duty and often involved weapons other than guns, including clubs and farm tools, such as pitchforks.

The 2nd Amendment was invoked in 1792 by a group of farmers in Pennsylvania who argued that the government had become tyrannical and thus they had a right to use their firearms to violently overthrow it. Neighboring states also invoked the 2nd Amendment to fight against the Farmers' Insurrection, by attempting to raise a militia to fight against the insurrectionists. The government found few people willing to join the militia and resorted to drafting people into the militia, which was an extremely unpopular decision. Eventually, President Washington personally led a militia of 7,000 men, who were able to put down the rebellion through negotiation. The lack of a standing army was criticized as allowing the insurrection to last longer than it should have and was blamed for the unpreparedness when British Canadians succeeded in burning down the White House during the War of 1812.

The burning of Washington during the War of 1812

Eventually, a standing army was adopted, and interpretation of the amendment shifted to emphasize the "bear arms" portion rather than the "militia" portion. Multiple legal scholars developed conflicting interpretations which continue to be controversial today. Some argue that gun ownership is dependent on being a member of a well-regulated militia, which implies that gun ownership is not an individual right but a collective one. This argument states that the 2nd Amendment means that individual states have a right to arm their militias. A deviation of this collective rights interpretation argues that individuals who are part of a well-regulated militia have the right to own guns personally, but if one is not part of such a militia, there is no individual right to gun ownership.

A third interpretation argues that the amendment outlines the right for individual Americans to own guns. This interpretation rejects the idea that the lack of existence of militias today invalidates the right to gun ownership and argues that the statements about a militia are merely a philosophical statement and not a dependent clause upon which gun ownership must rest. In 2001, a district court ruled that the individual rights approach should establish a future precedent, thus making gun ownership unlinked to militia membership. This individual rights interpretation was upheld by the Supreme Court in *District of Columbia v. Heller* (1998), taking the position that this right exists independently of belonging to a well-regulated militia. This interpretation by the Supreme Court remains extremely controversial today, as they have interpreted the amendment in such a way as to ignore the initial clause related to regulating militias.

Third Amendment

The 3rd Amendment states: "No Soldier shall, in time of peace be quartered in any house, without the consent of the Owner, nor in time of war, but in a manner to be prescribed by law." This amendment states that the government cannot force an individual to house soldiers in their home. While in today's context this sounds like a strange right to outline so high in the Bill of Rights, this was a symbolically important right in the time the amendment was adopted. In 1765, British Parliament had passed an act which required American colonists to pay the costs of quartering British soldiers in the thirteen colonies, and that if there were not enough space in the local military barracks, colonists would have to house soldiers for free at local inns and taverns.

After the Boston Tea Party, British Parliament passed another act which required American colonists to house British soldiers in their private homes if necessary. This act was listed as one of the Intolerable Acts cited by the American revolutionaries as the reason they were demanding independence from Britain. Thus, adding this to the Bill of Rights was a symbolic statement against the oppression of Britain before independence. The Supreme Court has never heard a case by the 3rd Amendment, and it is rarely a source of litigation at the district court level.

Throwing tea overboard during the Boston Tea Party

Fourth Amendment

The 4th Amendment states: "The right of the people to be secure in their persons, houses, papers, and effects, against unreasonable searches and seizures, shall not be violated, and no Warrants shall issue, but upon probable cause, supported by Oath or affirmation, and particularly describing the place to be searched, and the persons or things to be seized." This amendment is designed to protect against unreasonable searches and seizures of property and requires a court-ordered warrant based on probable cause to allow the police to search you. Practically this means that organs of government, in most cases the police, cannot simply search people at random and cannot take their things at random. For police to search you, they need to be issued a warrant by a neutral third party like a judge, and they need to present an argument to the judge that they have probable cause that you did something illegal and that the search will turn up evidence of that illegal activity.

The *Chandler v. Miller* (1997) Supreme Court ruling upheld that probable cause must be based on individual suspicion of wrongdoing. This ruling struck down a Georgia law requiring all state employees to undergo drug testing as an unreasonable search because it targeted a large group of people with no past evidence or future suspicion of drug use.

In *Katz v. United States* (1967) the court ruled that this amendment applies to "people and not places" and thus ruled that a wiretap on a public pay phone without a warrant be an unconstitutional search. This ruling also established the provisions for a general right to an expectation of privacy, as despite using a public pay phone, the person making the phone call had a reasonable expectation that the person would only hear the conversation on the other end of the line, and not the FBI or any wider audience. It is unclear so far as to whether the 4th Amendment applies to online activities and web browsing. Some civil liberties groups claim that government spying programs are a violation of the 4th Amendment, as they collect all information without a warrant and individual suspicion. Such a case has yet to be tried at the Supreme Court level.

Exceptions to the 4th Amendment should be noted. If an individual provides consent to be searched, then they can no longer claim a 4th Amendment violation. In 1973, the Supreme Court ruled in *Schneckloth v. Bustamonte* that the police do not need to inform an individual that they have the right to refuse a search without a warrant. In *United States v. Matlock* (1974), the Court ruled that a third-party occupant could give consent for police to search a house co-occupied by someone else. This means if the police want to search your house, your roommate can give them consent, and they can do so without a warrant or your explicit consent.

Police can also perform a "search" of objects in plain view without requiring a warrant. For example, if someone steals a car and parks it in his or her driveway and the police can see it while driving down the street, this can count as evidence for arrest without requiring a warrant. Motor vehicles are also an exception, as they are not considered a private residence. This means that police can search a car with probable cause and seize items in plain view but cannot search a driver or passenger without a warrant or consent. An important way that the 4th Amendment is enforced is through the Exclusionary Rule. This rule is the result of a 1914 Supreme Court ruling and states that any evidence obtained in violation of the 4th Amendment is not admissible in court. Before 1914, any evidence, even if obtained illegally, was allowed in a court trial.

Fifth Amendment

The 5th Amendment states: "No person shall be held to answer for a capital, or otherwise infamous crime, unless on a presentment or indictment of a Grand Jury, except in cases arising in the land or naval forces, or in the Militia, when in actual service in time of War or public danger; nor shall any person be subject for the same offence to be twice put in jeopardy of life or limb; nor shall be compelled in any criminal case to be a witness against himself, nor be deprived of life, liberty, or property, without due process of law; nor shall private property be taken for public use, without just compensation." This amendment does many things, it protects against self-incrimination and double jeopardy, guarantees due process in court and compensation in the event private property is seized by the government using eminent domain.

The double jeopardy clause is mainly meant to ensure that people cannot be punished for the same crime more than once. The clause does not prevent appeals or new trials if there is significant new evidence. The right against self-incrimination is used much more often than double jeopardy. This right means that the state cannot force someone to give testimony about a crime of which they are accused. Often called the right to remain silent, if one is asked a question about one's guilt in a crime, one can "plead the Fifth" and not answer the question by invoking the right not to incriminate oneself.

Originally, this right was meant to protect against confessions obtained under torture, but today is interpreted much more broadly. The right to not incriminate oneself and remain silent can also be invoked if the government impels testimony. For example, during the McCarthy era, the House Committee on Un-American Activities called many famous Hollywood actors to question them about Communist affiliations. Many invoked the Fifth Amendment when asked if they were communists, to avoid persecution.

House Committee on Un-American Activities

In *United States v. Sullivan* (1927) the Supreme Court ruled that the 5th Amendment could not be invoked to avoid paying income taxes. In a later 1976 case, the Supreme Court ruled that it not be a violation of the 5th Amendment for income tax records to be used in the trial. The case related to a man convicted of conspiracy to fix sports matches and illegal gambling who had declared on his income taxes that his profession was that of a professional gambler. He argued that this was self-incrimination, but the Supreme Court disagreed.

A more recent issue relates to computer passwords, as giving up one's password could produce incriminating evidence against oneself. The Supreme Court has yet to rule on this issue, but district courts have given conflicting interpretations. A Vermont court ruled that one cannot be forced to reveal one's passwords or to unencrypt data on a USB drive; however, another ruling required someone to hand over the password to an unencrypted drive. The trend so far has been that encrypting one's data protects it from authorities, but unencrypted data that is password protected can result in the court ordering someone to give up a password.

The 5th Amendment has also been used to justify eminent domain, which allows the government to seize private property when it is in the public interest, so long as the government provides fair compensation. This clause was most often invoked during the development of the railway system during the westward expansion. The public use clause has proven to be controversial and open to dispute. In a 5-4 decision in 2005's *Kelo v. City of New London* case, the Supreme Court ruled that a city which seized private land to hand it over to a private developer count as public use because it would provide housing and jobs. The dissenting opinion written by Sandra Day O'Connor was extremely critical of this rationale, arguing that this provided license for the rich to take property away from the poor in many cases, further arguing that public use was not justified as the property seizure was simply a transfer from one private agent to another private agent.

Sandra Day O'Connor, American jurist, and Supreme Court Justice

Sixth Amendment

The 6th Amendment states: "In all criminal prosecutions, the accused shall enjoy the right to a speedy and public trial, by an impartial jury of the State and district wherein the crime shall have been committed, which district shall have been previously ascertained by law, and to be informed of the nature and cause of the accusation; to be confronted with the witnesses against him; to have compulsory process for obtaining witnesses in his favor, and to have the Assistance of Counsel for his defense." This amendment outlines the rights to a fair trial and provides a legal framework for defendants in a criminal trial.

Given the vagueness of the notion of a speedy trial, in 1972 the Supreme Court set out concrete conditions which could be used to determine if a trial was sufficiently speedy or not. While the court did not set out any explicit time limits, it states that there should not be any delays in court proceedings of more than one year and that any such delay must be reasonable and not designed to advantage one side in the trial over the other. In 1973, the court further ruled that any case which violates the accused right to a speedy trial will simply be thrown out, and the accused cannot be tried at a later date or in a new trial. The impartial jury clause guarantees a jury trial for any crime which would result in a prison sentence of more than six months, and requires juries to reach a unanimous verdict, meaning each juror agrees. Unanimity does not apply to state-level jury trials, as only a majority is needed for such trials. Impartial jurors mean that lawyers from each side can vet the potential jury to ensure that jurors are not biased before the trial begins.

An important Supreme Court case based on the 6th Amendment was *Gideon v. Wainwright* in 1963. This decision ruled that those who could not afford legal representation would be provided a lawyer by the court and that the right to legal representation applied at the state and federal levels via the 14th Amendment. The case was prompted after a man in Florida who was too poor to afford a lawyer was forced to represent himself because the state court would not provide a lawyer for the relatively minor crime of petty burglary. The defendant in the burglary case was found guilty and appealed to the Supreme Court from his prison cell. After the Supreme Court ruled that everyone must be supplied with legal counsel, 2,000 people in Florida were freed, and the defendant in the original burglary case had a retrial, at which he was acquitted of all charges after his court-appointed lawyer successfully proved that the defendant could not have committed the robbery.

Seventh Amendment

The 7th Amendment states: "*In suits at common law, where the value in controversy shall exceed twenty dollars, the right of trial by jury shall be preserved, and no fact tried by a jury, shall be otherwise reexamined in any court of the United States, than according to the rules of the common law.*" This amendment is fairly self-explanatory, as it guarantees a jury trial in civil suits over twenty dollars and ensures that judges cannot overturn the decisions of juries. The twenty-dollar amount has not been indexed for inflation, which essentially means that all civil suits today will be tried by juries. Also of note is that this amendment has not been incorporated, which means it does not apply to state-level trials, which can be judge-only trials.

Eighth Amendment

The 8th Amendment states: "Excessive bail shall not be required, nor excessive fines imposed, nor cruel and unusual punishments inflicted." This amendment is inspired by the 1689 English Bill of Rights, which Madison had studied in detail. What excessive bail or an excessive fine entails is open to interpretation. One of the first rulings on this amendment came in 1951 in *Stack v. Boyle*. Under the Smith Act, some members of the Communist Party were arrested and had their bail set at $50,000 each. The Supreme Court ruled that this amounted to an excessive bail because, in previous arrests under the Smith Act, the bail had been set at a much lower level. This established the precedent of "excessive" bail as being relative to the bail that had been set in similar cases.

The first case in which the Supreme Court ruled that a fine was excessive did not occur until 1998 in *United States v. Bajakajian*. In the case, Hosep Krikor Bajakajian had attempted to leave the United States back in 1993 with the purpose of going to Cyprus to pay a large debt he owed. He was carrying $357,144 and failed to report it to customs, which requires declaring all cash exceeding $10,000. The government seized the entire $357,144. The Supreme Court ruled that this fine was grossly disproportionate to the crime of failing to report an international currency transaction and that there was no evidence to suggest that this money was intended for use in criminal activity. The ruling upheld the cash forfeiture as a violation of the 8th Amendment, even though it was not technically a fine.

What consists of cruel and unusual punishment was set out by the Supreme Court in *Furman v. Georgia* of 1972. The Court ruled that this amendment specifically outlawed torture, severe punishments inflicted arbitrarily, any severe punishment that is "clearly and totally rejected throughout society" and any punishment that is unnecessary. When it was discovered that the U.S. government was torturing prisoners in Guantanamo Bay and the Abu Ghraib prison in Iraq, many activists pointed out that this was a direct violation of the 8th Amendment.

Guard tower at Abu Ghraib Prison

Some legal scholars sympathetic to the Bush government, however, argued that the court had ruled that cruel and unusual punishment was dependent on society clearly and rejecting the punishment and that since the American public was divided on the issue, torture did not consist of cruel and unusual punishment.

Philosophers and ethicists saw this argument as extremely flimsy, as if the public were to become morally depraved, then there would be no limits on the government's ability to inflict cruel and unusual torture. Certain punishments are, however, banned in all situations. *Wilkerson v. Utah* in 1878 ruled that drawing and quartering, burning alive, dissection or disemboweling was cruel and unusual in any situations. *Thompson v. Oklahoma* in 1988 further ruled that executing people under the age of 16 amounted to cruel and unusual punishment, with this judgment being updated in 2005 to increase the age to 18. *Atkins v.*

Virginia in 2002 further ruled that executing someone with mental disabilities was cruel and unusual punishment.

In 1958, the Supreme Court ruled that stripping a natural born citizen of their citizenship is a cruel and unusual punishment worse than torture, as it deprives an individual of all legal rights. Even though taking illegal drugs is naturally against the law, in 1962, the court ruled that drug addicts could not be put in jail for being an addict in and of itself, as being addicted to illegal substances was not what was expressly prohibited.

A landmark 8th Amendment case came in 1988 with *Solem v. Helm*, which ruled for the first time that the length of a prison sentence could be construed as cruel and unusual if it was disproportionate to the crime. This case involved a man who had been convicted of writing a check from a fake account for one hundred dollars and received a life sentence. The court ruled that this sentence was cruel and unusual because it was grossly disproportionate to the crime.

A 1991 ruling, however, largely overturned the *Solem* precedent, as the Supreme Court upheld a life without parole sentence for the crime of possessing 1.5 pounds of cocaine. The court argued that although the punishment was cruel, it was not unusual, relying on the fact that the amendment places a dependency on cruel and unusual. This ruling was upheld again in 2003 on a challenge to the constitutionality of California's "Three Strikes" laws, finding that fifty years to life sentence for someone's third strike crime of shoplifting $150 worth of videotapes was not a violation of the 8th amendment. In 2010, the Supreme Court ruled that for those under the age of 18, any punishment of life in prison without parole was cruel and unusual except in the case of murder. Additional rulings in 1977 and 2008 found that the death penalty for cases other than murder amounted to cruel and unusual punishment.

The issue of whether or not the death penalty itself is cruel and unusual punishment was the subject of 1972's *Furman v. Georgia* ruling. In a split decision, the court ruled that capital punishment, as it was currently applied, consisted of cruel and unusual punishment. As a result, a moratorium on executions was placed in effect, and the death penalty became de facto illegal. In 1976 in *Gregg v. Georgia*, the Supreme Court reversed and reaffirmed the legality of the death penalty, ending the moratorium on executions. The ruling did add stipulations to death penalty eligible cases and requirements on how executions are to take place. The death penalty remains extremely controversial, especially as the rest of the world, except for a few dictatorships such as China, Saudi Arabia, and North Korea, has long since outlawed the death penalty.

Ninth Amendment

The 9th Amendment states: "The enumeration in the Constitution, of certain rights, shall not be construed to deny or disparage others retained by the people." The point of this amendment is to clarify that the rights listed in the Bill of Rights do not constitute an explicit and exhaustive list of the rights of the people. This amendment was adopted to appease the Federalists, who were worried that a listing of rights would be considered exhaustive and thus any right not listed in the Constitution would be assumed not to exist at all. Thus, this amendment was adopted to ensure that the government could not arbitrarily infringe on the rights of individuals in such a way that did not violate any of the listed rights but was publicly recognized as an infringement of individual liberty.

The Supreme Court has used the 9th Amendment to rule that Americans have a right to privacy. Even though this right is not explicitly outlined in the Bill of Rights, the court has argued that the 9th Amendment covers all rights, such as privacy, which are publicly recognized and not enumerated in the Constitution. The right to privacy was first established under the 9th Amendment in the 1965 ruling of *Griswold v. Connecticut*. Connecticut had passed a law banning all contraception, which was challenged in the Supreme Court. The court ruled that this law was an undue intrusion into the intimate lives of citizens, and thus violated the right to privacy. The majority decision in the case invoked the 5th Amendment's right against self-incrimination to justify the ruling, but more importantly a consenting opinion was written by Justice Arthur Goldberg which argued that the right to privacy was a constitutional right covered by the 9th Amendment. Goldberg's consenting opinion invoking the 9th Amendment for the protection of privacy has become an important precedent.

U.S. Justice Arthur Goldberg

The 9th Amendment, as it relates to the assurance of a right to privacy, was later invoked in the famous *Roe v. Wade* case in order to argue that women have a right to privacy under the 9th Amendment, and thus the state cannot pass laws against abortion which would make a woman's reproductive choices a matter of public record or concern. The 9th Amendment's right to privacy was also invoked in the 2003 *Lawrence v. Texas* ruling which legalized homosexual sex, holding that people had a right to privacy and the sex lives of citizens should not be public business. In the internet age, the 9th Amendment is often invoked as protection against electronic spying by the government. If citizens have a right to privacy, then the government should not be able to spy on what people assume are reasonably private activities. While internet activists such as the Electronic Frontiers Foundation often makes this 9th Amendment argument, the issue of online spying has yet to be tested in the Supreme Court.

Tenth Amendment

The 10th Amendment states: "The powers not delegated to the United States by the Constitution, nor prohibited by it to the States, are reserved to the States respectively, or to the people." This amendment reaffirms the separation of powers in the federal system and ensures that states can make their laws on matters not covered in the previous nine amendments. Madison generally saw this amendment as unnecessary but included it to ease the fears of Anti-Federalists and some state governments who thought the Bill of Rights would dramatically undercut their authority.

In the 1931 *United States v. Sprague* case, the Supreme Court ruled that this amendment was a truism which added nothing new to the Constitution, but merely reaffirmed what was already written elsewhere. Occasionally, state governments have attempted to invoke this amendment to argue that federal legislation should not apply to state governments, but the Supreme Court has consistently rejected this interpretation of the amendment. Rulings in the 1940s upheld the legality of federal minimum wage and labor standards legislation. The only occasions where the Supreme Court has struck down legislation for violating the 10th Amendment was in cases where legislation attempted to compel state governments to administer federal programs. One example was *Printz v. United States* in 1997, in which the Supreme Court ruled that a gun control law which required state officials to perform background checks violated the 10th Amendment because state officials were expected to carry out a federal program.

Later Amendments

In addition to the Bill of Rights and the Reconstruction Amendments (the 13th,14th,15th) banning slavery and racial discrimination, some later amendments were ratified which protected civil rights. The 19th Amendment of 1920 gave women the right to vote. The 23rd Amendment gave voting rights to residents of Washington, D.C. The court ruled that since residents of the capital district were citizens and had all the accompanying duties, such as military service and paying taxes, they could not be denied the right to vote. By 1960, Washington, D.C. had a larger population than thirteen of the states; thus, this was important legislation which also granted votes in the Electoral College to Washington, D.C.

The 24th Amendment was an important civil rights era amendment which made poll taxes illegal. Before this amendment, many southern states required a person to pay a sum of money to vote. These states used a poll tax to prevent poor white people from voting and as a means of discriminating against black people indirectly since they were disproportionately poor in the post-slavery era. President Lyndon B. Johnson called this amendment a "triumph of liberty over restriction" and a "verification of people's rights."

U.S. President Lyndon B. Johnson

The 24th Amendment significantly increased suffrage in the South, allowing poor white males and blacks equal access to the right to vote regardless of their ability to pay a poll tax. Although this amendment was meant to remove all undue obstacles to voting, Alabama retained a literacy test which was used to exclude people from voting. Congress eventually banned literacy tests in the Voting Rights Act of 1965 and an update to the act in 1970.

Finally, the 26th Amendment of 1971 lowered the national voting age from twenty-one to eighteen. The push for this amendment came from the upsurge in student activism in the late 1960s and early 1970s and protests against the Vietnam War. University students argued that they had become the most politically engaged segment of the population, yet they couldn't even vote. Congress agreed and passed the amendment.

While the Constitution and Bill of Rights provide a solid framework of rights and liberties which are meant to be held and exercised by all American citizens, the government and Supreme Court do not always apply these rights. As such, it is up to the people to constantly test their rights to ensure that the Constitution continues to be the supreme law. The political flavor of governments and courts changes with time, but the rights of the Constitution are meant to be a bulwark against government abuse. The long history of activism and litigation to ensure that the government and courts upheld these rights is evidence that Americans cannot simply take these rights for granted, they must be continually exercised and fought for.

The Impact of the Fourteenth Amendment on the Constitutional Development of Rights and Liberties

The 13th, 14th, and 15th Amendments are called the Reconstruction Amendments and were adopted in the wake of the Civil War. The goal of these amendments was to transform the United States from a country that was, as Abraham Lincoln put it, "half slave, half free" into a united country where freedom would be constitutionally guaranteed to all. The amendments were particularly meant to guarantee freedom to former slaves and their descendants.

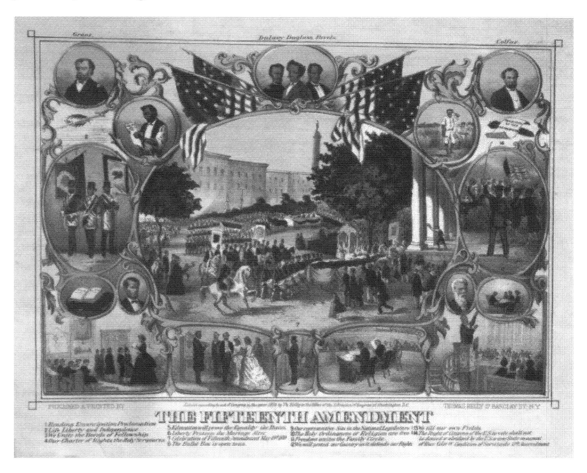

Print celebrating the passage of the Fifteenth Amendment to the United States Constitution

The 14th Amendment is especially important as it empowers the federal government to protect the rights of citizens and has been the basis of court challenges which have sought to bring new rights for American citizens. Section 1 of the amendment guarantees citizenship rights for natural born and naturalized persons and ensures that individual states cannot pass laws which violate these citizenship rights without due process. This section was important because it overturned the *Dred Scott v. Sandford* ruling of 1857, in which the Supreme Court had ruled that Americans descended from slaves could not be citizens.

The due process clause of this amendment gives the federal government the authority to ensure that states do not pass any legislation that violates the Bill of Rights. The equal protection clause states that all state governments must treat everyone equally under the law. This clause was important as it became the basis of the *Brown v. Board of Education* Supreme Court ruling in 1954 which ruled that racially segregated public schools be unconstitutional. The other four sections of the amendment have been less important for future court rulings but they did set out the proportion of representatives for each state in the legislature, bar people who have to participate in insurrections against the U.S. government from holding office, outlaw questioning of the validity of the public debt as related to putting down rebellions, and gave Congress the ability to enforce this amendment.

While the 14th Amendment was originally passed to ensure that the rights of former slaves were protected after emancipation, the amendment retains its importance as the basis for other groups acquiring rights which were once denied to them. This amendment was also extremely important in the wake of the Civil War, as it gave the federal government the power to enforce the Bill of Rights, something which it was unable to do before this amendment.

In the *Barron v. Baltimore* ruling of 1833, the Supreme Court decided that the Bill of Rights could not be applied to state governments. As such, slave states used this ruling as the basis of their claim that the Bill of Rights did not outlaw slavery because the Bill of Rights had no jurisdiction over state governments. Given the national unity problems caused by the *Barron v. Brown* ruling, the 14th Amendment was an important step both for the rights of individuals and for ensuring that the United States remained a single country and did not break up again as it had in the Civil War.

The three main protections outlined in the 14th Amendment became the basis for many Supreme Court decisions. Due process, which ensures the opportunity for trials to be heard fairly and without discrimination, was the basis of the 1973 *Roe v. Wade* ruling which legalized abortion. The court ruled that the 14th Amendment's due process clause establishes a right to personal privacy, which means that a state government cannot violate a woman's privacy by telling her whether or not she can terminate a pregnancy. In 2015 the *Obergefell v. Hodges* decision ruled that the liberty of individuals guaranteed by the due process clause and the equality of individuals guaranteed by the equal protection clause were both significantly burdened by state-level restrictions on same-sex marriage. The court ruled that states cannot pass laws banning same sex marriage, as doing so violated the 14th Amendment.

The equal protection clause, which guarantees that all citizens must be treated the same, has been the basis of famous rulings like *Brown v. Board of Education* which struck down racial segregation in schools. Equal protection was also the basis of the 1967 *Loving v. Virginia* which struck down laws against interracial marriage. *Eisenstadt v. Baird* was an important ruling in 1972 which invoked the equal protection clause to ensure that contraception was available to people who were not married. More recently, the equal protection clause of the 14th Amendment was used as the basis of the 2000 *Bush v. Gore* ruling related to recounts in Florida in the 2000 presidential election. The court ruled that a statewide recount of votes in Florida would violate the equal protection clause because of the way different counties counted votes. The result of the ruling was that recounts in progress were stopped, and the initial result of Bush winning the state was upheld.

Congressman John A. Bingham, a principal framer
of the Equal Protection Clause of the Fourteenth Amendment

The third most important clause of the 14th Amendment is the privileges and immunities clause which guarantees that all citizens have the same rights, regardless of which state they live in. In *United States v. Wheeler* (1920), the Supreme Court used this clause to rule that it was up to state governments to prosecute kidnappers. More importantly, this case set the standard for the legal right of citizens to travel freely within the United States. This right to travel between states was later upheld in the 1999 *Saenz v. Roe* case which found that although there was no constitutional right to free movement between states, the earlier case had set a precedent which had since enshrined free movement as a right.

In the 1940s, a ruling using this clause set a precedent which was used by the California Supreme Court to strike down laws against landownership by non-citizens, aimed at Japanese immigrants. The 14th Amendment remains the most actively litigated aspect of the entire Constitution. Given that it retains rights against discrimination, it is likely to continue to be the basis of future court challenges so long as discrimination continues to exist.

Please, leave your Customer Review on Amazon

Appendix

Court Systems Within the United States: Federal and State Courts

There are two kinds of courts in the USA – federal courts and state courts.

Federal courts are established under the U.S. Constitution by Congress to decide disputes involving the Constitution and laws passed by Congress. A state establishes state and local courts (within states there are also local courts that are established by cities, counties, and other municipalities, which are included here in the general discussion of state courts).

The differences between federal courts and state courts are further defined by jurisdiction.[1] Jurisdiction refers to the kinds of cases that a particular court is authorized to hear and adjudicate (i.e., pronouncement of a legally binding judgment upon the parties to the dispute).

Federal court jurisdiction is limited to the types of cases listed in the Constitution and specifically provided for by Congress. For the most part, federal courts only hear:

- cases in which the United States is a party[2];

- cases involving violations of the U.S. Constitution or federal laws (under federal-question jurisdiction[3]);

- cases between citizens of different states if the amount in controversy exceeds $75,000 (under diversity jurisdiction[4]); and

- bankruptcy, copyright, patent, and maritime law cases.

State courts, in contrast, have broad jurisdiction, so the cases individual citizens are likely to be involved in (e.g., robberies, traffic violations, contracts, and family disputes) are usually heard and decided in state courts. The only cases state courts are not allowed to hear are lawsuits against the United States and those involving certain specific federal laws: criminal, antitrust, bankruptcy, patent, copyright, and some maritime law cases.

In many cases, both federal and state courts have jurisdiction whereby the plaintiff (i.e., party initiating the suit) can choose whether to file their claim in state or federal court.

Criminal cases involving federal laws can be tried only in federal court, but most criminal cases involve violations of state law and are tried in state court. Robbery is a crime, but what law makes it is a crime? Except for certain exceptions, state laws, not federal laws, make robbery a crime. There are only a few federal laws about robbery, such as the law that makes it a federal crime to rob a bank whose deposits are insured by a federal agency.

Examples of other federal crimes are the transport of illegal drugs into the country or across state lines and use of the U.S. mail system to defraud consumers.

Crimes committed on federal property (e.g., national parks or military reservations) are also prosecuted in federal court.

Federal courts may also hear cases concerning state laws if the issue is whether the state law violates the federal Constitution. Suppose a state law forbids slaughtering animals outside of certain limited areas. A neighborhood association brings a case in state court against a defendant who sacrifices chickens in his backyard. When the court issues an order (i.e., an injunction[5]) forbidding the defendant from further sacrifices, the defendant challenges the state law in federal court as an unconstitutional infringement of his religious freedom.

Some kinds of conduct are illegal under both federal and state laws. For example, federal laws prohibit employment discrimination, and the states have added additional legal restriction. A person can file their claim in either federal or state court under the federal law or both the federal and state laws. A case that only involves a state law can be brought only in state court.

Appeals for review of actions by federal administrative agencies are also federal civil cases. Suppose, for example, that the Environmental Protection Agency issued a permit to a paper mill to discharge water used in its milling process into the Scenic River, over the objection of area residents. The residents could ask a federal court of appeals to review the agency's decision.

[1] *jurisdiction* – (1) the legal authority of a court to hear and decide a certain type of case; (2) the geographic area over which the court has the authority to decide cases.

[2] *parties* – the plaintiff(s) and defendant(s) in a lawsuit.

[3] *federal-question jurisdiction* – the federal district courts' authorization to hear and decide cases arising under the Constitution, laws, or treaties of the United States.

[4] *diversity jurisdiction* – the federal district courts' authority to hear and decide civil cases involving plaintiffs and defendants who are citizens of different states (or U.S. citizens and foreign nationals) and who meet certain statutory requirements.

[5] *injunction* – a judge's order that a party take or refrain from taking certain action. An injunction may be preliminary until the outcome of a case is determined, or permanent.

Organization of the Federal Courts

Congress has divided the country into 94 federal judicial districts with each having a U.S. district court. The U.S. district courts are the federal trial courts -- where federal cases are tried, witnesses testify, and juries serve. Each district has a U.S. bankruptcy court which is part of the district court that administers the U.S. bankruptcy laws.

Congress uses state boundaries to help define the districts. Some districts cover an entire state, like Idaho. Other districts cover just part of a state, like the Northern District of California. Congress placed each of the ninety-four districts in one of twelve regional circuits whereby each circuit has a court of appeals. The losing party can petition the court of appeals to review the case to determine if the district judge applied the law correctly. There is also a U.S. Court of Appeals for the Federal Circuit, whose jurisdiction is defined by subject matter rather than by geography. It hears appeals from certain courts and agencies, such as the U.S. Court of International Trade, the U.S. Court of Federal Claims, and the U.S. Patent and Trademark Office, and certain types of cases from the district courts (mainly lawsuits claiming that patents have been infringed).

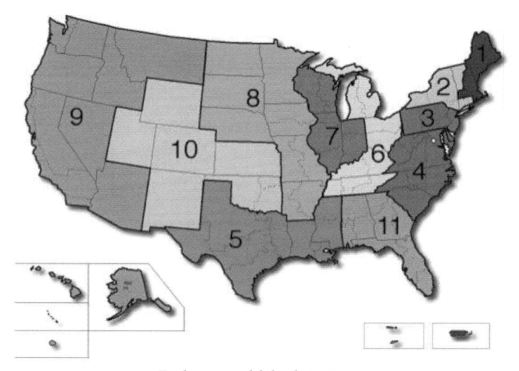

Twelve regional federal circuits

The Supreme Court of the United States, in Washington, D.C., is the highest court in the nation. The losing party can petition in a case in the court of appeals (or, sometimes, in a state supreme court), can petition the Supreme Court to hear an appeal. However, unlike a court of appeals, the Supreme Court doesn't have to hear the case. The Supreme Court hears only a very small percentage of the cases it is asked to review.

Judicial Independence

The founders of the United States recognized that the judicial branch must remain independent to fulfill its mission effectively and impartially. Article III of the Constitution protects certain types of judges by providing that they serve "during good behavior" and prohibits the reduction of their salary.

These constitutional protections allow judges to make unpopular decisions without fear of losing their jobs or having their pay cut. For example, the Supreme Court's decision in *Brown v. Board of Education* in 1954 declared racial segregation in public schools to be unconstitutional. This decision was unpopular with large segments of society at that time. Some members of Congress even wanted to replace the judges who made the decision, but this Constitutional protection wouldn't allow them to do so.

An Article III Judge

"Article III judge" denotes federal judges who under Article III of the Constitution are enabled to exercise "the judicial power of the United States" without fear of losing their jobs. They serve for "good Behaviour," which means they can be removed from office only by the rarely used process of impeachment and conviction. Article III further provides that their compensation cannot be reduced. From a practical standpoint, almost all of these judges hold office for as long as they wish. "Article III judges" are those on the U.S. Supreme Court, the federal courts of appeals and district courts, and the U.S. Court of International Trade.

Federal judges appointed under Article III of the Constitution are guaranteed what amounts to life tenure and unreduced salary so that they won't be afraid to make an unpopular decision. For example, in *Gregg v. Georgia*, the Supreme Court said it is constitutional for the federal and state governments to impose the death penalty if the statute is carefully drafted to provide adequate safeguards. Even though some people are opposed to the death penalty, Article III protections allowed the Judge to make this decision without fear of reciprocity.

The constitutional protection that gives federal judges the freedom and independence to make decisions that are politically and socially unpopular is one of the basic elements of our democracy. According to the Declaration of Independence, one reason the American colonies wanted to separate from England was that King George III "made judges dependent on his will alone, for the tenure of their offices, and the amount and payment of their salaries."

Federal Judges Other Than Article III Judges

Bankruptcy judges and magistrate judges conduct some of the proceedings held in federal courts. Bankruptcy judges handle almost all bankruptcy matters in bankruptcy courts that are technically included in the district courts but function as separate entities. Magistrate judges carry out various responsibilities in the district courts and often help prepare the district judges' cases for trial. They also may preside over criminal misdemeanor trials and may preside over civil trials when both parties agree to have the case heard by a magistrate judge instead of a district judge.

Unlike district judges, bankruptcy and magistrate judges do not exercise "the judicial power of the United States" but perform duties delegated to them by district judges. Bankruptcy and magistrate judges serve for fourteen and eight-year terms, respectively, rather than "during good Behaviour." Bankruptcy judges and magistrate judges don't have the same protections as judges appointed under Article III of the Constitution. Bankruptcy judges, in contrast, may be removed from office by circuit judicial councils, and magistrate judges may be removed by the district judges of the magistrate judge's district.

Appointment of Federal Judges

Congress authorizes a set number of judge positions, or judgeships, for each court level. Since the 1869 "Circuit Judges Act," Congress has mandated that the Supreme Court would consist of 9 judges. As of 2007, it had mandated 179 court of appeals judgeships and 678 district court judgeships. (In 1950, there were only 65 courts of appeals judgeships and 212 district judgeships). As of 2007, Congress had mandated 352 bankruptcy judgeships and 551 full-time and part-time magistrate judgeships. It is rare that all judgeships are filled at any one time as judges die or retire, causing vacancies until judges are appointed to replace them. In addition to judges occupying these positions, retired judges often continue to perform some judicial work.

Supreme Court justices and the court of appeals and district judges are appointed to office by the President of the United States, with the approval of the U.S. Senate. Presidents most often appoint judges who are members, or at least generally supportive, of their political party, but that doesn't mean that judges are given appointments solely for partisan reasons. The professional qualifications of prospective federal judges are closely evaluated by the Department of Justice, which consults with others, such as lawyers who can evaluate the prospect's abilities. The Senate Judiciary Committee undertakes a separate examination of the nominees. Magistrate judges and bankruptcy judges are not appointed by the President or subject to Congress's approval. The court of appeals in each circuit appoints bankruptcy judges for fourteen-year terms. District courts appoint magistrate judges for eight-year terms.

Although there are almost no formal qualifications for federal judges, there are some strong informal ones. For example, while magistrate judges and bankruptcy judges are required by statute to be lawyers, there is no statutory requirement that district judges, circuit judges, or Supreme Court justices be lawyers. However, there is no legal precedent for a president to nominate someone who is not a lawyer. Before their appointment, most judges were private attorneys, but many were judges in state courts or other federal courts. Some were government attorneys, and a few were law professors.

Most federal judges retire from full-time service at around sixty-five or seventy years of age and become senior judges. Senior judges are still federal judges, eligible to earn their full salary and to continue hearing cases if they and their colleagues want them to do so, but they usually maintain a reduced caseload. Full-time judges are known as active judges.

Judicial Conduct

Judges follow the ethical standards set out in the *Code of Conduct for United States Judges*, which contains guidelines to help them avoid situations that might limit their ability to be fair--or that might make it appear to others that their fairness is in question. It tells them, for example, to be careful not to do anything that might cause people to think they would favor one side in a case over another, such as giving speeches that urge voters to pick one candidate over another for public office or asking people to contribute money to civic organizations.

Additionally, Congress has enacted laws telling judges to withdraw or recuse themselves from any case in which a close relative is a party or in which they have any financial interest, even one share of stock. Congress requires judges to file an annual financial disclosure form, so that their stock holdings, board memberships, and other financial interests are a matter of public record.

Congress has also enacted a law that allows anyone to file a complaint alleging that a judge (other than a Supreme Court justice) has engaged in conduct "prejudicial to the effective and expeditious administration of the business of the courts" or that a judge has a mental or physical disability that makes him or her unable to adequately discharge the duties of the office. A complaint is filed with the clerk of the court of appeals of the respective judge's circuit and considered by the chief judge of the court of appeals. If the chief judge believes the complaint deserves attention, the chief judge appoints a special committee of the circuit judicial council to investigate it.

If the committee concludes that the complaint is valid, it may recommend various actions, such as temporarily removing the judge from hearing cases, but it may not recommend that an Article III judge be removed from office. Only Congress may do that, through the impeachment process.

Chief Judges dismiss the great majority of complaints filed under this law because the complaints involve judges' decisions in particular cases. This law may not be used to complain about decisions, even what may appear to be a very wrong decision or very unfair treatment of a party in a case. Parties in a lawsuit who believe the judge issued an incorrect ruling may appeal the case to a higher court, under the rules of procedure.

Each court with more than one judge must determine a procedure for assigning cases to judges. Most district and bankruptcy courts use random assignment, which helps to ensure a fair distribution of cases and also prevents "judge shopping," which refers to parties' attempts to have their cases heard by the judge whom they believe will act most favorably. Other courts assign cases by rotation, subject matter, or geographic division of the court. In courts of appeals, cases are usually assigned by random means to temporary three-judge panels.

The Supreme Court of the United States

The Supreme Court of the United States is the highest court in the nation. It's a different kind of appeals court; its major function is not correcting errors made by trial judges but clarifying the law in cases of national importance or when lower courts disagree about the interpretation of the Constitution or federal laws.

The Supreme Court does not have to hear every case that it is asked to review. Each year, losing parties ask the Supreme Court to review about 8,000 cases. Almost all these cases come to the Court as petitions for writ of certiorari. The court selects only about 80 – 120 of the most significant cases to review with oral arguments.

The decisions of the Supreme Court establish a precedent for the interpretation of the Constitution and federal laws, precedents that all state and federal courts must follow.

The power of judicial review makes the Supreme Court's role in our government vital. Judicial review is the power of any court when deciding a case, to declare that a law passed by a legislature or an action of the executive branch is invalid because it is inconsistent with the Constitution. Although district courts, courts of appeals, and state courts can exercise the power of judicial review, their decisions about the federal law are always subject, on appeal, to review by the Supreme Court. When the Supreme Court declares a law unconstitutional, its decision can only be overruled by a later decision of the Supreme Court or amendment to the Constitution. Seven of the twenty-seven amendments to the Constitution have invalidated decisions of the Supreme Court. However, most Supreme Court cases don't concern the constitutionality of laws, but the interpretation of laws passed by Congress.

Although Congress has steadily increased the number of district and appeals court judges over the years, the Supreme Court has remained the same size since 1869. It consists of a Chief Justice and eight associate justices. Like the federal court of appeals and federal district judges, the Supreme Court justices are appointed by the President with the advice and consent of the Senate. However, unlike the judges in the courts of appeals, the Supreme Court justices never sit on panels. Absent recusal, all nine justices hear every case, and a majority ruling decides cases.

The Supreme Court begins its annual session, or term, on the first Monday of October. The term lasts until the Court has announced its decisions in all of the cases in which it has heard argument that term—usually late June or early July. During the term, the Court, sitting for two weeks at a time, hears oral argument on Monday through Wednesday and then holds private conferences to discuss the cases, reach decisions, and begin preparing the written opinions that explain its decisions. Most decisions, along with their opinions, are released in the late spring and early summer.

THE U.S. NATIONAL ARCHIVES & RECORDS ADMINISTRATION

www.archives.gov

The Declaration of Independence: A Transcription

IN CONGRESS, July 4, 1776.

The unanimous Declaration of the thirteen united States of America,

When in the Course of human events, it becomes necessary for one people to dissolve the political bands which have connected them with another, and to assume among the powers of the earth, the separate and equal station to which the Laws of Nature and of Nature's God entitle them, a decent respect to the opinions of mankind requires that they should declare the causes which impel them to the separation.

We hold these truths to be self-evident, that all men are created equal, that they are endowed by their Creator with certain unalienable Rights, that among these are Life, Liberty and the pursuit of Happiness.--That to secure these rights, Governments are instituted among Men, deriving their just powers from the consent of the governed, --That whenever any Form of Government becomes destructive of these ends, it is the Right of the People to alter or to abolish it, and to institute new Government, laying its foundation on such principles and organizing its powers in such form, as to them shall seem most likely to effect their Safety and Happiness. Prudence, indeed, will dictate that Governments long established should not be changed for light and transient causes; and accordingly all experience hath shewn, that mankind are more disposed to suffer, while evils are sufferable, than to right themselves by abolishing the forms to which they are accustomed. But when a long train of abuses and usurpations, pursuing invariably the same Object evinces a design to reduce them under absolute Despotism, it is their right, it is their duty, to throw off such Government, and to provide new Guards for their future security.--Such has been the patient sufferance of these Colonies; and such is now the necessity which constrains them to alter their former Systems of Government. The history of the present King of Great Britain is a history of repeated injuries and usurpations, all having in direct object the establishment of an absolute Tyranny over these States. To prove this, let Facts be submitted to a candid world.

He has refused his Assent to Laws, the most wholesome and necessary for the public good.

He has forbidden his Governors to pass Laws of immediate and pressing importance, unless suspended in their operation till his Assent should be obtained; and when so suspended, he has utterly neglected to attend to them.

He has refused to pass other Laws for the accommodation of large districts of people, unless those people would relinquish the right of Representation in the Legislature, a right inestimable to them and formidable to tyrants only.

He has called together legislative bodies at places unusual, uncomfortable, and distant from the depository of their public Records, for the sole purpose of fatiguing them into compliance with his measures.

He has dissolved Representative Houses repeatedly, for opposing with manly firmness his invasions on the rights of the people.

He has refused for a long time, after such dissolutions, to cause others to be elected; whereby the Legislative powers, incapable of Annihilation, have returned to the People at large for their exercise; the State remaining in the mean time exposed to all the dangers of invasion from without, and convulsions within.

He has endeavoured to prevent the population of these States; for that purpose obstructing the Laws for Naturalization of Foreigners; refusing to pass others to encourage their migrations hither, and raising the conditions of new Appropriations of Lands.

He has obstructed the Administration of Justice, by refusing his Assent to Laws for establishing Judiciary powers.

He has made Judges dependent on his Will alone, for the tenure of their offices, and the amount and payment of their salaries.

He has erected a multitude of New Offices, and sent hither swarms of Officers to harass our people, and eat out their substance.

He has kept among us, in times of peace, Standing Armies without the Consent of our legislatures.

He has affected to render the Military independent of and superior to the Civil power. He has combined with others to subject us to a jurisdiction foreign to our constitution, and unacknowledged by our laws; giving his Assent to their Acts of pretended Legislation:

For Quartering large bodies of armed troops among us:

For protecting them, by a mock Trial, from punishment for any Murders which they should commit on the Inhabitants of these States:

For cutting off our Trade with all parts of the world:

For imposing Taxes on us without our Consent:

For depriving us in many cases, of the benefits of Trial by Jury:

For transporting us beyond Seas to be tried for pretended offences For abolishing the free System of English Laws in a neighbouring Province, establishing therein an Arbitrary government, and enlarging its Boundaries so as to render it at once an example and fit instrument for introducing the same absolute rule into these Colonies:

For taking away our Charters, abolishing our most valuable Laws, and altering fundamentally the Forms of our Governments:

For suspending our own Legislatures, and declaring themselves invested with power to legislate for us in all cases whatsoever.

He has abdicated Government here, by declaring us out of his Protection and waging War against us.

He has plundered our seas, ravaged our Coasts, burnt our towns, and destroyed the lives of our people.

He is at this time transporting large Armies of foreign Mercenaries to compleat the works of death, desolation and tyranny, already begun with circumstances of Cruelty & perfidy scarcely paralleled in the most barbarous ages, and totally unworthy the Head of a civilized nation.

He has constrained our fellow Citizens taken Captive on the high Seas to bear Arms against their Country, to become the executioners of their friends and Brethren, or to fall themselves by their Hands.

He has excited domestic insurrections amongst us, and has endeavoured to bring on the inhabitants of our frontiers, the merciless Indian Savages, whose known rule of warfare, is an undistinguished destruction of all ages, sexes and conditions.

In every stage of these Oppressions We have Petitioned for Redress in the most humble terms: Our repeated Petitions have been answered only by repeated injury. A Prince whose character is thus marked by every act which may define a Tyrant, is unfit to be the ruler of a free people.

Nor have We been wanting in attentions to our Brittish brethren. We have warned them from time to time of attempts by their legislature to extend an unwarrantable jurisdiction over us. We have reminded them of the circumstances of our emigration and settlement here. We have appealed to their native justice and magnanimity, and we have conjured them by the ties of our common kindred to disavow these usurpations, which, would inevitably interrupt our connections and correspondence. They too have been deaf to the voice of justice and of consanguinity. We must, therefore, acquiesce in the necessity, which denounces our Separation, and hold them, as we hold the rest of mankind, Enemies in War, in Peace Friends.

We, therefore, the Representatives of the united States of America, in General Congress, Assembled, appealing to the Supreme Judge of the world for the rectitude of our intentions, do, in the Name, and by Authority of the good People of these Colonies, solemnly publish and declare, That these United Colonies are, and of Right ought to be Free and Independent States; that they are Absolved from all Allegiance to the British Crown, and that all political connection between them and the State of Great Britain, is and ought to be totally dissolved; and that as Free and Independent States, they have full Power to levy War, conclude Peace, contract Alliances, establish Commerce, and to do all other Acts and Things which Independent States may of right do. And for the support of this Declaration, with a firm reliance on the protection of divine Providence, we mutually pledge to each other our Lives, our Fortunes and our sacred Honor.

The 56 signatures on the Declaration appear in the positions indicated:

Georgia:
Button Gwinnett
Lyman Hall
George Walton

North Carolina:
William Hooper
Joseph Hewes
John Penn

South Carolina:
Edward Rutledge
Thomas Heyward, Jr.
Thomas Lynch, Jr.
Arthur Middleton

Massachusetts:
John Hancock

Maryland:
Samuel Chase
William Paca
Thomas Stone
Charles Carroll of Carrollton

Virginia:
George Wythe
Richard Henry Lee
Thomas Jefferson
Benjamin Harrison
Thomas Nelson, Jr.
Francis Lightfoot Lee
Carter Braxton

Pennsylvania:
Robert Morris
Benjamin Rush
Benjamin Franklin
John Morton
George Clymer
James Smith
George Taylor
James Wilson
George Ross

Delaware:
Caesar Rodney
George Read
Thomas McKean

New York:
William Floyd
Philip Livingston
Francis Lewis
Lewis Morris

New Jersey:
Richard Stockton
John Witherspoon
Francis Hopkinson
John Hart
Abraham Clark

New Hampshire:
Josiah Bartlett
William Whipple

Massachusetts:
Samuel Adams
John Adams
Robert Treat Paine
Elbridge Gerry

Rhode Island:
Stephen Hopkins
William Ellery

Connecticut:
Roger Sherman
Samuel Huntington
William Williams
Oliver Wolcott

New Hampshire:
Matthew Thornton

THE U.S. NATIONAL ARCHIVES & RECORDS ADMINISTRATION

www.archives.gov

The Constitution of the United States: A Transcription

Note: The following text is a transcription of the Constitution as it was inscribed by Jacob Shallus on parchment (displayed in the Rotunda at the National Archives Museum.) Items that are hyperlinked have since been amended or superseded. The authenticated text of the Constitution can be found on the website of the Government Printing Office.

We the People of the United States, in Order to form a more perfect Union, establish Justice, insure domestic Tranquility, provide for the common defence, promote the general Welfare, and secure the Blessings of Liberty to ourselves and our Posterity, do ordain and establish this Constitution for the United States of America.

Article. I., Section. 1.

All legislative Powers herein granted shall be vested in a Congress of the United States, which shall consist of a Senate and House of Representatives.

Section. 2.

The House of Representatives shall be composed of Members chosen every second Year by the People of the several States, and the Electors in each State shall have the Qualifications requisite for Electors of the most numerous Branch of the State Legislature.

No Person shall be a Representative who shall not have attained to the Age of twenty five Years, and been seven Years a Citizen of the United States, and who shall not, when elected, be an Inhabitant of that State in which he shall be chosen.

Representatives and direct Taxes shall be apportioned among the several States which may be included within this Union, according to their respective Numbers, which shall be determined by adding to the whole Number of free Persons, including those bound to Service for a Term of Years, and excluding Indians not taxed, three fifths of all other Persons. The actual Enumeration shall be made within three Years after the first Meeting of the Congress of the United States, and within every subsequent Term of ten Years, in such Manner as they shall by Law direct. The Number of Representatives shall not exceed one for every thirty Thousand, but each State shall have at Least one Representative; and until such enumeration shall be made, the State of New Hampshire shall be entitled to chuse three, Massachusetts eight, Rhode-Island and Providence Plantations one, Connecticut five, New-York six, New Jersey four, Pennsylvania eight, Delaware one, Maryland six, Virginia ten, North Carolina five, South Carolina five, and Georgia three.

When vacancies happen in the Representation from any State, the Executive Authority thereof shall issue Writs of Election to fill such Vacancies.

The House of Representatives shall chuse their Speaker and other Officers; and shall have the sole Power of Impeachment.

Section. 3.

The Senate of the United States shall be composed of two Senators from each State, chosen by the Legislature thereof, for six Years; and each Senator shall have one Vote.

Immediately after they shall be assembled in Consequence of the first Election, they shall be divided as equally as may be into three Classes. The Seats of the Senators of the first Class shall be vacated at the Expiration of the second Year, of the second Class at the Expiration of the fourth Year, and of the third Class at the Expiration of the sixth Year, so that one third may be chosen every second Year; and if Vacancies happen by Resignation, or otherwise, during the Recess of the Legislature of any State, the Executive thereof may make temporary Appointments until the next Meeting of the Legislature, which shall then fill such Vacancies.

No Person shall be a Senator who shall not have attained to the Age of thirty Years, and been nine Years a Citizen of the United States, and who shall not, when elected, be an Inhabitant of that State for which he shall be chosen.

The Vice President of the United States shall be President of the Senate, but shall have no Vote, unless they be equally divided.

The Senate shall chuse their other Officers, and also a President pro tempore, in the Absence of the Vice President, or when he shall exercise the Office of President of the United States.

The Senate shall have the sole Power to try all Impeachments. When sitting for that Purpose, they shall be on Oath or Affirmation. When the President of the United States is tried, the Chief Justice shall preside: And no Person shall be convicted without the Concurrence of two thirds of the Members present.

Judgment in Cases of Impeachment shall not extend further than to removal from Office, and disqualification to hold and enjoy any Office of honor, Trust or Profit under the United States: but the Party convicted shall nevertheless be liable and subject to Indictment, Trial, Judgment and Punishment, according to Law.

Section. 4.

The Times, Places and Manner of holding Elections for Senators and Representatives, shall be prescribed in each State by the Legislature thereof; but the Congress may at any time by Law make or alter such Regulations, except as to the Places of chusing Senators.

The Congress shall assemble at least once in every Year, and such Meeting shall be on the first Monday in December, unless they shall by Law appoint a different Day.

Section. 5.

Each House shall be the Judge of the Elections, Returns and Qualifications of its own Members, and a Majority of each shall constitute a Quorum to do Business; but a smaller Number may adjourn from day to day, and may be authorized to compel the Attendance of absent Members, in such Manner, and under such Penalties as each House may provide.

Each House may determine the Rules of its Proceedings, punish its Members for disorderly Behaviour, and, with the Concurrence of two thirds, expel a Member.

Each House shall keep a Journal of its Proceedings, and from time to time publish the same, excepting such Parts as may in their Judgment require Secrecy; and the Yeas and Nays of the Members of either House on any question shall, at the Desire of one fifth of those Present, be entered on the Journal.

Neither House, during the Session of Congress, shall, without the Consent of the other, adjourn for more than three days, nor to any other Place than that in which the two Houses shall be sitting.

Section. 6.

The Senators and Representatives shall receive a Compensation for their Services, to be ascertained by Law, and paid out of the Treasury of the United States. They shall in all Cases, except Treason, Felony and Breach of the Peace, be privileged from Arrest during their Attendance at the Session of their respective Houses, and in going to and returning from the same; and for any Speech or Debate in either House, they shall not be questioned in any other Place.

No Senator or Representative shall, during the Time for which he was elected, be appointed to any civil Office under the Authority of the United States, which shall have been created, or the Emoluments whereof shall have been encreased during such time; and no Person holding any Office under the United States, shall be a Member of either House during his Continuance in Office.

Section. 7.

All Bills for raising Revenue shall originate in the House of Representatives; but the Senate may propose or concur with Amendments as on other Bills.

Every Bill which shall have passed the House of Representatives and the Senate, shall, before it become a Law, be presented to the President of the United States; If he approve he shall sign it, but if not he shall return it, with his Objections to that House in which it shall have originated, who shall enter the Objections at large on their Journal, and proceed to reconsider it. If after such Reconsideration two thirds of that House shall agree to pass the Bill, it shall be sent, together with the Objections, to the other House, by which it shall likewise be reconsidered, and if approved by two thirds of that House, it shall become a Law. But in all such Cases the Votes of both Houses shall be determined by yeas and Nays, and the Names of the Persons voting for and against the Bill shall be entered on the Journal of each House respectively. If any Bill shall not be returned by the President within ten Days (Sundays excepted) after it shall have been presented to him, the Same shall be a Law, in like Manner as if he had signed it, unless the Congress by their Adjournment prevent its Return, in which Case it shall not be a Law.

Every Order, Resolution, or Vote to which the Concurrence of the Senate and House of Representatives may be necessary (except on a question of Adjournment) shall be presented to the President of the United States; and before the Same shall take Effect, shall be approved by him, or being disapproved by him, shall be repassed by two thirds of the Senate and House of Representatives, according to the Rules and Limitations prescribed in the Case of a Bill.

Section. 8.

The Congress shall have Power To lay and collect Taxes, Duties, Imposts and Excises, to pay the Debts and provide for the common Defence and general Welfare of the United States; but all Duties, Imposts and Excises shall be uniform throughout the United States;

To borrow Money on the credit of the United States;

To regulate Commerce with foreign Nations, and among the several States, and with the Indian Tribes;

To establish an uniform Rule of Naturalization, and uniform Laws on the subject of Bankruptcies throughout the United States;

To coin Money, regulate the Value thereof, and of foreign Coin, and fix the Standard of Weights and Measures;

To provide for the Punishment of counterfeiting the Securities and current Coin of the United States;

To establish Post Offices and post Roads;

To promote the Progress of Science and useful Arts, by securing for limited Times to Authors and Inventors the exclusive Right to their respective Writings and Discoveries;

To constitute Tribunals inferior to the Supreme Court;

To define and punish Piracies and Felonies committed on the high Seas, and Offences against the Law of Nations;

To declare War, grant Letters of Marque and Reprisal, and make Rules concerning Captures on Land and Water;

To raise and support Armies, but no Appropriation of Money to that Use shall be for a longer Term than two Years;

To provide and maintain a Navy;

To make Rules for the Government and Regulation of the land and naval Forces;

To provide for calling forth the Militia to execute the Laws of the Union, suppress Insurrections and repel Invasions;

To provide for organizing, arming, and disciplining, the Militia, and for governing such Part of them as may be employed in the Service of the United States, reserving to the States respectively, the Appointment of the Officers, and the Authority of training the Militia according to the discipline prescribed by Congress;

To exercise exclusive Legislation in all Cases whatsoever, over such District (not exceeding ten Miles square) as may, by Cession of particular States, and the Acceptance of Congress, become the Seat of the Government of the United States, and to exercise like Authority over all Places purchased by the Consent of the Legislature of the State in which the Same shall be, for the Erection of Forts, Magazines, Arsenals, dock-Yards, and other needful Buildings;—And

To make all Laws which shall be necessary and proper for carrying into Execution the foregoing Powers, and all other Powers vested by this Constitution in the Government of the United States, or in any Department or Officer thereof.

Section. 9.

The Migration or Importation of such Persons as any of the States now existing shall think proper to admit, shall not be prohibited by the Congress prior to the Year one thousand eight hundred and eight, but a Tax or duty may be imposed on such Importation, not exceeding ten dollars for each Person.

The Privilege of the Writ of Habeas Corpus shall not be suspended, unless when in Cases of Rebellion or Invasion the public Safety may require it.

No Bill of Attainder or ex post facto Law shall be passed.

No Capitation, or other direct, Tax shall be laid, unless in Proportion to the Census or enumeration herein before directed to be taken.

No Tax or Duty shall be laid on Articles exported from any State.

No Preference shall be given by any Regulation of Commerce or Revenue to the Ports of one State over those of another: nor shall Vessels bound to, or from, one State, be obliged to enter, clear, or pay Duties in another.

No Money shall be drawn from the Treasury, but in Consequence of Appropriations made by Law; and a regular Statement and Account of the Receipts and Expenditures of all public Money shall be published from time to time.

No Title of Nobility shall be granted by the United States: And no Person holding any Office of Profit or Trust under them, shall, without the Consent of the Congress, accept of any present, Emolument, Office, or Title, of any kind whatever, from any King, Prince, or foreign State.

Section. 10.

No State shall enter into any Treaty, Alliance, or Confederation; grant Letters of Marque and Reprisal; coin Money; emit Bills of Credit; make any Thing but gold and silver Coin a Tender in Payment of Debts; pass any Bill of Attainder, ex post facto Law, or Law impairing the Obligation of Contracts, or grant any Title of Nobility.

No State shall, without the Consent of the Congress, lay any Imposts or Duties on Imports or Exports, except what may be absolutely necessary for executing it's inspection Laws: and the net Produce of all Duties and Imposts, laid by any State on Imports or Exports, shall be for the Use of the Treasury of the United States; and all such Laws shall be subject to the Revision and Controul of the Congress.

No State shall, without the Consent of Congress, lay any Duty of Tonnage, keep Troops, or Ships of War in time of Peace, enter into any Agreement or Compact with another State, or with a foreign Power, or engage in War, unless actually invaded, or in such imminent Danger as will not admit of delay.

Article. II., Section. 1.

The executive Power shall be vested in a President of the United States of America. He shall hold his Office during the Term of four Years, and, together with the Vice President, chosen for the same Term, be elected, as follows

Each State shall appoint, in such Manner as the Legislature thereof may direct, a Number of Electors, equal to the whole Number of Senators and Representatives to which the State may be entitled in the Congress: but no Senator or Representative, or Person holding an Office of Trust or Profit under the United States, shall be appointed an Elector.

The Electors shall meet in their respective States, and vote by Ballot for two Persons, of whom one at least shall not be an Inhabitant of the same State with themselves. And they shall make a List of all the Persons voted for, and of the Number of Votes for each; which List they shall sign and certify, and transmit sealed to the Seat of the Government of the United States, directed to the President of the Senate. The President of the Senate shall, in the Presence of the Senate and House of Representatives, open all the Certificates, and the Votes shall then be counted. The Person having the greatest Number of Votes shall be the President, if such Number be a Majority of the whole Number of Electors appointed; and if there be more than one who have such Majority, and have an equal Number of Votes, then the House of Representatives shall immediately chuse by Ballot one of them for President; and if no Person have a Majority, then from the five highest on the List the said House shall in like Manner chuse the President. But in chusing the President, the Votes shall be taken by States, the Representation from each State having one Vote; A quorum for this Purpose shall consist of a Member or Members from two thirds of the States, and a Majority of all the States shall be necessary to a Choice. In every Case, after the Choice of the President, the Person having the greatest Number of Votes of the Electors shall be the Vice President. But if there should remain two or more who have equal Votes, the Senate shall chuse from them by Ballot the Vice President.

The Congress may determine the Time of chusing the Electors, and the Day on which they shall give their Votes; which Day shall be the same throughout the United States.

No Person except a natural born Citizen, or a Citizen of the United States, at the time of the Adoption of this Constitution, shall be eligible to the Office of President; neither shall any Person be eligible to that Office who shall not have attained to the Age of thirty five Years, and been fourteen Years a Resident within the United States.

In Case of the Removal of the President from Office, or of his Death, Resignation, or Inability to discharge the Powers and Duties of the said Office, the Same shall devolve on the Vice President, and the Congress may by Law provide for the Case of Removal, Death, Resignation or Inability, both of the President and Vice President, declaring what Officer shall then act as President, and such Officer shall act accordingly, until the Disability be removed, or a President shall be elected.

The President shall, at stated Times, receive for his Services, a Compensation, which shall neither be encreased nor diminished during the Period for which he shall have been elected, and he shall not receive within that Period any other Emolument from the United States, or any of them.

Before he enter on the Execution of his Office, he shall take the following Oath or Affirmation:—"I do solemnly swear (or affirm) that I will faithfully execute the Office of President of the United States, and will to the best of my Ability, preserve, protect and defend the Constitution of the United States."

Section. 2.

The President shall be Commander in Chief of the Army and Navy of the United States, and of the Militia of the several States, when called into the actual Service of the United States; he may require the Opinion, in writing, of the principal Officer in each of the executive Departments, upon any Subject relating to the Duties of their respective Offices, and he shall have Power to grant Reprieves and Pardons for Offences against the United States, except in Cases of Impeachment.

He shall have Power, by and with the Advice and Consent of the Senate, to make Treaties, provided two thirds of the Senators present concur; and he shall nominate, and by and with the Advice and Consent of the Senate, shall appoint Ambassadors, other public Ministers and Consuls, Judges of the supreme Court, and all other Officers of the United States, whose Appointments are not herein otherwise provided for, and which shall be established by Law: but the Congress may by Law vest the Appointment of such inferior Officers, as they think proper, in the President alone, in the Courts of Law, or in the Heads of Departments.

The President shall have Power to fill up all Vacancies that may happen during the Recess of the Senate, by granting Commissions which shall expire at the End of their next Session.

Section. 3.

He shall from time to time give to the Congress Information of the State of the Union, and recommend to their Consideration such Measures as he shall judge necessary and expedient; he may, on extraordinary Occasions, convene both Houses, or either of them, and in Case of Disagreement between them, with Respect to the Time of Adjournment, he may adjourn them to such Time as he shall think proper; he shall receive Ambassadors and other public Ministers; he shall take Care that the Laws be faithfully executed, and shall Commission all the Officers of the United States.

Section. 4.

The President, Vice President and all civil Officers of the United States, shall be removed from Office on Impeachment for, and Conviction of, Treason, Bribery, or other high Crimes and Misdemeanors.

Article III., Section. 1.

The judicial Power of the United States, shall be vested in one supreme Court, and in such inferior Courts as the Congress may from time to time ordain and establish. The Judges, both of the supreme and inferior Courts, shall hold their Offices during good Behaviour, and shall, at stated Times, receive for their Services, a Compensation, which shall not be diminished during their Continuance in Office.

Section. 2.

The judicial Power shall extend to all Cases, in Law and Equity, arising under this Constitution, the Laws of the United States, and Treaties made, or which shall be made, under their Authority;—to all Cases affecting Ambassadors, other public Ministers and Consuls;—to all Cases of admiralty and maritime Jurisdiction;—to Controversies to which the United States shall be a Party;—to Controversies between two or more States;—between a State and Citizens of another State,—between Citizens of different States,—between Citizens of the same State claiming Lands under Grants of different States, and between a State, or the Citizens thereof, and foreign States, Citizens or Subjects.

In all Cases affecting Ambassadors, other public Ministers and Consuls, and those in which a State shall be Party, the supreme Court shall have original Jurisdiction. In all the other Cases before mentioned, the supreme Court shall have appellate Jurisdiction, both as to Law and Fact, with such Exceptions, and under such Regulations as the Congress shall make.

The Trial of all Crimes, except in Cases of Impeachment, shall be by Jury; and such Trial shall be held in the State where the said Crimes shall have been committed; but when not committed within any State, the Trial shall be at such Place or Places as the Congress may by Law have directed.

Section. 3.

Treason against the United States, shall consist only in levying War against them, or in adhering to their Enemies, giving them Aid and Comfort. No Person shall be convicted of Treason unless on the Testimony of two Witnesses to the same overt Act, or on Confession in open Court.

The Congress shall have Power to declare the Punishment of Treason, but no Attainder of Treason shall work Corruption of Blood, or Forfeiture except during the Life of the Person attainted.

Article. IV., Section. 1.

Full Faith and Credit shall be given in each State to the public Acts, Records, and judicial Proceedings of every other State. And the Congress may by general Laws prescribe the Manner in which such Acts, Records and Proceedings shall be proved, and the Effect thereof.

Section. 2.

The Citizens of each State shall be entitled to all Privileges and Immunities of Citizens in the several States.

A Person charged in any State with Treason, Felony, or other Crime, who shall flee from Justice, and be found in another State, shall on Demand of the executive Authority of the State from which he fled, be delivered up, to be removed to the State having Jurisdiction of the Crime.

No Person held to Service or Labour in one State, under the Laws thereof, escaping into another, shall, in Consequence of any Law or Regulation therein, be discharged from such Service or Labour, but shall be delivered up on Claim of the Party to whom such Service or Labour may be due.

Section. 3.

New States may be admitted by the Congress into this Union; but no new State shall be formed or erected within the Jurisdiction of any other State; nor any State be formed by the Junction of two or more States, or Parts of States, without the Consent of the Legislatures of the States concerned as well as of the Congress.

The Congress shall have Power to dispose of and make all needful Rules and Regulations respecting the Territory or other Property belonging to the United States; and nothing in this Constitution shall be so construed as to Prejudice any Claims of the United States, or of any particular State.

Section. 4.

The United States shall guarantee to every State in this Union a Republican Form of Government, and shall protect each of them against Invasion; and on Application of the Legislature, or of the Executive (when the Legislature cannot be convened), against domestic Violence.

Article. V.

The Congress, whenever two thirds of both Houses shall deem it necessary, shall propose Amendments to this Constitution, or, on the Application of the Legislatures of two thirds of the several States, shall call a Convention for proposing Amendments, which, in either Case, shall be valid to all Intents and Purposes, as Part of this Constitution, when ratified by the Legislatures of three fourths of the several States, or by Conventions in three fourths thereof, as the one or the other Mode of Ratification may be proposed by the Congress; Provided that no Amendment which may be made prior to the Year One thousand eight hundred and eight shall in any Manner affect the first and fourth Clauses in the Ninth Section of the first Article; and that no State, without its Consent, shall be deprived of its equal Suffrage in the Senate.

Article. VI.

All Debts contracted and Engagements entered into, before the Adoption of this Constitution, shall be as valid against the United States under this Constitution, as under the Confederation.

This Constitution, and the Laws of the United States which shall be made in Pursuance thereof; and all Treaties made, or which shall be made, under the Authority of the United States, shall be the supreme Law of the Land; and the Judges in every State shall be bound thereby, any Thing in the Constitution or Laws of any State to the Contrary notwithstanding.

The Senators and Representatives before mentioned, and the Members of the several State Legislatures, and all executive and judicial Officers, both of the United States and of the several States, shall be bound by Oath or Affirmation, to support this Constitution; but no religious Test shall ever be required as a Qualification to any Office or public Trust under the United States.

Article. VII.

The Ratification of the Conventions of nine States, shall be sufficient for the Establishment of this Constitution between the States so ratifying the Same.

The Word, "the," being interlined between the seventh and eighth Lines of the first Page, The Word "Thirty" being partly written on an Erazure in the fifteenth Line of the first Page, The Words "is tried" being interlined between the thirty second and thirty third Lines of the first Page and the Word "the" being interlined between the forty third and forty fourth Lines of the second Page.

Attest William Jackson Secretary, done in Convention by the Unanimous Consent of the States present the Seventeenth Day of September in the Year of our Lord one thousand seven hundred and Eighty seven and of the Independance of the United States of America the Twelfth In witness whereof We have hereunto subscribed our Names, G°. Washington, *Presidt and deputy from Virginia*

Delaware
Geo: Read
Gunning Bedford jun
John Dickinson
Richard Bassett
Jaco: Broom

Maryland
James McHenry
Dan of St Thos. Jenifer
Danl. Carroll

Virginia
John Blair
James Madison Jr.

North Carolina
Wm. Blount
Richd. Dobbs Spaight
Hu Williamson

South Carolina
J. Rutledge
Charles Cotesworth Pinckney
Charles Pinckney
Pierce Butler

Georgia
William Few
Abr Baldwin

New Hampshire
John Langdon
Nicholas Gilman

Massachusetts
Nathaniel Gorham
Rufus King

Connecticut
Wm. Saml. Johnson
Roger Sherman

New York
Alexander Hamilton

New Jersey
Wil: Livingston
David Brearley
Wm. Paterson
Jona: Dayton

Pensylvania
B Franklin
Thomas Mifflin
Robt. Morris
Geo. Clymer
Thos. FitzSimons
Jared Ingersoll
James Wilson
Gouv Morris

Notes

Bill of Rights of the United States of America (1791)

The first ten amendments to the Constitution make up the Bill of Rights. Written by James Madison in response to calls from several states for greater constitutional protection for individual liberties, the Bill of Rights lists specific prohibitions on governmental power. The Virginia Declaration of Rights, written by George Mason, strongly influenced Madison.

One of the many points of contention between Federalists and Anti-Federalists was the Constitution's lack of a bill of rights that would place specific limits on government power. Federalists argued that the Constitution did not need a bill of rights, because the people and the states kept any powers not explicitly given to the federal government. Anti-Federalists held that a bill of rights was necessary to safeguard individual liberty.

Madison, then a member of the U.S. House of Representatives, went through the Constitution itself, making changes where he thought most appropriate. However, several Representatives, led by Roger Sherman, objected that Congress had no authority to change the wording of the Constitution itself. Therefore, Madison's changes were presented as a list of amendments that would follow Article VII.

The House approved 17 amendments. Of these 17, the Senate approved 12. Those 12 were sent to the states for approval in August of 1789. Of those 12, ten were quickly ratified. Virginia's legislature became the last to ratify the amendments on December 15, 1791. These amendments are known as the Bill of Rights.

The Bill of Rights is a list of limits on government power. For example, what the Founders saw as the natural right of individuals to speak and worship freely was protected by the First Amendment's prohibitions on Congress from making laws establishing a religion or abridging freedom of speech. Another example is the Fourth Amendment's warrant requirements safeguarded the natural right to be free from the government's unreasonable intrusion in one's home.

Other precursors to the Bill of Rights include English documents such as the Magna Carta[1], the Petition of Right, the English Bill of Rights, and the Massachusetts Body of Liberties.

The Magna Carta illustrates Compact Theory[1] as well as initial strides toward limited government. Its provisions address individual rights and political rights. Latin for "Great Charter," the Magna Carta was written by Barons in Runnymede, England and forced on the King. Although the protections were generally limited to the prerogatives of the Barons, the

Magna Carta embodied the general principle that the King accepted limitations on his rule. These included the fundamental acknowledgment that the king was not above the law.

Included in the Magna Carta are protections for the English church, petitioning the king, freedom from a forced quarter of troops and unreasonable searches, due process and fair trial protections, and freedom from excessive fines. These protections can be found in the First, Third, Fourth, Fifth, Sixth, and Eighth Amendments to the Constitution.

The Magna Carta is the oldest example of a compact in England. The Mayflower Compact, the Fundamental Orders of Connecticut, and the Albany Plan are examples from the American colonies. The Articles of Confederation was a compact among the states, and the Constitution creates a compact based on a federal system between the national government, state governments, and the people. The Hayne-Webster Debate focused on the compact created by the Constitution.

[1] Philosophers including Thomas Hobbes, John Locke, and Jean-Jacques Rousseau theorized that peoples' condition in a "state of nature" (that is, outside of a society) is one of freedom, but that freedom inevitably degrades into war, chaos, or debilitating competition without the benefit of a system of laws and government. They reasoned, therefore, that for their happiness, individuals willingly trade some of their natural freedom in exchange for the protections provided by the government.

The Bill of Rights

Amendment I

Congress shall make no law respecting an establishment of religion, or prohibiting the free exercise thereof; or abridging the freedom of speech, or of the press; or the right of the people peaceably to assemble, and to petition the government for a redress of grievances.

Amendment II

A well regulated militia, being necessary to the security of a free state, the right of the people to keep and bear arms, shall not be infringed.

Amendment III

No soldier shall, in time of peace be quartered in any house, without the consent of the owner, nor in time of war, but in a manner to be prescribed by law.

Amendment IV

The right of the people to be secure in their persons, houses, papers, and effects, against unreasonable searches and seizures, shall not be violated, and no warrants shall issue, but upon probable cause, supported by oath or affirmation, and particularly describing the place to be searched, and the persons or things to be seized.

Amendment V

No person shall be held to answer for a capital, or otherwise infamous crime, unless on a presentment or indictment of a grand jury, except in cases arising in the land or naval forces, or in the militia, when in actual service in time of war or public danger; nor shall any person be subject for the same offense to be twice put in jeopardy of life or limb; nor shall be compelled in any criminal case to be a witness against himself, nor be deprived of life, liberty, or property, without due process of law; nor shall private property be taken for public use, without just compensation.

Amendment VI

In all criminal prosecutions, the accused shall enjoy the right to a speedy and public trial, by an impartial jury of the state and district wherein the crime shall have been committed, which district shall have been previously ascertained by law, and to be informed of the nature and cause of the accusation; to be confronted with the witnesses against him; to have compulsory process for obtaining witnesses in his favor, and to have the assistance of counsel for his defense.

Amendment VII

In suits at common law, where the value in controversy shall exceed twenty dollars, the right of trial by jury shall be preserved, and no fact tried by a jury, shall be otherwise reexamined in any court of the United States, than according to the rules of the common law.

Amendment VIII

Excessive bail shall not be required, nor excessive fines imposed, nor cruel and unusual punishments inflicted.

Amendment IX

The enumeration in the Constitution, of certain rights, shall not be construed to deny or disparage others retained by the people.

Amendment X

The powers not delegated to the United States by the Constitution, nor prohibited by it to the states, are reserved to the states respectively, or to the people.

Constitutional Amendments 11-27

Amendment XI

Passed by Congress March 4, 1794. Ratified February 7, 1795.

Note: Article III, section 2, of the Constitution was modified by amendment 11.

The Judicial power of the United States shall not be construed to extend to any suit in law or equity, commenced or prosecuted against one of the United States by Citizens of another State, or by Citizens or Subjects of any Foreign State.

Amendment XII

Passed by Congress December 9, 1803. Ratified June 15, 1804.

Note: The 12th amendment superseded a portion of Article II, section 1 of the Constitution.

The Electors shall meet in their respective states and vote by ballot for President and Vice-President, one of whom, at least, shall not be an inhabitant of the same state with themselves; they shall name in their ballots the person voted for as President, and in distinct ballots the person voted for as Vice-President, and they shall make distinct lists of all persons voted for as President, and of all persons voted for as Vice-President, and of the number of votes for each, which lists they shall sign and certify, and transmit sealed to the seat of the government of the United States, directed to the President of the Senate; -- the President of the Senate shall, in the presence of the Senate and House of Representatives, open all the certificates and the votes shall then be counted; -- The person having the greatest number of votes for President, shall be the President, if such number be a majority of the whole number of Electors appointed; and if no person have such majority, then from the persons having the highest numbers not exceeding three on the list of those voted for as President, the House of Representatives shall choose immediately, by ballot, the President. But in choosing the President, the votes shall be taken by states, the representation from each state having one vote; a quorum for this purpose shall consist of a member or members from two-thirds of the states, and a majority of all the states shall be necessary to a choice. [And if the House of Representatives shall not choose a President whenever the right of choice shall devolve upon them, before the fourth day of March next following, then the Vice-President shall act as President, as in case of the death or other constitutional disability of the President. --]* The person having the greatest number of votes as Vice-President, shall be the Vice-President, if such number be a majority of the whole number of Electors appointed, and if no person have a majority, then from the two highest numbers on the list, the Senate shall choose the Vice-President; a quorum for the purpose shall consist of two-thirds of the whole number of Senators, and a majority of the whole number shall be necessary to a choice. But no person constitutionally ineligible to the office of President shall be eligible to that of Vice-President of the United States.

Superseded by section 3 of the 20th amendment.

Amendment XIII

Passed by Congress January 31, 1865. Ratified December 6, 1865.

Note: The 13th amendment superseded a portion of Article IV, section 2, of the Constitution.

Section 1.
Neither slavery nor involuntary servitude, except as a punishment for crime whereof the party shall have been duly convicted, shall exist within the United States, or any place subject to their jurisdiction.

Section 2.
Congress shall have power to enforce this article by appropriate legislation.

Amendment XIV

Passed by Congress June 13, 1866. Ratified July 9, 1868.

Note: Section 2 of the 14th amendment modified article I, section 2, of the Constitution.

Section 1.
All persons born or naturalized in the United States, and subject to the jurisdiction thereof, are citizens of the United States and of the State wherein they reside. No State shall make or enforce any law which shall abridge the privileges or immunities of citizens of the United States; nor shall any State deprive any person of life, liberty, or property, without due process of law; nor deny to any person within its jurisdiction the equal protection of the laws.

Section 2.
Representatives shall be apportioned among the several States according to their respective numbers, counting the whole number of persons in each State, excluding Indians not taxed. But when the right to vote at any election for the choice of electors for President and Vice-President of the United States, Representatives in Congress, the Executive and Judicial officers of a State, or the members of the Legislature thereof, is denied to any of the male inhabitants of such State, being twenty-one years of age,* and citizens of the United States, or in any way abridged, except for participation in rebellion, or other crime, the basis of representation therein shall be reduced in the proportion which the number of such male citizens shall bear to the whole number of male citizens twenty-one years of age in such State.

Section 3.
No person shall be a Senator or Representative in Congress, or elector of President and Vice-President, or hold any office, civil or military, under the United States, or under any State, who, having previously taken an oath, as a member of Congress, or as an officer of the United States, or as a member of any State legislature, or as an executive or judicial officer of any State, to support the Constitution of the United States, shall have engaged in insurrection or rebellion against the same, or given aid or comfort to the enemies thereof. But Congress may by a vote of two-thirds of each House, remove such disability.

Section 4.
The validity of the public debt of the United States, authorized by law, including debts incurred

for payment of pensions and bounties for services in suppressing insurrection or rebellion, shall not be questioned. But neither the United States nor any State shall assume or pay any debt or obligation incurred in aid of insurrection or rebellion against the United States, or any claim for the loss or emancipation of any slave; but all such debts, obligations and claims shall be held illegal and void.

Section 5.
The Congress shall have the power to enforce, by appropriate legislation, the provisions of this article.

*Changed by section 1 of the 26th amendment.

Amendment XV

Passed by Congress February 26, 1869. Ratified February 3, 1870.

Section 1.
The right of citizens of the United States to vote shall not be denied or abridged by the United States or by any State on account of race, color, or previous condition of servitude.

Section 2.
The Congress shall have the power to enforce this article by appropriate legislation.

Amendment XVI

Passed by Congress July 2, 1909. Ratified February 3, 1913.

Note: Article I, section 9, of the Constitution was modified by amendment 16.

The Congress shall have power to lay and collect taxes on incomes, from whatever source derived, without apportionment among the several States, and without regard to any census or enumeration.

Amendment XVII

Passed by Congress May 13, 1912. Ratified April 8, 1913.

Note: The 17th amendment modified article I, section 3, of the Constitution.

The Senate of the United States shall be composed of two Senators from each State, elected by the people thereof, for six years; and each Senator shall have one vote. The electors in each State shall have the qualifications requisite for electors of the most numerous branch of the State legislatures.

When vacancies happen in the representation of any State in the Senate, the executive authority of such State shall issue writs of election to fill such vacancies: *Provided*, That the legislature of any State may empower the executive thereof to make temporary appointments until the people fill the vacancies by election as the legislature may direct.

This amendment shall not be so construed as to affect the election or term of any Senator chosen before it becomes valid as part of the Constitution.

Amendment XVIII

Passed by Congress December 18, 1917. Ratified January 16, 1919. Repealed by amendment 21.

Section 1.

After one year from the ratification of this article the manufacture, sale, or transportation of intoxicating liquors within, the importation thereof into, or the exportation thereof from the United States and all territory subject to the jurisdiction thereof for beverage purposes is hereby prohibited.

Section 2.

The Congress and the several States shall have concurrent power to enforce this article by appropriate legislation.

Section 3.

This article shall be inoperative unless it shall have been ratified as an amendment to the Constitution by the legislatures of the several States, as provided in the Constitution, within seven years from the date of the submission hereof to the States by the Congress.

Amendment XIX

Passed by Congress June 4, 1919. Ratified August 18, 1920.

The right of citizens of the United States to vote shall not be denied or abridged by the United States or by any State on account of sex.

Congress shall have power to enforce this article by appropriate legislation.

Amendment XX

Passed by Congress March 2, 1932. Ratified January 23, 1933.

Note: Section 2 of this amendment modified article I, section 4, of the Constitution. Also, a portion of the 12th amendment was superseded by section 3.

Section 1.

The terms of the President and the Vice President shall end at noon on the 20th day of January, and the terms of Senators and Representatives at noon on the 3d day of January, of the years in which such terms would have ended if this article had not been ratified; and the terms of their successors shall then begin.

Section 2.

The Congress shall assemble at least once in every year, and such meeting shall begin at noon on the 3d day of January, unless they shall by law appoint a different day.

Section 3.

If, at the time fixed for the beginning of the term of the President, the President elect shall have died, the Vice President elect shall become President. If a President shall not have been chosen before the time fixed for the beginning of his term, or if the President elect shall have failed to qualify, then the Vice President elect shall act as President until a President shall have qualified; and the Congress may by law provide for the case wherein neither a President elect nor a Vice President elect shall have qualified, declaring who shall then act as President, or the manner in which one who is to act shall be selected, and such person shall act accordingly until a President or Vice President shall have qualified.

Section 4.

The Congress may by law provide for the case of the death of any of the persons from whom the House of Representatives may choose a President whenever the right of choice shall have devolved upon them, and for the case of the death of any of the persons from whom the Senate may choose a Vice President whenever the right of choice shall have devolved upon them.

Section 5.

Sections 1 and 2 shall take effect on the 15th day of October following the ratification of this article.

Section 6.

This article shall be inoperative unless it shall have been ratified as an amendment to the Constitution by the legislatures of three-fourths of the several States within seven years from the date of its submission.

Amendment XXI

Passed by Congress February 20, 1933. Ratified December 5, 1933.

Section 1.

The eighteenth article of amendment to the Constitution of the United States is hereby repealed.

Section 2.

The transportation or importation into any State, Territory, or possession of the United States for delivery or use therein of intoxicating liquors, in violation of the laws thereof, is hereby prohibited.

Section 3.

This article shall be inoperative unless it shall have been ratified as an amendment to the Constitution by conventions in the several States, as provided in the Constitution, within seven years from the date of the submission hereof to the States by the Congress.

Amendment XXII

Passed by Congress March 21, 1947. Ratified February 27, 1951.

Section 1.

No person shall be elected to the office of the President more than twice, and no person who has held the office of President, or acted as President, for more than two years of a term to which some other person was elected President shall be elected to the office of the President more than once. But this Article shall not apply to any person holding the office of President when this Article was proposed by the Congress, and shall not prevent any person who may be holding the office of President, or acting as President, during the term within which this Article becomes operative from holding the office of President or acting as President during the remainder of such term.

Section 2.

This article shall be inoperative unless it shall have been ratified as an amendment to the Constitution by the legislatures of three-fourths of the several States within seven years from the date of its submission to the States by the Congress.

Amendment XXIII

Passed by Congress June 16, 1960. Ratified March 29, 1961.

Section 1.

The District constituting the seat of Government of the United States shall appoint in such manner as the Congress may direct:

A number of electors of President and Vice President equal to the whole number of Senators and Representatives in Congress to which the District would be entitled if it were a State, but in no event more than the least populous State; they shall be in addition to those appointed by the States, but they shall be considered, for the purposes of the election of President and Vice President, to be electors appointed by a State; and they shall meet in the District and perform such duties as provided by the twelfth article of amendment.

Section 2.

The Congress shall have power to enforce this article by appropriate legislation.

Amendment XXIV

Passed by Congress on August 27, 1962. Ratified January 23, 1964.

Section 1.

The right of citizens of the United States to vote in any primary or other election for President or Vice President, for electors for President or Vice President, or for Senator or Representative in Congress, shall not be denied or abridged by the United States or any State by reason of failure to pay any poll tax or other tax.

Section 2.

The Congress shall have power to enforce this article by appropriate legislation.

Amendment XXV

Passed by Congress July 6, 1965. Ratified February 10, 1967.

Note: Article II, section 1, of the Constitution was affected by the 25th amendment.

Section 1.
In case of the removal of the President from office or of his death or resignation, the Vice President shall become President.

Section 2.
Whenever there is a vacancy in the office of the Vice President, the President shall nominate a Vice President who shall take office upon confirmation by a majority vote of both Houses of Congress.

Section 3.
Whenever the President transmits to the President pro tempore of the Senate and the Speaker of the House of Representatives his written declaration that he is unable to discharge the powers and duties of his office, and until he transmits to them a written declaration to the contrary, such powers and duties shall be discharged by the Vice President as Acting President.

Section 4.
Whenever the Vice President and a majority of either the principal officers of the executive departments or of such other body as Congress may by law provide, transmit to the President pro tempore of the Senate and the Speaker of the House of Representatives their written declaration that the President is unable to discharge the powers and duties of his office, the Vice President shall immediately assume the powers and duties of the office as Acting President.

Thereafter, when the President transmits to the President pro tempore of the Senate and the Speaker of the House of Representatives his written declaration that no inability exists, he shall resume the powers and duties of his office unless the Vice President and a majority of either the principal officers of the executive department or of such other body as Congress may by law provide, transmit within four days to the President pro tempore of the Senate and the Speaker of the House of Representatives their written declaration that the President is unable to discharge the powers and duties of his office. Thereupon Congress shall decide the issue, assembling within forty-eight hours for that purpose if not in session. If the Congress, within twenty-one days after receipt of the latter written declaration, or, if Congress is not in session, within twenty-one days after Congress is required to assemble, determines by two-thirds vote of both Houses that the President is unable to discharge the powers and duties of his office, the Vice President shall continue to discharge the same as Acting President; otherwise, the President shall resume the powers and duties of his office.

Amendment XXVI

Passed by Congress March 23, 1971. Ratified July 1, 1971.

Note: section 1 of the 26th amendment modified amendment 14, section 2, of the Constitution.

Section 1.
The right of citizens of the United States, who are eighteen years of age or older, to vote shall not be denied or abridged by the United States or by any State on account of age.

Section 2.
The Congress shall have power to enforce this article by appropriate legislation.

Amendment XXII

Originally proposed Sept. 25, 1789. Ratified May 7, 1992.

No law, varying the compensation for the services of the Senators and Representatives, shall take effect, until an election of Representatives shall have intervened

We want to hear from you
Your feedback is important to us because we strive to provide the highest quality prep materials. Email us if you have any questions, comments or suggestions, so we can incorporate your feedback into future editions.

Customer Satisfaction Guarantee
If you have any concerns about this book, including printing issues, contact us and we will resolve any issues to your satisfaction.

info@sterling-prep.com

We reply to all emails – please check your spam folder

Thank you for choosing our products to achieve your educational goals!

Glossary

A

Absent vote — a vote cast by those who are out of their division but still within their State or Territory; which may be cast at any polling place in that State or Territory.

Absentee ballot — a ballot, usually sent in the mail, that allows those who cannot go to their precinct on election day to vote.

Absolute majority — a term used to compare the least votes a winning candidate may need in a preferential, single-member voting system (also known as "50% + 1 vote"); this is compared to first-past-the-post systems of other countries, where a "majority" may be less than 50%; this concept is used in some parliamentary votes where a simple majority of all members present is not enough.

Absolutism — the belief that the government should have all the power and be able to do whatever it wants.

Accord — a diplomatic agreement that does not have the same binding force as a treaty.

Acquisitive model — a view of bureaucracies that argues agency heads will always seek to expand the size, budget, and power of their agency.

Actual malice — knowingly publishing falsehoods (whether in print, on radio, TV or the internet) to harm a person's reputation.

Ad hominem — Latin for "to the man," attacking the presenter of an argument rather than the argument itself (also known as "playing the man, not the ball").

Adjournment — temporary interruption during a parliamentary session.

Administrative adjudication — the bureaucratic function of settling disputes by relying on rules and precedents.

Administrative law — the segment of public law that is used to challenge the decisions of government officials and/or delegated legislation; excluding policy decisions made by the people's elected representatives where it is deemed that electoral popular support authorizes office holders to be unrestrained in their decision making as long as it is within the law, all civil/public servants can be challenged in court (as long as the plaintiff has standing) on the "reasonableness" of their administrative actions or on a failure to act; over time, the authority of A.L. has been extended to so-called public bodies (e.g., NGOs, Quangos and other organizations which otherwise have discretionary power over the rights of their members).

Affirm — an action by the Supreme Court to uphold a ruling by a lower court; that ruling now becomes the legally binding one.

Affirmative action — legislative programs which aim to create minority equality in employment, university placements, housing, and other government-influenced beneficial situations.

Agency capture — the gaining of control (direct or indirect) over a government regulatory agency by the industry it regulates.

Agency representation — a type of representation in which the representative is seen as an agent acting on behalf of the voters of their district and who is held accountable if they do not do as the constituents wish.

Agenda-setting — the power of the media to determine which issues will be discussed and debated.

Agitprop — less-than-subtle political propaganda disseminated through the media and performing arts; the term derived from the Department of Agitation and Propaganda of the Soviet Union.

Agrarian socialist — originally applying to non-urban, pre-Industrial Revolution people with traditional, conservative attitudes; believe in the collective ownership and control of primary industries and, to a lesser extent, secondary industries for the benefit of all; otherwise are not that committed to other socialist beliefs such as progressive/liberal approaches to domestic or international social concerns.

Saul Alinsky — described by opponents as an organizational genius, an American political activist never aligned with any political party; through his book *Rules for Radicals*, propagated ideas for poor communities to successfully politically organize; widely used in the 1960s by college students and other counter-culture movements, his book is now popular with both sides of the political divide.

Altruism — the devotion to the interests of others above that of the self; the opposite of egotism.

Amendment — a change to the Constitution.

American conservatism — the belief that freedom trumps all other political considerations; the government should play as small a role as possible in people's lives.

American exceptionalism — the view that the United States is markedly different from and better than other countries.

American liberalism — the belief that the government should actively promote equality in politics and economics.

Americans with Disabilities Act — the major law banning discrimination against the disabled; requires employers to make all reasonable accommodations to disabled workers; passed in 1990.

Amicus curiae **brief** — a "friend of the court" brief; a brief submitted to the court by a group not involved in the case; presents further arguments for one side in the case.

Anarchism — the belief that all governments are repressive and should be dismantled.

Anarchy — a condition of lawlessness and disorder brought about in the absence of any controlling authority.

Androcracy — a state or society ruled by men where moral authority and, usually, control of property are exclusively in the hands of males (also known as andrarchy or phallocracy).

Anti-clericalism — opposition to the influence of religion in government and legislative affairs.

Anti-Federalists — group opposed to the ratification of the Constitution because it gave too much power to the national government at the expense of the states; later became one of the first two major political parties in America; see *Federalists*.

Antitrust policy — a collection of national and state laws (including the Sherman Antitrust Act of 1890) aimed at preventing a single business from gaining monopoly control over a particular sector of the economy.

Apparatchik — a member of the Communist Party machine; derogatory term for a political party zealot.

Appellate jurisdiction — authority to hear appeals of cases arising in a particular geographic area or sphere of the law. The Supreme Court has appellate jurisdiction over all cases arising under the Constitution of the United States; see *Original jurisdiction*.

Appointment power — the president's power to appoint people to key federal offices.

Appropriation — the act of Congress formally specifying the amount of money that an agency is authorized to spend.

Approval voting — first-past-the-post voting with the added concept that one can vote for as many candidates' names as one wishes; a simpler form of preferential voting eliminating the chances of minority candidates winning when too many mainstream candidates are running against each other.

Articles of Confederation — a document that established a "firm league of friendship" or weak national congress between the original thirteen states during the Revolutionary War.

Attack journalism — journalism that aims to undermine political leaders.

Authoritarian regime — a government that can do whatever it wants, without limits.

Authority — the ability of the government to exercise power without resorting to violence.

Authorization — a formal declaration by a congressional committee that a certain amount of money is available to an agency.

Autocracy — a form of government where one single individual or regime hold unlimited power.

B

Backbencher — a member of Parliament (whether the government or the opposition) who is not in a leadership role in their party and who sits on the back bench.

Bad tendency doctrine — interpretation of the First Amendment that would allow the Congress or state legislatures to prohibit or limit speech or expression that tends to incite illegal activity.

Bad-tendency rule — a rule to judge if speech can be limited (i.e., if the speech could lead to some "evil," it can be prohibited).

***Bakke* case** — this Supreme Court Case decided in 1978 that affirmative action is legal as long as race is not the only factor considered.

Balance of power — the leverage a small party in the legislature possesses in being able to give or hold back voting support to a large (albeit still minority) party to allow it to have a majority on a vote.

Balanced budget — when a government spends exactly as much as it takes in.

Ballot — a method of secret voting, normally in a written form; a form provided to each voter on election day to be marked, showing the names of the candidates (and sometimes the parties) who are standing for election.

Ballot initiative — a public policy question to be decided by a vote of the people; the placement of the question on the ballot is initiated by the people (usually by petition); used only at the state level.

Bell the cat — an impractical suggestion that highlights the short-sightedness of the theorist advocating a problem's solution which will not in work in practice or would be politically lethal for the party proposing it; derived from a fable about a group of mice who decide the best way to be warned when the cat is near is for someone to place a bell around its neck, only to find there are no volunteers to perform that task.

Bellwether — a small entity whose characteristics happen to reflect that of the whole state or nation (a bellwether is a ram with a bell attached to indicate to the farmer where the flock is when not in sight); for example, the American state of Nevada is a bellwether state for presidential elections in that it has voted the same as the whole country for a century with only one exception.

The Beltway — a term to describe the politically and socially insular community of Washington, D.C.; derived from Interstate Highway 495 which circumnavigates Washington, forming a "belt;" the term is sometimes used in other countries, although in Britain the equivalent is "the Westminster Bubble."

Bicameral (legislature) — a term describing a legislative branch that is divided into two houses (e.g., the United States Congress, which consists of the House of Representatives and the Senate).

Bigot — a person who refuses to discuss, consider or listen to beliefs or theories contrary to their own; derived from the French term of abuse in the Middle Ages for religious Normans who would frequently use the term "By God."

Bilateral — a state acting in cooperation with another state.

Bill — the name for proposed legislation entered into the house/houses of Parliament or Congress to be debated and then voted upon for approval; if approved at all stages it then becomes an act and law.

Bill of attainder —a no-longer practiced ancient writ or act of Parliament to declare someone guilty of a crime and/or subject to punishment without benefit of trial; attainder, meaning tainted-ness, also meant that any party guilty of a capital crime lost all civil rights including property and, if not life, then right to reputation; a bill passed by a legislature imposing a penalty or inflicting a detriment on a particular individual or group of individuals; forbidden by Article I, Section 9 of the U.S. Constitution.

Bill of Rights —a list of entrenched fundamental human rights as perceived by the declarer (also known as Charter of Rights or Declaration of Rights); whereas a nation's enacted laws are deemed to protect people from the malevolent deeds of their fellow citizens, a Bill of Rights is deemed to protect the citizenry from the excesses of their rulers; term derived from the 1689 Bill of Rights enacted by the British Parliament after the Glorious Revolution; the first ten Amendments to the U.S. Constitution which safeguard some specific rights of the American people and the states.

Bipartisan(ship) — cooperation and collaboration between members of the two major political parties (e.g., Republicans and Democrats) to agree on an initiative.

Bipartisan Campaign Finance Reform Act — a law passed in 2002 that banned soft money, put limits on issue advertising and increased the amount that people can donate to candidates; see *McCain-Feingold bill.*

Bipolar system — an international system characterized by two superpowers that roughly balance each other.

Blanket primary — a primary in which voters can choose candidates from more than one party; declared unconstitutional by the Supreme Court.

Block grant — a grant-in-aid with few restrictions or rules about how it can be spent.

Block voting — in multi-member electorates, each voter having the same number of votes as the number of vacant seats; this has the effect of minimizing the chances of minority candidates winning seats.

Boondoggle — a wasteful government-financed infrastructure developed at a cost much greater than its value, undertaken for local or political gain.

Bourgeois — Marxist term now used to describe middle-class professionals living a relatively luxurious lifestyle.

Brief — a document submitted to a court that presents one side's argument in a case.

Brinksmanship — belligerent diplomatic relations where at least one party is prepared to risk all and go to the brink of war, economic ruin or whatever calamitous situation to get what they want (e.g., the present government of North Korea).

Broadcast media — media that is distributed over the airwaves.

Brown v. Board of Education — Supreme Court case that ended segregation and declared "separate but equal" schools and facilities to be unconstitutional.

Bundling — the practice of lumping campaign donations from several donors together, sometimes to disguise the identities of contributors.

Bureaucracy — an administrative way of organizing large numbers of people to work together; usually relies on specialization, hierarchy and standard operating procedure.

Buying power — one's ability to purchase things; it is undermined by inflation.

By-law — not a law but a government rule or regulation; see *Delegated legislation*.

C

Cabinet — a group, composed of the heads of federal departments and key agencies that advises the president; made up of the President or Prime Minister as chairman and each director as the Secretary or (in the U.K.) Minister responsible for the relevant government departments (e.g., Defense, Environment, Commerce, etc.).

Caesaropapism — the belief that the powers of church and state should be united in one person.

Candidate — an individual who stands for election to political office.

Candidate-centered politics — campaigns and politics that focus on the candidates, not party labels.

Capitalism — an economic system based on the recognition of private property rights, where prices are dictated by supply and demand and the means of production and distribution of goods and services derived from privately owned resources, or capital, operating within a minimally regulated or unregulated market.

Caretaker government — a type of governance where those in power refrain from significant actions, such as undertaking major legislative programs or senior judicial or public service appointments, and only maintain necessary normal administrative duties; the reason for this is that power would be in transition due to an election or some other situation where legitimate democratic government has to be restored.

Carpetbagger — a pejorative term to describe outsiders taking advantage of a situation where others would normally be expected to benefit. A carpet bag was a fashionable form of luggage of the time used by northern "Yankees," political appointees or opportunistic businessmen who moved down to southern states during the American post-Civil War Reconstruction era, taking advantage of the instability, power vacuum and fire sale prices of the property market.

Case law — the collection of court decisions that shape the law.

Casework — work was done by a member of Congress or their staff on behalf of constituents.

Casus belli — the alleged justification for acts of war.

Categorical grants — money was given for a specific purpose that comes with restrictions concerning how the money should be spent; there are two types of categorical grants: project grants and formula grants.

Caucus (legislative) — a group of legislators unified by common goals or characteristics; the largest congressional caucuses are the Republican and Democratic party caucuses; other caucuses include the Black Caucus, the Hispanic Caucus and a variety of issue-oriented caucuses.

Caucus (local party) — a closed meeting of members of a political party or faction to make decisions, such as which candidate to nominate for an office; to set policy and to plot strategy; also the term for a group of people within an establishment with a common political leaning.

Cause célèbre — French for "famous case," a controversy (often a court case) arousing high public interest because of "sensitive" policy issues at stake (e.g., the Dreyfus affair, the Scopes Monkey Trial and the American *Roe v. Wade* Supreme Court case).

Census — counting the population to determine representation in the House of Representatives; the Constitution mandates one every ten years.

Central bank — the institution with the power to implement monetary policy.

Centralization — the process by which law and policymaking become centrally located.

Centrally planned economy — an economy where the government makes all decisions.

Charter — a document issued by state government granting certain powers and responsibilities to a local government.

Chatham House Rules — rules or undertakings, sometimes declared at public meetings, where the identity or affiliation of a speaker cannot later be made public when and if mentioning what was said; the alternative to "on the record" discussions.

Checks and balances — the ability of different branches of government to stop each other from acting; designed to prevent one branch from gaining too much power (e.g., the president's ability to veto legislation and the judicial authority to declare a legislative action or presidential order unconstitutional).

Chief diplomat — the role of the President as the primary point of contact between the United States of America and other nations.

Chief of state — the ceremonial head of government; in the United States, the president serves as chief of state.

Citizen — a legal member of a political unit.

Citizens initiated referendum — a democratic vehicle for legislative or constitutional enactment which bypasses Parliament; as exists in Switzerland and some states of the U.S., if a petition for a certain proposition can raise a certain number of signatures, then the legislature is compelled to put it to the people at a referendum and enact it in law if passed.

Civic education — education geared toward training the young to be good citizens.

Civil liberties — individual freedoms that the government cannot take away, including free speech, freedom of religion and the rights of the accused.

Civil Rights Act of 1964 — the major civil rights legislation in the modern era; banned discrimination and segregation in public accommodations.

Civil Rights Cases — a Supreme Court decision in 1883 that said the Fourteenth Amendment only made discrimination by the government illegal; private citizens could do as they pleased.

Civil service — government employees hired and promoted based on merit, not political connections.

Civil Service Commission — the first federal personnel agency; an impartial, independent board that hears and decides appeals filled by certain state and municipal workers and those who are seeking civil service employment opportunities.

Civil Service Reform Act of 1883 — a law that established the federal civil service; see *Pendleton Act.*

Civil Service Reform Act of 1978 — a law that updated and reformed the civil service.

Civil society — the network of community relationships that builds social capital.

Civil war — a war fought within a single country between or among different groups of citizens who want to control the government and do not recognize another group's right to rule.

Civis Romanus sum — Latin for "I am a Roman Citizen," the claim by ancient Romans that wherever they travel in foreign lands, they should be afforded full rights and protection with the understanding that the Roman military would respond to any violations; justification used by UK Prime Minister Lord Palmerston in 1850 when blockading Athens to ensure a British citizen there was compensated for the property damage inflicted by a violent Greek mob.

Classical conservatism — a view that arose in opposition to classical liberalism; it claimed that tradition was very valuable, human reason limited and stability essential.

Classical liberalism — a political philosophy that arose in the early modern era in Europe that individual human beings are autonomous agents with inviolable rights and that the powers of government arise from the people; argues for the value of the individual, the necessity for freedom, the importance of rationalism and the value of the free market.

Clear and present danger — a concept in American constitutional law to describe a situation where fundamental constitutional principles can be ignored in exigent circumstances.

Client state — a country that is economically or militarily dependent upon another but not controlled politically by the patron state, as in the case of a "puppet state."

Closed rule — a rule in the House of Representatives which limits or forbids any amendments to a bill being considered on the floor

Closed primary — a primary election in which only voters who belong to a particular political party are permitted to vote (e.g., only registered Democrats can vote in a closed Democratic party primary election).

Closed shop — a place of work where the union has arranged that the employer will only employ those who are its members.

Cloture — a motion to end debate in the Senate; must be approved by sixty votes.

Coattail effect — a boost in electoral support realized by candidates lower down the ballot when a successful candidate of their party runs strong at the top of the ballot (e.g., a popular Democratic presidential candidate who wins a large percentage of the vote might carry other Democratic Party candidates into office on his or her "coattails").

Codetermination — a policy in some countries with strong social democratic parties that forces large corporations to have substantial representation from their workers on the board of directors.

Cold war — the "war" between the United States and the former Soviet Union which involved no direct conflict between the two nations but instead was characterized by a multibillion-dollar nuclear arms race and numerous aggressive acts against secondary (or "satellite") nations backed (sometimes publicly, sometimes secretly) by each nation.

Commander-in-Chief — formal constitutional role of the President as leader of the nation's armed forces.

Command economy — as compared to the free market, an economy which is mostly under the command of the government.

Commerce clause — a clause in Article I, Section 8 of the U.S. Constitution that grants Congress the power to regulate interstate commerce.

Common-carrier role — the media's role as an intermediary between the people and the government.

Common law — the law of the land which comes from neither the statute books nor the constitution but from court law reports; originally, that body of law which was common to all parts of England (not customary or local law) and developed over centuries by the English courts, subsequently adopted by and further developed in countries using that system; in contrast to democratically maintained law, common law is judge-maintained and modified law and is valid unless it conflicts with statute law.

Communism — an extreme form of socialism that advocated violent revolution to create a socialist state.

Communitarianism — the concept of collective, rather than individual, ownership of all the nation's assets, as well as the duty by those able to create and manage those assets.

Comparative advantage — the ability of a state to produce a particular good or service at a lower marginal or opportunity cost than another (e.g., if country A can produce both apples and oranges cheaper than country B, with apples significantly cheaper, it is more efficient for it to concentrate on growing and exporting only apples while importing oranges, even though the imported oranges would not be as cheap as the homegrown).

Comparative politics — an academic discipline that compares states to understand how they work.

Concurrent powers — powers shared and exercised jointly under the Constitution by both national and state governments (e.g., taxation and law enforcement).

Concurrent resolution — a statement of the "sense" or opinion of the Congress, passed by both the House and the Senate; not binding as a matter of law.

Concurring opinion — an opinion issued by a judge who votes with the winning side but in some way disagrees with the majority or plurality opinion.

Confederacy — a loose relationship among some smaller political units.

Confederalism — a form of federalism where the individual regions that make up the sovereign state exercise a larger degree of autonomy; often claiming the right to secede and the sole right to raise taxes, with the funding of the central government coming from the confederated regions; the pre-Civil War slave states of America united to form the Confederate States of America to maintain their states' rights.

Confederate system — a system of government with a very weak central government and strong states.

Conference committee — a committee comprised of both House and Senate members charged with reconciling the differences between the House and Senate versions of a bill.

Conformism — a tendency for people to act the same way (e.g., watch the same television programs, read the same books, etc.).

Conservatism —political philosophy that favors limited government with minimal regulation and governmental interference in the economy and other aspects of social life; in general, conservatives favor giving power to state and local governments rather than to the national government; often taken as synonymous with "right-wing," with a penchant for censorship and state control to protect against "immoral" personal behavior, but technically an attitude of belief in the established order and suspicious of change.

Constituent — a citizen, residing in a particular legislator's area or district.

Constituency — the people in a district represented by a legislator.

Constitution — the structures and fundamental principles of how power will be distributed and used legitimately in a state, usually in written form (Great Britain is notable for its "unwritten" constitution); the United States Constitution is the supreme law of the land, meaning that all other laws (including state laws), executive actions and judicial decisions must be consistent with it; granting power to the government from the people, the Constitution of the United States can only be changed by the people (through their representatives).

Constitutional amendment — a formally proposed and ratified a change to the Constitution that becomes a fully binding provision of the Constitution itself.

Constitutional democracy — a system of governance based on popular sovereignty in which the structures, powers, and limits of government are set forth in a constitution.

Constitutional government — a regime in which the use of power is limited by law.

Constitutional law — a law that finds its basis in the Constitution; more particularly, "constitutional law" is the sum of the interpretations of constitutional questions rendered by the Supreme Court and subsidiary courts in their written and published decisions.

Constitutional powers — the powers of the president granted explicitly by the Constitution.

Constitutional convention —a gathering for the purpose of writing a new constitution or amending an existing constitution.

Consumer price index — a measurement of inflation arrived at by comparing, at regular intervals, the price (taking weighting into account) of a set of basic consumer goods and services purchased by households.

Consumption tax — a tax levied on goods and services such as sales tax, GST, VAT or an excise tax; a tax on the spending of income rather than the earning of it, so as to include people who might otherwise evade income tax, such as those in the black economy or those with successful tax avoidance schemes.

Continuing resolution — a temporary spending bill which funds government programs until funds are appropriated for them.

Continuing resolution — a measure passed by Congress that temporarily funds an agency while Congress completes its budget.

Conventional participation — political participation in activities deemed appropriate by most people (e.g., voting, donating to a campaign, writing letters to officeholders).

Convention delegate — a party member or official who goes to the national convention to vote for who will be the party's presidential nominee and to ratify the party's platform.

Cooperative federalism — a term used to describe federalism for most of the twentieth century (and into the twenty-first), where the federal government and the states are partners, not competitors, in the exercise of governmental authority; see *Marble-cake federalism*.

Corrupt practices acts — a series of laws in the early twentieth century that were the first attempts to regulate campaign finance.

Coup d'état — the sudden and often violent overthrow of a government.

Credentials committee — party officials who decide which delegates may participate in the national convention.

Critical election — an election that marks the advent of a realignment.

Crossing the floor — a legislator crossing the floor of Parliament or Congress to vote with the opposition party. An act rarely forgiven in Commonwealth countries but common in the U.S.

Crossover voting — members of one party voting for candidates of another; encouraged by open primaries; see *Split-ticket voting*.

Cumulative voting — a type of block voting; where the voter can choose from a list of (for example) ten candidates running for four seats, their preferred four, two or even one; in such decisions, the selected candidates would get one quarter of a vote each, half a vote or, where only one candidate received the vote, the whole vote.

D

Damage control — the concerted defensive mode of response a political player sometimes adopts to offset negative publicity when an embarrassing "situation" develops, such as a controversial comment, evidence of a scandal, egregious hypocritical actions or abuse of public position.

Dark horse candidate — an unexpected, somewhat unknown candidate with little public exposure who has potential to win an election against established candidates; term originated by British prime minister and author Benjamin Disraeli.

Dealignment — the loosening of party ties as more voters see themselves as independents.

Debt — the accumulated amount of unpaid budget deficits.

Decision — a document issued by the court stating who wins the case.

Declaration of Independence — the document written by Thomas Jefferson in 1776 that formally broke the colonies away from British rule.

Deficit — the shortfall in any one year of a nation's income as compared to its expenditure and the total unpaid accumulated debt of the government over time; see *National debt*.

Deficit spending — government intentionally spending more money than has been raised in taxes in a fiscal year.

De facto **segregation** — segregation that exists due to economic status and residential patterns, not because of law.

Defamation of character — unfairly hurting a person's reputation.

De jure **segregation** — segregation imposed by law.

Delegate — a representative who bases their votes on the majority opinions of the people they represent.

Delegated legislation — rules, regulations, by-laws, ordinances, etc. made by a government official under the authority of a specific act of parliament; sets out the broad purpose of what is desired but delegates to that official's office the authority to create the minutiae (the delegated legislation) necessary; whereas all parliamentary legislation is final and cannot be challenged in court (apart from constitutional inconsistencies) delegated legislation can be challenged in court if it can be shown to violate the purpose of the original act; see *Enabling legislation*.

Delegated powers — powers granted by Congress to help the president fulfill their duties.

Demagogue — a leader who gains popularity by baldly appealing to prejudice and basic instincts; often considered manipulative and dangerous.

Demand-side economics — an approach to economic policy that stresses the stimulation of demand by putting more money in the hands of consumers.

Democracy — a form of government in which policy alternatives are voted on by the people with the majority determining the outcome (i.e., rule by the people); from the Greek "demos" for the ordinary, common people and "kratos" for power or strength.

Democratic socialism — a peaceful form of socialism that works within democratic governments to attain socialism gradually.

Demosclerosis — the inability of the U.S. government to get anything significant done because interest groups block all major change.

Denial of power — declaring that a certain person or group does not have a particular power.

Deontology — the concept of moral obligation and binding duty; as compared to consequentialism, where an act is judged by its consequences (the ends justify the means), deontology is where goodness or righteousness is judged by the act alone (the means justify the means).

Depression — a severe economic downturn that lasts a long time; more serious than a recession.

Deregulation — the repeal or reduction of regulations to boost efficiency, increase competitiveness and benefit consumers.

Descriptive / normative ethics —the study of what people think is moral; normative, or prescriptive, ethics is the study of what is moral; meta-ethics is the study of what "moral," or any other term, actually means.

Deterrence — threatening to use military force to prevent another state from taking a particular course of action.

Devolution — the process of the national government giving increased responsibilities and powers to the state, local or regional governments.

Dictatorship — an absolute government in which one person holds all the power and uses it for their self-interest.

Diplomacy — the act of negotiating and dealing with other nations in the world; trying to achieve goals without force.

Direct democracy — a system or process that depends on the voice of the people (and not representatives), usually through referendums or initiatives, to make public policy decisions; government by the people in fact rather than merely in principle, with the citizenry themselves voting on all issues affecting them (practiced in ancient Greece and to some degree in some cantons of Switzerland and some small towns in the New England states of America); considered by most to be a highly impractical form of government.

Discharge petition — a measure in the House that forces a bill out of a committee for consideration by the whole House.

Direct primary — an election in which rank-and-file members (and not the leaders) of a political party select nominees to represent their party in the general election.

Dirigisme — from the French "diriger" to direct, direct government control of a country's economic and social institutions.

Discretionary spending — spending that can be raised, lowered, kept even or eliminated by the Congress as it sees fit.

Disinformation — information that is false or misleading deliberately disseminated for strategic gain (also known as "black propaganda").

Dissenting opinion — a court opinion written by the losing side that explains why it disagrees with the decision.

Diversity — a mix of different cultural, ethnic and religious traditions and values.

Divided government — a situation in which one party controls the presidency while the other controls at least one house of Congress (also known as "divided-party government").

Divine right theory of kingship — the view that the monarch is chosen by God to rule with absolute power over a country.

Division of labor — the practice of dividing a job into smaller parts and assigning one person or group to do each part.

Donkey vote — the excess votes a candidate at the top of the ballot paper will get because of those voters who don't bother to consider their decision but tick the first box in sight (also known as the "unthinking vote")

Doublespeak — using language that intentionally distorts or obscures the meaning of unpalatable information or policy; sometimes the real meaning is the exact opposite; allegedly the amalgam of two terms invented by George Orwell in his novel *1984*, "doublethink" and "newspeak."

Dual federalism — the view that the national government and state governments have distinct realms of authority which do not overlap and into which the other should not intrude; a term to describe federalism throughout most of the nineteenth century, when the federal and state governments each had their separate issue areas that rarely overlapped; see *Layer-cake federalism*.

Duchess — to court or curry favor for political or another advantage.

Due process clause — part of the Fourteenth Amendment which declares that no person can be deprived of life, liberty or property without due process of law.

Duopoly — a term to describe the overwhelming power of the two major parties in American politics.

Duumvirate / triumvirate / quadrumvirate — Latin terms to describe a group of two, three or four people (respectively) joined in authority or office.

Duverger's Law — a theory attributed to French political scientist Maurice Duverger which asserts a nexus in the number of political parties in a democratic state with the electoral system used; proportional representation nurtures a growth in parties catering to most people's needs while the single-member system (SMV) restrict parties to only two over time.

Dynasty — a sequence of hereditary rulers.

Dystopia — a nightmare vision of society beyond that of even a failed, dysfunctional state where the system is planned by those in power, creating (most often) a totalitarian society (fictional examples are Jack London's *The Iron Heel* and George Orwell's *1984*); alternative to "utopia."

E

Earned Income Tax Credit — a federal welfare program that refunds all or part of a low-income family's social security tax.

Economic aid — assistance to other countries designed to help the recipient's economy.

Economic group — an interest group that seeks material benefits for its members.

Economic growth — the expansion of the economy, leading to the creation of more jobs and more wealth.

Effective tax rate — the actual percentage of one's income paid in taxes after deductions and tax credits.

Elastic clause — clause in Article I, Section 8 of the Constitution that says the Congress has the power to do anything that is necessary and proper to carry out its explicit powers; see *Necessary and proper clause.*

Elector — a member of the Electoral College; in practice, the name often given by governments to voters in normal elections or to those who have been appointed to a certain level so as to vote their choice to a higher office (e.g., members of the American Electoral College that choose the president); technically, a voter who is successful in helping to get their preferred candidate elected; term possibly used to disguise the fact that approximately half of all voters in SMV systems end up not electing anyone.

Electorate — all the people in a country, state or district who are entitled to vote in an election.

Electoral College — the body that elects the president of the United States; composed of electors from each state equal to that state's representation in Congress; a candidate must get a majority of electoral votes to win.

Elitism/elite theory — the view that a small, capable group should rule over the rest.

Émigré — one who leaves their home country for political reasons.

Emergency powers — inherent powers exercised by the president to deal with emergencies.

Empire — a state that governs more than one national group, usually as a result of conquest.

Enabling legislation — a law passed by Congress that lays out the general purposes and powers of an agency but grants the agency the power to determine the details of how it implements policy.

The Enlightenment — the 18th century epoch of intellectual advances where it was thought that "humanity was brought into the light of reason out of the darkness of tradition and prejudice" (also known as "the Age of Reason"); originated in the U.K. but developed most fully in continental countries such as France, with thinkers such as Spinoza, Voltaire, and Rousseau.

Entitlement programs — benefits extended to individuals who meet legislatively-established eligibility requirements; any individual who meets the requirements is considered "entitled" to the benefit, regardless of the overall amount spent on providing the benefit to all eligible individuals.

Enumerated powers — the powers specifically given to Congress in Article I, Section 8 of the Constitution.

Environmental impact statement — a statement that must be prepared by the federal government before acting that describes how the environment will be affected.

Environmentalism — the belief that humans must protect the world from the excesses of human habitation, including pollution and the destruction of wilderness.

Equality of opportunity — when all people are given the same chances to compete and achieve so that those with talent and diligence will succeed, whereas others will not.

Equality of finish — equality of outcomes, generally measured regarding socioeconomic status; the "finish" in question generally refers to accomplishments after entering adulthood.

Equality of outcome — when all people achieve the same result, regardless of talent or effort.

Equality of start — equality of opportunity, generally measured regarding equal access to quality education and training.

Equal protection clause — a provision in the 14th Amendment to the Constitution that guarantees all people "equal protection under the law."

Equal Rights Amendment — a proposed amendment that would have ended gender discrimination; it failed to be ratified.

Equal time rule — a broadcast media regulation that requires media outlets to give equal amounts of time to opposing candidates in an election.

Equity — when all parties to a transaction are treated fairly.

Equity law — an auxiliary part of the common law where the courts not only have the authority to modify existing common law to adapt to modern times but also have the power to create original law, overriding existing common law in circumstances where it is deemed that without it "unconscionable" conduct would occur.

Establishment clause — a part of the First Amendment that forbids government establishment of religion.

Excess demand — an economic situation in which the demand for something exceeds the supply.

Exchange rate — the relationship between the values of any two countries' currencies; any one-off reading is informative when taking into account what each country's unit of currency will buy in its domestic market; also relevant is when the rate changes over time, indicating one country's economy is not doing as well as the other.

Exclusionary rule — a legal rule that excludes from a trial any evidence obtained in an illegal search.

The Executive — that part of the government which executes the law of the land, as compared to the legislature which creates and maintains the law; comprises public service officials from the Prime Minister or President on down and is responsible for the daily administration of the state.

Executive agreement — an agreement made between the President of the United States and the leader of another country or countries; has the same effect as a treaty but does not need to be ratified by the Senate.

Executive branch — a branch of government charged with "executing" or implementing and enforcing the laws.

Executive leadership — the view that the president should have a strong influence over the bureaucracy.

Executive Office of the President — a set of agencies that work closely with the president to help them perform their job.

Executive order — an order issued by the president that has the effect of law.

Executive privilege — claim that the president, as the leader of the Executive Branch, has the prerogative to divulge or refuse to divulge information in a manner that they believe most consistent with the national interest; the right of officials of the executive branch to refuse to disclose some information to other branches of government or to the public.

Ex officio — Latin meaning "by virtue of one's office," the power to do something or hold an office because one holds an earlier office (e.g., the American Vice President is, ex officio, the President of the Senate).

Ex post facto **law** — a law that declares something illegal after it has been done.

Expressed powers — the specific powers given to Congress or the president by the Constitution; see *Enumerated powers.*

F

Fabian Society — a movement founded in 1884 by intellectuals Sidney and Beatrice Webb and George Bernard Shaw who believed the only possible way to introduce socialism would be in an incremental way using education and gradual legislative changes; named after the Roman general Fabius Cunctator ("the delayer") who possessed the patience to defeat the Carthaginian Hannibal by engaging in a slow war of attrition and harassment.

Faction — a group of individuals united in the pursuit of shared political values; a political party is a large faction.

Fairness doctrine — a broadcast media regulation that requires broadcast media airing a controversial program to also provide airtime to those with an opposing view.

Faithless elector — an elector who votes for someone other than the candidate who won the most votes in the state.

Fascism — an authoritarian and nationalist political ideology that embraces strong leadership, singular collective identity and the will to commit violence or wage war to further the interests of the state; averse to concepts such as individualism, pluralism, multiculturalism or egalitarianism.

Federal budget — a document detailing how the federal government will spend money during a fiscal year.

Federal Communications Commission — the federal agency that regulates the broadcast media.

Federal Election Campaign Act — a law, passed in 1971, that limited expenditures on media advertising and required disclosure of donations above $100; made more stringent following the Watergate scandal.

Federal Election Commission — the independent agency established in 1974 to enforce campaign finance laws.

Federal Register — a federal publication that lists all executive orders.

Federal Reserve Bank — the name of the central bank of the United States; often called the Fed.

Federal system — a system of government where power is shared between the central government and state and local governments; see *Federalism*.

Federalism — a system under which governmental powers are divided (e.g., national, state and local) between the central government and the states or provinces, all within the same geographical territory; opposite to a unitary system as exists in the U.K., New Zealand and Japan.

Federalist Papers — a series of essays written in support of ratifying the Constitution; written by Alexander Hamilton, John Jay, and James Madison.

Federalists —supporters of the Constitution during the battle for its ratification; one of the first two major political parties in the United States (opposed by the Anti-Federalists).

Fellow traveler — mid-20th-century term to describe someone who allegedly sympathized with Communism, but would not go so far as to declare themselves a Communist or join the party.

Feminism — the belief that women are equal to men and should be treated equally by the law.

Fence mending — a politician, returning to his electorate hoping to restore his reputation with the voters.

Fifth columnist — in a military or political environment, a person who surreptitiously undermines a group or entity from within; term derived from a Nationalist General during the Spanish Civil War who boasted he had four columns of troops attacking Madrid, together with the fifth column of sympathizers inside the city; sometimes described as "entryism;" the Alec Guinness character in the film *Dr. Zhivago* was a wartime fifth columnist.

Filibuster — a form of legislative obstruction by a Member of Parliament by prolonging a speech for merely the sake of preventing a vote (as the clerk of Parliament sets an agenda calendar allocating certain bills for certain days, if the business of reading, debating and voting on one bill is not completed on its allotted day it may be a long time before it again comes before the house); a Senate tactic in which a senator in the minority opposing a bill holds the floor, speaking endlessly (in effect shutting down the Senate) until the majority backs down and kills the bill.

First Continental Congress — a gathering of representatives from all thirteen colonies in 1774; called for a total boycott of British goods in protest against taxes.

First-past-the-post — an electoral system where the winning candidate needs only the most votes, even if well below a majority (also known as "pluralist voting").

Fiscal federalism — the practice of states spending federal money to help administer national programs.

Fiscal policy — policies and programs establishing budgetary policy, including types and rates of taxation and types and amounts of spending.

Fiscal year — a twelve-month period which does not coincide with the calendar year (beginning October 1 and ending September 30 in the U.S.); used for accounting and budget purposes by the federal government.

527 groups — a political organization, not affiliated with a party that can raise and spend soft money; named after a section of the Internal Revenue Code.

Fixed term — concept to describe the set term of office of representatives (e.g., U.S. House of Representatives is a strict two years) as compared to other democracies like the U.K., where the House of Commons term of office is for a maximum of five years but can be shorter at the discretion of the Prime Minister.

Flat tax — tax collected at the same rate or percentage regardless of income level.

Food stamps — coupons issued by the government that can be used to purchase food.

Foreign policy — a state's international goals and its strategies to achieve those goals.

Formalized rules — another term for the standard operating procedure.

Formula grants — grants in which a formula is used to determine how much money each state receives.

Fourth estate — the unofficial political institution and authority comprising the press and other forms of the media; the term comes from the first three estates of the French States-General: the church, the nobility, and the townsmen.

Framers — the men who wrote the Constitution.

Franchise — the right to vote; see *Suffrage*.

Franking — the ability of members of Congress to mail informational literature to constituents free of charge.

Free exercise clause — the part of the First Amendment that forbids the government from interfering in the free exercise of religion.

Free rider — someone who can receive the benefits of government policy without incurring any of the costs; an individual who chooses not to join or contribute to an interest group, but benefits from the existence and activities of the group.

Free vote — In Commonwealth countries, the rare instance where a Member of Parliament is not obliged to vote according to their party's call (e.g., the 1996 Victorian drug law reform or the 1995 Northern Territory's euthanasia law); also known as a "conscience vote."

Friday news dump — the practice of governments releasing embarrassing or unpopular news just before the weekend, as it is believed few people pay attention to the news on a Saturday (is not only the timing effective for what the government wants to hide, but also the act of lumping together as many stories as possible so as to minimize the effect of each one); also known as "take out the trash day."

From each according to his ability . . . — "From each according to his ability, to each according to his needs;" slogan made popular by Karl Marx in an 1875 publication highlighting a fundamental tenet of communism; allegedly a riposte to the capitalist concept of private property.

Front-loading — moving primaries up in the campaign calendar so that many primaries are held early in the campaign.

Front-runner — the candidate perceived to be in the lead in an election campaign.

Full faith and credit clause — a clause in Article IV of the Constitution that declares that state governments must give full faith and credit to other state governments' decisions.

Fundamentalism — the belief that a religious document is infallible and true.

G

Gag order — an order by a court to block people from talking or writing about a trial.

Gauche caviar — a "left-wing caviar eater" is a French derogatory term for a supposed socialist who nonetheless maintains a luxurious lifestyle (British equivalent: Champagne socialist, Bollinger Bolshevik; American: limousine liberal; Italian: radical chic; Australian: Chardonnay socialist).

Gender discrimination — treating people differently and unequally because of gender.

Gender gap — the difference between women and men in political ideology or political party preferences; in recent years, for example, women have been more likely than men to support the Democratic Party.

General election — either an election that is not local but is for the state or national governments or an election that is the final arbiter after the preliminary ones have been dispensed with; can be contrasted to the council, primary or by-elections.

General jurisdiction — a court's power to hear cases, which is mostly unrestricted.

Georgism —a philosophy created by the 19th century American economist Henry George which advocated that things found in nature, such as land, always remain property of the state; government revenue would be raised by rents on land (at an unimproved rate), mineral and mining rights, fishing licenses, etc. to such an extent that hopefully no other taxes might be needed.

Gerrymander — how a significant number of equally sized, single-member electorates are redrawn and repopulated with both party voters to significantly different degrees; intended to have a partisan and unfair effect on the total vote.

Gerrymandering — the redrawing of a political district to favor a particular candidate or kind of candidate (e.g., an incumbent, a member of a particular political party or a racial minority).

Gibbons v. Ogden — an 1824 Supreme Court case that gave the federal government extensive powers through the commerce clause.

Gideon v. Wainwright — Supreme Court case of 1963 that ordered governments to provide an attorney to criminal defendants who cannot afford one.

Glad-hander — an excessively "friendly" person, typically a politician, who greets another effusively but insincerely in an attempt to gain popularity.

Glasnost — Russian for "publicness," a policy that commits the government to greater accountability and visibility, such as freedom of information laws.

Globalization — the trend toward the breakdown of state borders and the rise of international and global organizations and government bodies.

Godwin's Law — theory by American journalist Mike Godwin that as an online discussion or argument grows longer, the probability of one party comparing the other to Nazis approaches.

Going negative — a campaigning style where an election candidate will emphasize the negative attributes of the opponent rather than their positive ones or plans for future governance; sometimes a legitimate action if the opponent has serious character or competency issues, but otherwise often used to compensate for the fact the candidate has little to offer the electorate in experience, vision or concrete plans.

Government — the organization of power within a country.

Government Accountability Office — Congress's main investigative agency; investigates operations of government agencies as part of congressional oversight.

Government bond — a promissory note issued by the government to pay back the purchase price plus interest.

Government corporation — a federal agency that operates like a corporation (following business practices and charging for services) but receives some federal funding.

Grandfather clause —a voting law that stated that a person could vote if their grandfather were eligible to vote prior to 1867; designed to keep African-Americans from voting; an exemption to a new law which accommodates already existing entities (metaphoric "grandfathers") not having to comply (e.g., existing buildings not required to be rebuilt in accordance with new building or environmental codes, or a law increasing the drinking age from 18 to 21 but exempting those under 21 who were at this point legally entitled to consume alcohol).

Grant-in-aid — a general term to describe federal aid given to the states for a particular matter.

Grant of power — declaring that a certain person or group has a specific power.

Grassroots activism — efforts to influence the government by mobilizing large numbers of people.

Grassroots — the ordinary and common people, often agrarian; the term generally refers to movements or political parties created by them rather than by professionals, elitists or established leaders.

Great Compromise — the compromise plan on representation in the constitutional convention; created a bicameral legislature with representation determined by population in one house and compelling equality in the other (with each state getting two Senators); see *Connecticut Compromise*.

Grievance debate — short speeches allowed to any Member of Parliament on any subject; only granted at a specific time per week for a few hours.

Gross domestic product (GDP) — monetary value of all economic activity (goods and services produced, etc.) in a nation during one calendar year; the total amount produced on shore, whether by local or foreign entities; the total value of all economic transactions within a state.

Gross national product (GNP) — monetary value of the goods and services produced in a nation during one calendar year; the total output of goods and services annually produced by a country, whether on or offshore.

Group benefits — incentives such as mementos (e.g., calendars, mugs) or financial benefits (e.g., insurance discounts) given to people who join a group; these benefits are often unrelated to the primary purposes and goals of the group.

Groupthink — an attitude is often existing in academia or the media where there is found to be unanimity in approaches to certain issues, either due to laziness in research or fear of the consequences of going against the prevailing wisdom.

Gubernatorial — of or relating to a state governor or the office of the state governor.

Guerrilla war — a war in which one or both combatants use small, lightly armed militia units rather than professional, organized armies; guerrilla fighters usually seek to topple their government, often having the (sometimes covert) support of the people.

Gun control — policies that aim at regulating and reducing the use of firearms.

H

Habeas corpus — Latin for "deliver the body," a writ, issued by a court upon request, for a government authority to present a person it is detaining to the court and give justification as to why they should continue to be detained.

Hack — derogatory term for a writer or journalist of very ordinary, unexceptional talents employed to do routine work; derived from the term for an old saddle horse still performing basic duties.

Hansard — the official parliamentary record of whatever is said in Parliament.

Hatch Act — a law passed in 1939 that restricts the participation of federal civil servants in political campaigns.

Hegemony — dominance or leadership of one state or social group over another.

Hierarchy — an arrangement of power with a small number of people at the top issuing orders through a chain of command to lower-level workers; each person is responsible to someone above them.

Hoi polloi — the common people, as compared to the wealthy, higher educated or elite.

Hollow men — conviction-free, consensus-driven politicians who live by the polls and whose only goal appears to be to achieve and maintain political power; found in major parties on both sides of the political divide but generally more prevalent with conservative parties; term derived from the T.S. Eliot poem of that name in referring to the "men of straw" it described.

Home rule — the granting of significant autonomy to local governments by state governments.

Homestyle — the way a member of Congress behaves in their district.

Honeymoon — period shortly after an election, particularly a presidential election, during which the winning candidate enjoys a surge in public and political support; see *Honeymoon period*.

Honeymoon period — the first few months of an administration in which the public, members of Congress and the media tend to give the president their goodwill.

Horizontal federalism — how state governments relate to one another.

House of Representatives (U.S.) — the lower house of the U.S. Congress which consists of at most 435 members, each state having some members proportional to its population; the lower house of a U.S. state legislature.

House Rules Committee — the committee in the House of Representatives that creates a "rule" for each bill to be debated on the floor; the rule establishes the time for and extent of debate and what, if any, amendments can be offered.

Huey P. Long — the quintessential populist, corrupt demagogue of modern times who served as governor of the U.S. state of Louisiana from 1928 to 1932 and as Senator until 1935; a master of political patronage who became the model for the Robert Penn Warren novel and the film adaptation *All the Kings Men*; eventually assassinated by a relative of one of his victims.

Humanism — cultural movement during the Renaissance emphasizing secularism and classical learning from ancient Greece and Rome; the doctrine that emphasizes the human capacity for self-fulfillment without religion.

The hustings — involved in political campaigning, especially making speeches; the husting was originally a place of assembly at which to speak; U.S. equivalent is "on the stump," derived from the 19th-century practice of speaking while standing on a tree stump.

Hyperpluralism — the idea that there are too many interest groups competing for benefits.

I

Idealism — the view that states should act in the global arena to promote moral causes and use ethical means to achieve them.

Identity politics — political theories or advocacy which, rather than proposing better ways to fight crime, improve the economy or save the environment, etc., orient themselves towards the victimhood (or alleged victimhood) of certain people because of their demographics (e.g., their age, religion, gender, race, etc.).

Ideologue — an individual with strong philosophical or ideological leanings; generally unwilling to budge to compromise or work with others with differing views.

Ideology — a set of beliefs a person holds that shapes the way they behave and see the world.

Illegal participation — a political activity that includes illegal actions, such as sabotage or assassination.

Impeachment — the legislative equivalent of a criminal prosecution, where a high government official is subject, by a house of Parliament or Congress, to an investigation, indictment and subsequent trial; in the United States, it is the power of the House of Representatives to charge an officeholder with crimes; the Senate then holds a trial to determine if the officeholder should be expelled from office.

Implementation — the act of putting laws into practice.

Implied powers — powers not explicitly stated in the Constitution but which are suggested or implied by the "general welfare," the "necessary and proper" and the commerce clauses in the Constitution.

Income distribution — the way income is distributed among the population.

Income transfer — a government action that takes money from one part of the citizenry and gives it to another part; usually the transfer goes from the well-off to the poor.

Incorporation — the practice of federal courts forcing state governments to abide by the Bill of Rights.

Incrementalism — the tendency of policy in the United States to change gradually, rather than dramatically.

Incumbent — the current holder of a seat in the legislature or an office of authority.

Independent — a person who does not profess affiliation for any party.

Independent executive agency — a federal agency that is not part of any department; its leader reports directly to the president.

Independent regulatory agency — a federal agency charged with regulating some part of the economy; in theory, such agencies are independent of Congress and the president.

Individualism — the idea that all people are different and should be able to make their own choices.

Inflation — the increase in prices that accompanies a decline in the purchasing power of the currency.

Informational benefits — the educational benefits people derive from belonging to an interest group and learning more about the issues they care about.

Inherent powers — powers not explicitly delegated to the president or Congress but are nonetheless reasonable and logical derivatives needed to carry out national objectives; see *Implied powers*.

Initiative — a public policy question that is initiated by the people, usually by petition, and decided by the people at the ballot box.

In-kind subsidies — government aid to poor people that are not given as cash but in forms such as food stamps and rent vouchers.

Inside game — interest groups' efforts to influence government policy by direct and close contact with government officials (also known as "lobbying").

Interest group — an organization of people who share a common interest and work together to protect and promote that interest by influencing the government.

International agreement — an understanding between states to restrict their behavior and set up rules governing international affairs.

Internationalism — the view that the United States should play an active role in world affairs.

International law — a set of agreements, traditions, and norms built up over time that restricts what states can do; not always binding.

International organization — an institution set up by agreements between nations, such as the United Nations and the World Trade Organization.

International system — the basic structures that affect how states relate to one another, including rules and traditions.

Internet media — media that is distributed online.

Interpretive reporting — reporting that states the facts and also provides analysis and interpretation.

Interregnum — an interval of seemingly "directionless" government, such as between administrations.

Intervention — when a state sends military forces to help a country that is already at war.

Invisible hand — the free market theory of the 18th-century economist Adam Smith that there is an "invisible hand" which guarantees that, without government intervention, there will always be a supply to placate demand.

Iron triangle — an alliance of groups with interest in a particular policy area (e.g., bureaucrats from the relevant agency, legislators from the appropriate committee, and interest groups affected by the issue).

Isolationism — a policy of isolating one's country from military alliances or other commitments with all other countries as the best resort to avoiding foreign entanglements; historically, a strong sentiment in the USA; President Woodrow Wilson won a second term in 1916 by promising to keep America out of WWI, which it subsequently entered; the U.S. was conspicuous for not joining the newly formed League of Nations after the War.

Issue advertising — advertising paid for by outside groups that can criticize or praise a candidate but cannot explicitly say to vote for or against them.

Issue network — a collection of actors who agree on policy and work together to shape it.

J

Jim Crow laws — laws passed by southern states that imposed inequality and segregation on African Americans.

Jingoism — a nineteenth and twentieth-century term to describe chauvinistic, bellicose expressions of nationalism, especially in warlike pursuits; the term is often associated with U.S. President Teddy Roosevelt; derives from the bellicose British slang expression "By Jingo."

Jobs for the boys — a type of political nepotism where prestigious government jobs are given to those in the party family (often those voted out of office or otherwise unemployed) rather than those deserving them due to merit; the term once had a legitimate meaning in the early 20th century, when it was used to express public gratitude for demobilized soldiers returning home from war; see *Nomenklatura*.

Joint committee — a committee with members from both the House and Senate; such committees are generally advisory or oversight committees, not legislative (law-making) committees.

Joint Chiefs of Staff — a group that helps the president make strategy decisions and evaluates the needs and capabilities of the military.

Judicial activism — a judicial philosophy advocating that courts are allowed to take an active role not supported by existing law to remedy alleged wrongs in society.

Judicial branch — the branch of government that hears and settles legal disputes.

Judicial implementation — the process of enforcing a court's ruling.

Judicial philosophy — a set of ideas that shape how a judge or lawyer interprets the law and the Constitution.

Judicial restraint — a judicial philosophy that believes the court's responsibility is to interpret the law, not set policy.

Judicial review — the power of the courts to declare laws and presidential actions unconstitutional.

Junta — a clique, faction or cabal, often military, taking power after an overthrow of the government; from the Latin "*juncta*," meaning "join."

Jurisdiction — a court's power to hear cases of a particular type.

Jus ad bellum — the alleged justification a country will use to go to war.

Justiciable question — a matter that the courts can review.

Just-war theory — a theory of ethics that defines when war is morally permissible and what means of warfare are justified.

K

Keynesianism — the theories of a very influential economist of the twentieth century, John Maynard Keynes, who advocated government taxing and spending to keep the economy under control; in times of recession, he advocated greatly increased government spending on public works as well as intervention in the economy whenever it was necessary.

Keynesian economics — a demand-side economic policy, first presented by John Maynard Keynes after World War I, that encouraged deficit spending by governments during economic recessions to provide jobs and boost income.

Kitchen Cabinet — an informal name for the chief executive's closest advisers.

Kleptocracy — a cynical term used to describe highly corrupt governments where politicians, bureaucrats, and their protected friends engage in sales of government licenses, perquisites and other frauds.

Kyoto Protocol — an international treaty aimed at reducing greenhouse gas emissions.

L

Laissez-faire — French for, "allow to do," an economic system with total or near-total abstinence of state interference.

Laissez-faire capitalism — the economic philosophy that the government should not interfere with the economy.

Lame duck — a political office holder who, because of term limits, retirement or defeat, will not be returning to the office after the end of their present term of office; presidents serving in their second terms are not eligible to run for a third term and are, therefore "lame duck" presidents.

Lawmaking — the power to make rules that are binding on all people in a society.

Layer-cake federalism — a term used to describe federalism through most of the nineteenth century in which the federal and state governments each had their issue areas that rarely overlapped; see *Dual federalism*.

Leader of the House — a lower house MP of the ruling party who has been appointed to organize and arrange the various proceedings of that house.

Left-wing — the liberal, socialist or radical side of a political system.

Legislative agenda — a series of laws a person wishes to pass.

Legislative branch — branch of government with authority to make a change the laws of the land.

Legitimacy — acceptance by citizens of the government.

Lemon test — a three-part test to determine if the establishment clause of the First Amendment has been violated; named for the 1971 case *Lemon v. Kurtzman*.

Levelers — an early grassroots, neo-libertarian, an urban political group which existed in the U.K. during and after the English Civil War; they advocated self-ownership, electoral reform, separation of powers, limited use of the death penalty, religious toleration, and removal of government restrictions on trade and land use; were so named, pejoratively, by the privileged aristocracy and wealthy traders who feared their estates would be leveled.

Libel — printing false statements that defame a person's character.

Liberal democracy — a vague term to reflect democracy controlled by restraints that only allow the seemingly good (e.g., a constitution or entrenched common law that protects such institutions as freedom of speech, freedom of the press, a moderately free market, an independent judiciary, the rule of law, separation of powers, minority rights and the notion of the individual).

Liberalism — a theory of international relations that deemphasizes the importance of military power in favor of economic power, trade, and international institutions.

Liberalism (classic) — a philosophy advocating the rights of the individual against the state or church as espoused by such eighteenth-century English writers like John Locke and J.S. Mill; causes advocated would be laissez-faire economics, freedom of speech, the rule of law, an extension of the franchise, amelioration in penal practices and changing views on relations between the sexes and the upbringing of children; in modern times Classic Liberals have become either libertarians or "small 'l'" liberals.

Liberalism (small 'l') — loosely described as a modern philosophy which favors change for change's sake; also encompasses a compromising and compassionate attitude to personal lifestyle, law and order, foreign affairs and immigration; policy decisions often tilt toward those in more straitened circumstances.

Libertarianism — a political philosophy of self-reliance, reason and maximum non-interference by the state in matters of both economic and personal affairs (i.e., "limited government"); straddling both left and right, a libertarian would believe in the right to bear arms, access to IVF or hallucinatory drugs for any adult, a free market capitalist economy and the abolition of censorship.

Liberty — the freedom to do what one chooses as long as it does not harm or limit the freedom of other people.

Limited government — a right-wing concept that espouses the practice that any public service that could reasonably be solely supplied by the market, or any potentially harmful action that could be self-regulated or otherwise controlled by public censure, should be.

Limited jurisdiction — a court's power to hear only certain kinds of cases.

Limited war — a war, often not formally declared, fought to obtain specific political or territorial objective, rather than to obtain the unconditional surrender of the enemy.

Line-item veto — a veto used to reject only specific items or parts of legislation passed by the Congress; Congress attempted to give the president a line-item veto authority in 1995, however the Supreme Court ruled the effort unconstitutional because it transferred legislative authority from the Legislative Branch to the Executive Branch (it had been the hope of the Congress that the president would use the line-item veto to remove or lower excessive spending measures from legislation passed by Congress).

Line organization — in the government bureaucracy, an agency whose head reports directly to the president.

List system P.R. — above and below the line proportional representation voting; voters do not have to cast preferences but can vote "above the line" for the candidates or parties of their choice whom themselves choose (before the election) the list of preferred other candidates to which their unused votes will go.

Literacy test — historically, a test that must be passed before a person can vote; designed to prevent African-Americans from voting.

Lobbying — the practice of talking with members of Congress to persuade them to support a particular position or piece of legislation; originally conducted in the "lobbies" just off the Parliament chambers in the U.K.; see *Inside game.*

Lobbyist — someone who acts professionally to serve as a go-between for people or businesses with a strongly pro or con attitude about specific legislation and the members of the legislature who will vote on it; sometimes also with the relevant government Minister or Secretary; it is in the interests for politicians to not only keep abreast of the possibly problematic effects of legislation but also to have that communicated to them quickly and efficiently by an experienced and knowledgeable operator (the fact that corruption often occurs in the lobbying process does not invalidate lobbying as a generally legitimate function).

Logrolling — a practice in Congress where two or more members agree to support each other's bills.

Loophole — a part of a tax code that allows individuals or businesses to reduce their tax burden.

Loose constructionism — a judicial philosophy that believes the Constitution should be interpreted openly and not be limited to things explicitly stated.

Lower house — the House of Representatives or (statewide) the Legislative Assembly.

Luddites — nineteenth-century British tradesman who rebelled against the technology of the industrial revolution that was making them obsolete by organizing riots to destroy the textile machinery of the day; named after the mythical King Ludd; the term now used to describe those opposed to technological progress.

Lumpenproletariat — a term for those in society Marx identified as miscreants, lacking class consciousness and useless to the revolutionary struggle (e.g., beggars, prostitutes, gangsters, racketeers, swindlers, petty criminals, tramps, the chronically unemployed or unemployable).

Luvvie — derogatory British term for pretentious artistic or theatrical people claiming and receiving special benefits or privileges.

M

Mace — large and intimidating medieval hand-held weapon; appears with the speaker in lower houses and used as a symbol of authority.

Machine — a very strong party organization that turns favors and patronage into votes.

Machiavellian — adjective to describe manipulative and cynical political activity in which morals and principles figure but little; somewhat unfairly attributed to Renaissance political theorist Niccolo Machiavelli who wrote in an age where government and statecraft had urgent life or death consequences.

Madisonian Model — a structure of government proposed by James Madison that avoided tyranny by separating power among different branches and building checks and balances into the Constitution; see *Separation of powers*.

Maiden speech — the first ever speech given by an MP in Parliament, traditionally granted the courtesy of no interjections.

Majority leader — in the House, the second-ranking member of the majority party; in the Senate, the highest-ranking member of the majority party.

Majority opinion — a court opinion that reflects the reasoning of the majority of justices.

Majority party — in a legislative body, the party with more than half of the seats.

Majority preferential — preferential voting in single-member electorates.

Majority rule — the idea that the government should act by the will of the majority of the people.

Malapportionment — an apportionment of seats in Congress that is unfair due to population shifts; violating the concept of "one person one vote," the existence of electorates of unequal population sizes that still have the same number of representatives, whereby a partisan political party advantage can very often develop; the practice is still very common in the United Kingdom.

Thomas Malthus — clergyman and political economist of the eighteenth century who theorized that the world's population always grows faster than its food supply, and, rather than attempting to alleviate perpetual hunger by misguided compassion, allow the inevitable famine, disease, and war to act as natural retardants to population growth; Malthus argued from an empiricist point of view against the ideological, theoretical ideas of the philosopher William Godwin and other supporters of the French Revolution who believed in the perfectibility of humankind.

Mandate — when the federal government requires states to do certain things; the alleged command and authority a winning political party has to institute its promised pre-election policies because of the fact it had a convincing win.

Mandatory retirement — an employment policy that states that when an employee reaches a certain age, they must retire.

Mandatory spending — spending that is largely out of the control of the Congress; primarily "entitlements" which are paid to people on a formula basis regardless of how much money is available.

Marble-cake federalism — a term used to describe federalism for most of the twentieth century (and into the twenty-first), where the federal government and the states work closely together and are intertwined; see *Cooperative federalism*.

Marginal seat — a single-member vote electorate where the winning candidate or party only just barely won the last election and could well lose the next.

Markup — when a Congressional committee revises a bill in session.

Material incentive — the lure of a concrete benefit, usually money, that attracts people to join a group.

McCain-Feingold bill — the popular informal name for the Bipartisan Campaign Finance Reform Act of 2002; it is named after its sponsors, Republican John McCain, and Democrat Russell Feingold.

McCulloch v. Maryland — a Supreme Court case in 1819 that granted the federal government extensive power to carry out its enumerated powers.

Means testing — limiting government benefits, such as a baby bonus or health care, to those below a certain income or accumulated wealth; basing benefits from a policy on a person's financial status so that poor people get more benefits than rich people.

Media — information and the organizations that distribute that information to the public.

Media bias — occurs when the media (individually or collectively) reports something that is inaccurate or one-sided because of ideology, political favoritism (not treating both sides equally) or other factors; bias can show up in coverage (or lack thereof) or the content and analysis of stories.

Media consolidation — the trend toward a few large corporations owning most of the media outlets in the country.

Mediating institution — an institution which stands between and connects people with the government (e.g., the media, political parties, and interest groups).

Mercantilism — a broad, command type economic doctrine, practiced from the 16th to the 18th centuries, which predicated state power in international affairs as the predominant goal; policies utilized would be export subsidies, maintaining a positive balance of payments, developing colonies, forbidding trade to be carried in foreign ships, restricting colonies' trade to only the mother country, maintaining a large as possible precious metal reserve and limiting domestic consumption, such as with sumptuary laws.

Merit system — the practice of hiring and promoting people based on skill.

Merit System Protection Board — a board that investigates charges of wrongdoing in the federal civil service.

Midterm election — a congressional election that does not coincide with a presidential election.

Military aid — assistance to other countries designed to strengthen the recipient's military.

Military-industrial complex — the alliance of defense contractors, military elites and some members of Congress that promotes ever-larger defense budgets to profit themselves.

Minority leader — an individual elected to lead a party in the House or Senate that does not hold the majority of seats in the body.

Minority party — in a legislative body, the party with fewer than half of the seats.

Miranda v. Arizona — a 1966 case in which the Supreme Court ruled that police must inform suspects of their rights when arrested.

Mixed economy — an economic system which embraces some aspects of the free enterprise together with elements of socialism.

Monarchy — a regime in which all power is held by a single person (a king or queen).

Monetarism — the theory that the economy can be controlled by increasing or reducing the money supply.

Monetary policy — policies aimed at controlling inflation and unemployment through manipulation of the money supply and interest rates; primarily established by the Federal Reserve Board.

Monocracy — rule by one person; not necessarily anti-democratic.

Monopoly — a situation where there is only one seller of a good or service due to either protection by legislation or it being impractical for other parties to compete in this market.

Monopolistic model — a view of the bureaucracy that says bureaucracies have no incentive to reform or improve performance because they face no competition.

Monopsony — where there is but a single buyer market for goods or services; the opposite of a monopoly.

Monroe Doctrine — an American policy, promulgated by President James Monroe in 1823, that claims America's right to intervene in the affairs of Western Hemisphere nations and a reluctance to intervene in the Eastern Hemisphere (e.g., Europe).

Moral relativism — loosely described as a philosophical concept whereby an act universally identified as immoral in the home country is excusable when observed in another because of the culture or history of that country.

Motherhood statement — a "feel good" platitude supporting an uncontroversial case that few would dare disagree with.

Muckraker — a journalist or author whose primary goal is to uncover the negative character traits or history of their subject; a term coined by Teddy Roosevelt about a *Pilgrim's Progress* character with a muckrake who could only look down.

Multiculturalism — the perspective that all cultures within a society are of equal merit and should be respected.

Multilateralism — the idea that nations should act together to solve problems.

Multinational corporation — a business that operates in more than one country.

Multiple-member district — a legislative district that sends more than one person to the legislature.

Multipolar system — an international system with more than two major powers.

N

Nation — a large group of people who are linked by a similar culture, language, and history.

National convention — a convention held by a political party every four years to nominate candidates for president and vice president and to ratify the party platform.

National debt — money owed by a government.

National interest — things that will benefit and protect a state.

Nationalism — a belief in the goodness of one's nation and a desire to help make the nation stronger and better.

National Security Council — a part of the White House Staff that advises the president on security policy.

Nation-building — the task of creating a national identity through the promotion of a common culture, language, and history.

Nation-state — a state that rules over a single nation.

Nazism — political ideology originating in 1930s Germany that stressed the superiority of the German race, authoritarian rule by one party, military expansion and taking inspiration from a mythical past.

Necessary and proper clause — a clause at the end of Article I, Section 8 of the U.S. Constitution that grants Congress the power to do whatever is necessary and proper to carry out its duties; it strongly suggests that the national government has powers other than those explicitly stated in the Constitution; see *Elastic Clause.*

Necessary evil — something that is believed to be needed but not good in and of itself; many Americans see the federal government as a necessary evil.

Negative rights / positive rights — the right to do, or refrain from, an action or otherwise be free from interference, as compared to the right to gain a specific benefit that would have a monetary value; the right to speak freely and the right to having legal representation supplied when in court; a positive obligation to supply the cost of a lawyer while there is no (negative) cost to allow someone the right of free association; term derives from the obligation on society for supplying those rights.

Negotiated rule-making — a federal rule-making process that includes those who will be affected by the rules.

Neoconservatism — a recent development in American conservatism that believes the power of the state should be used to promote conservative goals.

New Deal coalition — the supporters of Franklin Roosevelt's New Deal; the coalition included labor unions, Catholics, southern whites and African-Americans; helped the Democrats dominate politics from the 1930s until the 1960s.

New federalism — an American movement, starting in the 1970s, to return power to state and local governments, thereby decreasing the amount of power held by the federal government.

New Jersey Plan — a plan at the constitutional convention that gave each state equal representation in the legislature.

NGO — a non-profit, non-government organization.

Nihilism — the belief that life and all of the things that make it up are meaningless; the rejection of all moral and religious notions.

Nimby — stands for "Not - In - My – Backyard;" a pejorative term used to describe opposition to any public policy decision, which in itself is considered beneficial but may happen to cause discomfort for geographical or other reasons when it is actually put into practice (e.g., airports, prisons or nuclear power plants placed in one's own vicinity or austerity measures which may cause budget cuts affecting those who thought they would be excluded).

Nineteenth Amendment — passed in 1920, it gave women the right to vote.

No Child Left Behind Act — a law passed in 2001 that expanded federal funding to schools while linking them to increased testing and accountability.

Nomenklatura — from the Latin *nomenclatura* for "list of names," the system of patronage for Party members applied during the existence of the USSR; a list of individuals drawn up by the Communist Party from which candidates for vacant senior positions in the state, party and other important organizations were selected.

Nomination — a prerequisite to standing as a political candidate; made only after the writ for an election has been issued; a financial deposit, which will be returned on the candidate receiving a reasonable number of votes, must also be lodged.

Noneconomic group — an interest group that works on noneconomic issues; also called a "citizens' group."

Nongovernmental actor — a participant in the international arena that is not part of a government (e.g., nongovernmental organizations, multinational corporations, and international organizations).

Nongovernmental organization — a political actor that is not affiliated with a particular government; many NGOs are nonprofit institutions run by private citizens, such as the Red Cross, Doctors Without Borders and the Catholic Church.

Nonprobability sampling — a non-random selection of respondents for a survey; problematic because the group of people chosen to respond to the survey is unlikely to be representative of the larger population.

Nuclear Non-Proliferation Treaty — an international treaty, signed in 1968, intended to prevent the spread of nuclear weapons.

O

Objective reporting — reporting only the facts with no opinion or bias.

OECD — Organization for Economic Co-operation and Development; founded in 1961 to stimulate world trade and economic progress; a group of 34 first world countries committed to democracy and the market economy who organize mutual plans to maintain taxation conventions and fiscal stability, combat corruption and bribery, as well as other endeavors such as issuing annual publications on the world economic outlook.

Office-block ballot — a ballot that groups candidates by the office (all candidates for an office are listed together); also called "the Massachusetts ballot."

Office of Management and Budget (OMB) — the federal agency that compiles and reviews budget figures on the president's behalf.

Office of Personnel Management — the central federal personnel office, created in 1978.

Oligarchy — a form of government where the rule is by the few and in their interest.

Ombudsman — a concept, originally Swedish, where parliament appoints a person to act as an official watchdog over bureaucracy on behalf of the public; on its initiative or from public complaints, the Ombudsman will investigate government officials or departments and report its findings to the government, whereupon action may be taken; the office of the Ombudsman itself has no power to penalize, although in some jurisdictions the Ombudsman can launch criminal prosecutions.

Ombudsperson — a person who investigates complaints against government agencies or employees.

Open primary — election held to choose the nominee for a particular political party in which voters of any party are eligible to vote.

Open rule — a rule in the House of Representatives which allows an unlimited number of amendments to be made to a bill being considered on the floor.

Opinion — a document issued by a court explaining the reasons for its decision.

Opinion leader — a person whose opinion can shape the opinions of many others.

Optional preferential voting — preferential voting where one has the option to choose to mark off only the number of preferences as one wishes.

Ordinary vote — a vote cast at a polling place in the elector's home division on polling day, as compared with a postal vote.

Original intent — a judicial philosophy that states that judges should seek to interpret the law and the Constitution in line with the intent of the founders.

Original jurisdiction — authority to hear a case for the first time in a particular geographic area or sphere of the law; courts of original jurisdiction are generally trial courts in which juries make decisions; see *Appellate jurisdiction*.

Outside game — a term used to describe grassroots activism and other means to influence elections and policymaking.

Overregulation — an excess of regulation that hurts efficiency.

Oversight — Congress's power to make sure laws are being properly enforced.

The Overton window — modern concept advanced by political theorist Joseph Overton, whereby there is a small window of acceptable political approaches on any given subject at any time and any approaches or ideas not within the window are likely to be considered "extreme" and politically unsafe for a politician to uphold; most mainstream politicians will only admit to supporting policies within the window at the moment and only publicly declared more "extreme" policies they believe in if and when the window is seen to be moving in that direction.

P

Pack journalism — the tendency of journalists and news outlets to cover the same stories, driven by the fear of being "scooped" by other reporters or news outlets; the idea that journalists frequently copy and imitate each other rather than doing independent reporting.

Pairing — an informal practice occurring in Parliamentary systems (where voting cannot be by proxy) where a member of one party will agree not to vote on a specific bill if an opposing member would prefer not to be present; the understanding is that the favor may be reciprocated at a later date.

Palm tree justice — expedient justice applied in good faith but absent of the rule of law; paying little or no attention to the existing law, precedent or fundamental principles; comes from primitive societies where justice was dispensed by a wise old man sitting under a palm tree; a U.S. example is Judge Roy Bean.

Parachute in (a candidate) — when the central office of a political party appoints the candidate for a certain electorate at the next election, rather than the usual practice of being appointed by the local branch.

Paradox of participation — when many people vote because they wish to make a difference, but the actual chances of making a difference are infinitesimally small.

Pardon — a release from punishment for a criminal conviction; the president has the power to pardon.

Parliamentary democracy — a regime in which the legislature chooses the executive branch.

Parliamentary government — a system of government where ultimate authority is vested in the legislative body; the cabinet, including the chief executive, is from, appointed by and responsible to the legislature (the Parliament); alternative to what is known as a presidential system, where the voters independently appoint both the legislature and the executive.

Parliamentary privilege — the privilege while (physically) in Parliament that allows a Member of Parliament to say anything without fear of prosecution for slander; also Parliament itself has the privilege to summon, cross-examine, judge and punish entities that have deemed to offend against it; in Italy, Parliamentary privilege grants a Member of Parliament immunity from arrest for criminal charges.

Participation rate — the share of the potential workforce (15-65, not institutionalized) working or seeking work.

Partisan journalism — journalism that advances the viewpoint of a political party.

Party activist — a person who is deeply involved with a party; usually more ideologically committed than an average party voter.

Party-centered politics — campaigns and politics that focus on party labels and platforms.

Party-column ballot — a ballot that groups candidates by party; also called "the Indiana ballot."

Party identification — feeling connected to a political party.

Party in government — the role and function of parties in government, particularly in Congress.

Party in the electorate — party identification among voters.

Party line voting — despite the fact that MPs in Parliament "represent" the residents of their specific electorates, at voting time they will almost always vote (unless an independent) strictly according to their party's call (i.e., as directed by their leader rather than according to the wishes of their own constituents).

Party-list voting — "above the line" only proportional representation voting; voters do not cast preferences, but the candidates or parties themselves choose (before the election) the list of preferred other candidates to which their unused votes will go.

Party organization — the formal structure and leadership of a political party.

Party platform — an official statement and proclamation of the beliefs, values and policy positions of a political party; specific statements or positions in a platform are sometimes called "planks" (e.g., the "abortion plank" of a party's platform).

Party platform — the collection of issue positions endorsed by a political party.

Party reform — measures aimed at opening up party leadership adopted by the major parties following the 1968 election.

Patronage — the practice of rewarding jobs in official governmental posts to one's political allies after an electoral victory; government jobs and contracts given out to political allies in exchange for support.

Payroll tax — paid in equal amounts (7.65%) by employers and employees to fund Social Security and Medicare; also known as FICA.

Pendleton Act — another name for the Civil Service Reform Act of 1883.

Perestroika — a term denoting political, bureaucratic or economic restructuring; first coined by Mikhail Gorbachev about the former Soviet Union.

Pericles — esteemed Athenian leader of ancient Greece who, while advancing the material and cultural aspects of his city-state, also did much to enhance democracy.

Permissive federalism — view that because the national government is supreme, the states only have those powers which the national government permits them to exercise.

Per Curiam — an unsigned decision issued by an appellate court; reaffirms the lower court's ruling.

Pettifogging — a member of the legislature holding up a debate by quibbling or fussing over trivial, irrelevant matters.

Photo op — a situation where a politician arranges or accepts an invitation to an event (or pseudo-event) where the setting and circumstances are such that they will attract the media and give the politician exposure.

Pigeonholing — the ability of a committee to kill a bill by setting it aside and not acting on it.

Platform — the political agenda of a candidate or party.

Plausible deniability — the position a member of the executive or some person in charge of an organization attempts to maintain; created by keeping a distance from certain operations or practices such that, if an operation "goes south" and attracts unfavorable publicity, there should be no evidence linking them to the chain of command.

Plebeian / patrician — the two citizen classes of ancient Rome; the allegedly coarse and crude ordinary plebeians and the wealthy, educated and aristocratic "born to rule" patricians; both terms used today in a derogatory manner (e.g., U.S. President G.H.W. Bush was often described as a patrician due to his being born into a wealthy political family, treating political life as a duty rather than as an opportunity for reformist zeal and allegedly not being in touch with the concerns of ordinary Americans).

Plebiscite — a public vote to gauge public opinion on an issue (such as conscription) which does not affect the constitution nor is otherwise legally binding.

Plessy v. Ferguson — the Supreme Court case of 1896 that upheld a Louisiana law segregating passengers on trains created the "separate but equal" doctrine.

Pluralism — the view that society contains numerous centers of power and many people participate in making decisions for society.

Plurality — more votes than any other candidate but not a majority.

Plurality opinion — an opinion written by the majority of the justices on the winning side.

Plutocracy — government, controlled by, or greatly influenced by, the wealthy.

Pocket veto — if Congress adjourns before ten days have passed since the passage of a bill, the president can allow the legislation to die simply by neither signing nor vetoing the bill; see *Veto*.

Poison the well — when made aware of a new topic or program your opponent is about to discuss, to get in early and do your best to publicly criticize or deride the issue to "poison" the public against having an open mind to your opponent's suggestion.

Political action committee (PAC) — an arm of an interest group legally permitted to give money to political candidates competing for federal elected office.

Political appointees — federal bureaucrats appointed by the president, often as a reward for loyalty.

Political culture — the set of beliefs, values, shared myths and notions of a good polity that a group of people holds.

Political economy — the study of how politics and economics interact.

Political efficacy — the belief that the government listens to ordinary people and that their participation can make a difference in government.

Political equality — treating everyone the same way in the realm of politics.

Political participation — engaging in actions to achieve political goals.

Political party — a team of office-seekers and their supporters; generally unified by a common ideology, philosophy, set of values and political beliefs; usually outlined in a party platform.

Political party status — candidates with a common cause can register at an election as a party and enjoy certain privileges such as "above the line" placement and public funding if they attain a certain percentage of the vote (as long as they can present to officials the signatures and addresses of a sufficient number of supporters); certain P.P.S. privileges also apply to the winning candidates of a party if their numbers reach a certain threshold.

Political science — the systematic, rigorous study of politics.

Political socialization — the process by which political culture is passed on to the young.

Politico — one interested or engaged in politics.

Politics — the process by which government decisions are made.

Polity — form or process of civil government; organized society; the state.

Poll — a research survey; another word for an election.

Polling — assessing public opinion by asking people what they think and feel.

Polling place/booth — numerous centers set up in each division to take the votes of the local people.

Pollster — a person who conducts polls.

Poll tax — a fee for voting; designed to keep poor people, particularly African-Americans, from voting.

Popular sovereignty — notion that political power or the power to govern is derived from the people; as such, the people retain the right to rescind any grant of power to the government; a regime in which the government must respond to the wishes of the people.

Populace — the people living in a certain area.

Populism — political campaigning oriented toward true democracy (soliciting votes by promising specific benefits, liberties, law and order programs, etc.) rather than representative democracy where one votes for a team of (allegedly) responsible candidates who will, at a measured pace and after due deliberation, institute a program under some general theme (even if specific legislation is mentioned); populists will promise to bring about their agenda despite whatever institutional obstructions may exist, while non-populists will take a more conservative approach respecting the judiciary, the constitution, the bureaucracy and the examples of international approaches to the same issues.

Populist democracy — ultimate democracy not restricted by a constitution or any other reviewing authority to the passage of legislation or executive orders; an alternative to liberal democracy.

Populist politician — a politician who offers the people what they want irrespective of how moral, feasible or practical it is for such promises to be carried out; cynically, it is how a losing candidate is likely to describe the candidate he lost to.

Populists — a political movement in the late nineteenth century that fought on behalf of the poor workers and farmers; fused with the Democratic Party in 1896.

Pork / *Pork-barrel* / Pork-barrel spending — politicians arranging for big-spending government contracts in their electorates to enhance their reputation with their constituents; not in the interest of the nation as a whole; more prevalent in governments with SMV electoral systems.

Positivist / naturalist law — two opposing branches of legal philosophy, either of which judges use to aid decision making; naturalist law theory is that law is the ageless, unchanging law of nature, as deduced by the reasoning process of the interpreter or the teachings of God and should be followed even in instances where it conflicts with duly constituted legislation; positivist law theory is simply following the democratically instituted law of the land no matter how rational and just it may, or may not, appear to be.

Poverty line — the minimal income one needs to cover the necessities of a healthy life (e.g., fuel, food, clothing, shelter and basic household and personal items); as in "relative poverty," whereby the line is set as a percentage of the country's median income (the OECD and the European Union use 60%), immaterial of how much it would fluctuate with the nation's GDP.

Power — the ability held by individuals or institutions to create and enforce policies and manage resources for society.

Power of the purse — the ability of Congress to create and raise taxes and to authorize the spending of the money raised through them; all federal expenditures must be authorized by Congress.

Pragmatism — a non-ideological approach to political issues where "the merits of the particular case" may take a higher than normal precedence.

Pravda — Russian for "truth," state-owned and controlled newspaper of the Soviet Union and an official organ of the Central Committee of the Communist Party between 1921 and 1991; derogatory term for media organs such as TV or newspapers which are owned by, or to some degree supported by, government.

Precedent — a court ruling bearing on subsequent court cases.

Preemption — the practice of the national government overriding state and local laws in the name of the national interest.

Preferential voting — when voters do not simply vote for one candidate or party but a number of candidates in order of their preference with the intention that at least one choice will be elected.

Pre-poll votes — voting before election day by post or appearing at a special AEC office; permitted when the voter will be elsewhere on election day.

Presidential Commission — a body that advises the president on some problem and makes recommendations; some are temporary; others are permanent.

Presidential democracy — a regime in which the president and the legislators must be entirely separate.

President pro tempore — acting president of the United States Senate in the absence of the Vice President, who is the constitutionally authorized president of the body.

Presidential system — as opposed to parliamentary government, a constitutional framework where the executive is directly chosen by and responsible to the people (e.g., France, South Korea, the Philippines, and the U.S.).

Primary election — mostly occurring in America, an election where the successful candidate wins no actual office but becomes eligible to run in the upcoming official election as the candidate of a particular party.

Primary election — an election within a party to choose the party's nominee for the office.

Primary vote — the number of first choice votes that a candidate receives in preferential voting systems; see *Two-party-preferred*.

Print media — media distributed via printed materials.

Prior restraint — stopping free expression on a sensitive (usually "national security") issue before it can happen.

Private bill — a bill that offers benefit or relief to a single person named in the bill.

Private good — a good that benefits only some people, such as members of a group.

Private member's bill — proposed legislation introduced in Parliament by neither the government nor the opposition but by an individual MP.

Privatization — the practice of private companies providing government services.

Privileges and immunities clause — part of the Fourteenth Amendment, which forbids state governments from taking away any of the privileges and immunities of American citizenship.

Probability sample — a sampling technique in which each member of the population has a known chance of being chosen for the sample.

Professional legislature — a state legislature that meets in session for long periods, pays its members well and hires large support staffs for legislators.

Progressive / flat /regressive tax — progressive income tax, as espoused in "plank" two of Karl Marx's *The Communist Manifesto*, is a graduated tax where the rate increases as the income of the taxpayer gets higher; a flat tax is where all taxpayers pay the same rate of their income to the state (e.g., 15%); regressive taxation is where the rate decreases as the income of the payer increases; in all three situations, high earners pay more actual tax than low earners, but under a progressive tax system more cunning and resources are spent on creating tax avoidance schemes.

Prohibited powers — the powers specifically denied to the national government by the Constitution.

Project grants — categorical grant programs in which states submit proposals for projects to the federal government and the national government chooses which to fund on a competitive basis.

Proletariat — a term used in Marxist ideology to describe the working class who don't own property and whose only value is their labor.

Property right — the right to use, control, benefit and exclude others from any tangible or intangible object.

Proportional representation — an electoral system in which each party gets a number of seats in the legislature proportionate to its percentage of the vote; a voting system where the whole state is just one electorate and parties win seats in proportion to the total votes they receive in an election (hybrid systems often exist where the state is divided up into a number of multi-member electorates whereby seats won are approximately proportional to the votes cast).

Pro tem — the phrase to describe a person who temporarily takes the role of an absent superior; abbreviation of the Latin *pro tempore*, meaning "for the time being."

Prorogue — to temporarily bring Parliament to an end (such as for a summer break), as compared with a dissolution which occurs before an election.

Prospective voting — voters choosing by looking to the future; voters choose the candidate(s) they believe will help the country the most in the next few years.

Provisional vote — votes cast at an election in circumstances where a voter's name cannot be found on the roll or has already been marked off the roll; they are not counted until a careful check of enrollment records has been made.

Proxy war — a war instigated by enemy states in which third parties fight rather than the enemy states themselves.

Psephology — Greek for "voting with pebbles," the statistical and predictive study of elections.

Public administration — the task of running the government and providing services through policy implementation.

Public assistance — government benefits provided to those who meet certain criteria (e.g., low income).

Public choice theory — the study of politics from an economic perspective; rather than assuming that politicians, civil servants, and voters are all motivated by "what should be done," the analysis of how all three very often take self-interest into account when making decisions.

Public education — informing the public about key issues and what Congress is doing about those issues.

Public good — a good that benefits everyone, not just some; also called a "collective good."

Public interest group (or PIG) — a group that exists for the express purpose of promoting public interests that would not otherwise be pursued (e.g., Common Cause, a group that promotes campaign finance reform, and Public Citizen, a broad consumer advocacy group).

Public opinion — the basic attitudes and opinions of the general public.

Public policy — any rule, plan or action about issues of domestic national importance.

Public representative role — the role of the media acting as a representative of the public, holding government officials accountable to the people.

Pundit — Hindi for "learned one," a commentator with supposedly keen knowledge of contemporary politics.

Purposive incentive — a lure designed to promote a cause that might otherwise not have much appeal.

Q

Quadratic voting — a theory created by economics academic Glen Weyl that has yet to be put into practice; for referenda or plebiscites, those wishing to vote must not only pay the state for the privilege but have the option to pay a higher amount for multiple votes, accommodating a greater input for those with a greater stake in the issue at hand; to prevent simple vote buying, the cost of each extra vote is not linear, but quadratic (e.g., if the cost of one vote was set at a dollar then two votes would cost the square of two, four dollars; three votes, nine dollars; four votes 16 dollars, etc.); not a counter to "the tyranny of the majority" but a counter to the tyranny of the indifferent majority.

Quango — Quasi-Autonomous Non-Government Organization; a body financed by a government but not under its direct control.

Question Time — one of the tenets of Responsible Government whereby, for a set period each sitting day in Parliament, government ministers must answer any MP's questions, though in practice there is nothing to prevent them from giving evasive answers.

Quota preferential — preferential voting used in conjunction with proportional representation.

R

Rally 'round the flag effect — a significant boost in presidential popularity when a foreign crisis or threat of war arises.

Random sampling — the selection of individuals to participate in a public opinion poll (or another kind of study) in a way that is unbiased.

Random selection — a sampling technique to ensure that each person in the population has an equal chance of being selected for the sample.

Ranking member — the senior committee member from the minority party.

Rapprochement — the renewal or establishment of friendly relations between states which were previously hostile towards each other.

Ratings game — the practice of organizations rating members of Congress based on how they voted on issues of concern to the organizations and their members, usually expressed as a percentage (e.g., a Senator given a 100% rating always voted the way the organization rating them wanted).

Rational choice theory — an approach that assumes people act rationally in their self-interest, seeking to maximize value.

Rationalism — the belief that human reason can find solutions to many of our problems.

Reaganomics — economic strategy promoted by Ronald Reagan during his time in office based on the supposition that cutting taxes would make individual taxpayers more productive and more wealthy; consequently, the taxes paid by the wealthy, although collected at a lower percentage, would, in theory, be equal to or greater than before the tax cuts.

Realignment — a dramatic shift in the balance between the two parties that changes where they stand on the key issues dividing them.

Realism — a theory of international relations that stresses the importance of power (particularly military power) and claims that states act in their national interest.

Realpolitik — the politics of realism; rather than from principle, a self-interested approach to politics either from the standpoint of what will benefit one's party or, in international affairs, one's country.

Reapportionment — the process of reallocating representation in the House of Representatives after a census; some states (the more newly populous) will gain seats, while others (with dwindling populations) will lose them.

Recall — electoral procedure practiced in Canada and in many American states whereby an elected official, including the chief executive, can be recalled from office by the voters if there are sufficient signatures on a petition; there is no provision for a recall at the national level.

Recession — a country's economic status achieved following two consecutive quarters of a drop in real GNP; milder than a depression.

Redistribution — in SMV systems, the periodical redrawing of electoral boundaries to ensure each electorate conforms to the prerequisites of the electoral laws, making the number of representatives consistent with the district's current population.

Redistributive policy — a government action that takes money from one part of the citizenry and gives it to another part; usually the transfer goes from the well-off to the poor; see *Income transfer*.

Redistricting — redrawing district boundaries so that a state either loses or gains seats in the House of Representatives.

Referendum — a public policy decision referred to the vote of the people by a legislative body; used only at the state level.

Regime — a word used to describe a particular government.

Regressive tax — tax collected at increasingly lower rates or percentages as income level increases; a taxation system that costs the poor a larger portion of their income than it does the rich because the amount of tax gets smaller as the amount to which the tax is applied gets larger.

Regulated federalism — the practice of the national government imposing standards and regulations on state governments.

Regulatory policy — government policies that limit what businesses can do (e.g., minimum wages, workplace safety measures and careful monitoring of stock sales).

Remand — sending a case back to a lower court for a new trial or proceeding.

Rent-seeker — term created by American economist Anne Krueger; someone who attempts to make an income by manipulating the social, political or economic environment to their advantage in the form of political lobbying, rather than actually creating goods or services themselves; the "rent" coming to them is usually from government-enforced monopoly privileges or government grants paying for "services" which the free market might not otherwise see as of any value.

Rent voucher — a voucher issued by the government that can be used to pay all or part of a poor person's rent.

Repatriation — the sending back of someone to their country of origin, such as an illegal immigrant or prisoner of war.

Representative democracy — a system of government where citizens do not directly vote on actual issues and laws but surrender that right to their duly elected representatives; in modern times, it is commonly known as a democracy.

Representative sample — a sample that resembles the population as a whole.

Reprieve — a formal postponement of the execution of a criminal sentence; the president has the power to grant reprieves.

Republic — a regime that runs by representative democracy; form of government in which decisions are made by representatives who are chosen by the people; defined by some sources as simply a democracy but otherwise loosely described as a form of government where, in word or deed, rule is constrained by institutional frameworks and is not by the selected few; it is not an oligarchy but not necessarily a democracy; the Roman Republic was the original precedent for republicanism; apartheid South Africa, by this definition, was a republic.

Reregulation — significantly changing government regulations on industry.

Reserved powers — the powers reserved to the states and the people in the Tenth Amendment.

Responsible government — when government evolved from an independent authoritarian monarch in conjunction with a people's parliament to a merely symbolic monarch together with a prime minister and parliament, it was said that government (the executive in the form of the prime minister and his cabinet) had become responsible to parliament; now taken to be synonymous with parliamentary government.

Responsible party — a party that is strong enough to carry out a specific platform if elected to office.

Retention election — a state election, held in states using the merit plan for selecting judges, in which voters are asked to decide whether a judge should keep his or her job.

Retrospective legislation — laws defining behavior upon which one can be held criminally liable or responsible in civil court or otherwise liable for payment (such as taxation), even when that behavior may have happened before the enactment of said laws; more prevalent in autocracies as it violates the traditional concept of the rule of law, although is known to sometimes happen in democracies; see *Ex post facto laws*.

Retrospective voting — making a vote choice by looking to the past; voters support incumbents if they feel that the country has done well over the past few years.

Revenue agency — a government agency that raises money by collecting taxes or fees.

Revenue sharing — the practice of the federal government giving money to the states with no strings attached; started by the Nixon Administration and ended by the Reagan Administration.

Reverse — when a court overturns a lower court's ruling, declaring it void.

Reverse discrimination — discrimination against majority-status people due to affirmative action policies.

Revolution — a major event causing a fundamental change in a state.

Rider — an attachment to a piece of legislation that is generally unrelated to the rest of the bill.

Right of rebuttal — a media regulation that requires broadcasters to give people an opportunity to reply to criticisms aired on the outlet.

Rights of the minority — rights held by the minority that must be respected by the majority.

Right-wing / left-wing — "on the right" can be loosely described as a political philosophy favoring conservative, pro-market attitudes with a preference for (some) individual rights as opposed to "interventionist" government, a strict approach to law and order, a strong defense force and a sense of nationalism; "on the left" would be, loosely, opposite to the above together with a so-called "womb to tomb" (or "cradle to grave") approach to social welfare and an internationalist worldview; the terms originated in the French Estates General in 1789 when the nobility who favored complacency sat on the King's right and those who wanted change and amelioration of the peasant's conditions sat on the left.

Robson Rotation — an electoral method practiced in places such as Tasmania where multiple printings of ballot papers are made to rotate the first spot equally amongst all the candidates; an attempt to eliminate the *Donkey Vote*.

Roe v. Wade — a 1973 Supreme Court case that legalized abortion during the first trimester.

Rogue state — a state that does not follow international law or unspoken rules of the global arena.

Roll — the list of voters eligible to vote at an election.

Roll-call vote — occurs when each member's vote is recorded.

Rotten boroughs — an accident of circumstances in the U.K. up until 1832 whereby population movements over time left some electorates with as few as seven voters (a wealthy patron could then often bribe the constituents to elect whomever that person chose); also known as "pocket boroughs."

Royal Commission — a one-off, open inquiry into a specific issue which has raised public concern, instigated by the executive government but operated independently from it; the commissioner is often a retired judge and his given terms of reference strictly limiting the bounds of the investigation; despite that, the commissioner has considerable powers, from the summoning of witnesses, the granting of indemnity, allowing evidence not normally allowed in a court of law such as hearsay or government classified documents, even forcing testimony from officials of the government itself.

Rugged individualism — a form of individualism that emphasizes self-reliance and ignoring what others want and think.

Rule-making — the bureaucratic function of creating rules needed to implement policy.

Rule of law — the traditional legal concept, dating back as far as Aristotle, that we live under a set of predetermined rules rather than the arbitrary "wise guidance" of any contemporary judge, king or chief executive; does not necessarily imply democratic or just rule, but simply stable government where the law is proclaimed, followed and applied equally to all; term derived by the 19th century British jurist A.C. Dicey.

- All people are subject equally to the privileges and penalties of the law.

- The people are ruled by laws and not by individuals (both the judiciary and the executive are to act only according to the law rather than to their own beliefs of what is justice).

- The law shall be prospective, visible, clear and relatively stable.

- Due process must be afforded to all those before the law (following the letter and procedures of the law).

Rule of four — an informal rule in the Supreme Court in which four of the nine justices must agree to hear a case for the Court to issue a writ of certiorari.

S

Safe seat — a congressional seat that is very likely to be held by the incumbent (the current occupant of the seat) after the next election; also known as a "blue ribbon seat."

Sample — a group of people who are taken to stand for the whole population in a poll.

Sampling error — an error that arises as a matter of chance in the process of selecting individuals for participation in a public opinion poll or another study.

School vouchers — government money given to parents to help pay for tuition at private schools.

Scrutiny — the checking and counting of ballot papers to ascertain the result of an election; political parties are allowed representatives on such occasions.

Second Continental Congress — the governing body over the colonies during the American Revolution that drafted the Articles of Confederation to create the first national government.

Selective incentives — the lure of benefits that only group members will receive.

Selective incorporation — forcing states to abide by only certain parts of the Bill of Rights, not the whole thing.

Self-selected candidate — a person who chooses to run for office on their initiative.

Semantic infiltration — a concept first highlighted by Daniel Patrick Moynihan where political players succeed in persuading opponents to accept their terms in the discussion of specific subjects and, by extension, the policies and beliefs that accompany them (e.g., freedom fighters/terrorists, benefits/entitlements or illegal immigrants/asylum seekers).

Senate (U.S.) — the upper legislative chamber in the bicameral legislature of the United States, and together with the House of Representatives makes up the U.S. Congress; consists of 100 elected U.S. Senators, two from each state.

Senatorial courtesy — a tradition in which a Senator, if they are of the president's party, is allowed to have input into whom the president will nominate for federal judgeships in their state.

Separation of powers — derived by Charles Montesquieu, a traditional concept of liberalism where, for the sake of limiting abuse of power, the three branches of government (the executive, the legislature and the judiciary) remain independent; in modern times, the best examples are some American states where all branches have tangible power and, because of separate elections, no branch is appointed by nor can be removed by another branch; less than perfect examples would be parliamentary systems where the executive is directly appointed and can be removed by the legislature and the judiciary is directly appointed by the executive; see *Madisonian Model*.

Sexual harassment — unwanted and inappropriate physical or verbal conduct of a sexual nature that interferes with doing one's job or creates a hostile work environment.

Shadow cabinet — the "would be" cabinet of the opposition party in Parliament.

Shared powers — powers which are held and exercised by more than one level of government.

Shays' Rebellion — a 1786 uprising of Massachusetts farmers against high taxes and debt.

Signing message — a message attached to a bill that the president signs, explaining their understanding of the bill, sometimes with specific instructions as to how it should be implemented.

Single-member district — a legislative district that sends only one person to the legislature.

Single-member voting (SMV) — as opposed to proportional representation, the system where only one candidate represents all the citizens of an electorate or geographical area (also known as Majoritarian voting when preferences are allowed on the ballot paper).

Single transferable vote (STV) — a proportional representation voting system where there is no "above the line" option to vote for a party but only for individual candidates in preferred order; a party's winning candidates may not be in the same order as on the party's "ticket," and the voters' preferences may not necessarily be what the party would have liked; due to the relative complexity of voting and vote counting, there are likely to be more invalid ballot papers and the election results would take longer to ascertain.

Skewed sample — a sample that is not representative and leads to inaccurate polling results; a deceptive practice used to manipulate public opinion.

Slander — publicly stating things that the speaker knows to be untrue that hurt a person's reputation.

Social capital — mutual trust and habits of cooperation that are acquired by people through involvement in community organizations and volunteer groups.

The Social Contract — an 18th century philosophical concept used to attempt to explain the understanding by which people originally left their solitary, wilderness existence and came together under the auspices of government; theorist Thomas Hobbes first posited that the "contract" entailed each surrendering all their rights, save that of life, in exchange for the protection of the Crown; a half-century later, philosopher John Locke modified that to the proposition that the people retained not only life, but certain other fundamental rights and that they were legitimate in overthrowing any state that violated those rights.

Socialism — a method of government in which the means of planning and producing goods and services are controlled by a central government which also seeks to collect the wealth of the nation and distribute it evenly amongst its citizens; philosophy based on the notion that the governmental authority ought to be used to promote fair and equal socioeconomic outcomes in terms of education, income distribution and other important ways; socialistic governments generally own or exercise substantial control over sectors of the economy that impact large portions of the population and maintain significant wealth and income redistribution programs.

Social engineering — the practice that it is not enough for governments to create an environment for the citizenry where there is an adequate standard of living together with good health care, minimum crime and basic freedoms; governments must also engineer or program the beliefs, attitudes, and practices of the citizenry to conform to what is decreed, at the time, to be socially, physiologically and intellectually acceptable.

Social security — a social insurance program that aims to keep retired people and the disabled out of poverty.

Sociological representation — a type of representation in which the representative resembles most of their constituents in ethnicity, religion, race or social or educational background.

Soft money — political contributions not regulated by federal campaign finance laws; money is given directly to political parties for "party building;" not to be used for or given directly to candidates in support of election efforts; banned by the 2002 Bipartisan Campaign Reform Act, also known as the *McCain-Feingold bill*.

Solicitor general — a high-ranking Justice Department official who submits requests for writs of certiorari to the Supreme Court on behalf of the federal government; they also usually argue cases for the government in front of the Court.

Solidarity incentive — the lure of a social benefit, such as friendship, gained by members of an organization.

Sortition — an electoral system whereby candidates do not win office by popular choice but by lottery; popular in ancient Greece but rarely used today, though occasionally advocated by reformists.

Sovereignty — the right to exercise political power in a territory.

Speaker — an individual selected by the House to preside over the proceedings of the House in formal session; the Speaker of the House is almost always a member of the majority party.

Speaker of the House — the leader of the House of Representatives, elected by the majority party.

Special district — a type of local government designed to meet a very specific need.

Special election — an election to replace a member of Congress who leaves office in between regular elections.

Specialization — the practice of a group or person becoming extremely knowledgeable and skilled at one specific task.

Spin — to frame a news story in such a way as to shift the emphasis in the most politically favorable direction.

Splinter party — a third party, created when a faction from a major party breaks off and forms its party.

Split-ticket voting — the practice of casting votes for candidates of different political parties on the same ballot (e.g., casting a vote for the Democratic presidential candidate while voting for the Republican congressional candidate).

Spoiler — a losing candidate who costs another candidate the election.

Spoils system — the practice of elected officials rewarding supporters and allies by giving them government jobs.

Staffer — a person who works for a Senator or Congressman in a supporting capacity.

Standard operating procedure — a set of rules established in a bureaucracy that dictates how workers respond to different situations so that all workers respond in the same way.

Standing — the legal right to bring a suit before a court; to have standing, an individual must show that they have been harmed in a real way, not merely that they might be harmed in the future.

Standing committees — permanent legislative committees in the House and Senate with established issue and policy jurisdictions.

Stare decisis — Latin for "let the decision stand," a general practice followed by the Supreme Court of adhering to previous decisions when it makes new ones.

State — a political unit that has sovereign power over a particular piece of land.

State of nature — the natural condition of humankind living in a primitive environment before governments developed; existence was a perpetual struggle for sustenance, shelter and protection from potential harm by others and life was, to quote the English philosopher Thomas Hobbes, "solitary, poor, nasty, brutish and short."

Statecraft — the exercise of power, guided by wisdom, in pursuit of the public good.

State of the Union address — a constitutionally mandated message, given by the president to Congress, in which the president lays out plans for the coming year.

Statute — a law passed by Congress, a state legislature or some other government body.

Stewardship theory — a view of presidential power put forward by Theodore Roosevelt, arguing that the president is uniquely suited to act for the well-being of the whole nation because the whole nation has elected them.

Straight-ticket voting — voting for only candidates from one party.

Straw man (argument) — addressing and refuting an argument your opponents didn't make, even though at first glance it might appear they could make it (a human-like figure made of straw such as a military target dummy or scarecrow is always easily destroyed or knocked down).

Strict constructionism — a judicial philosophy that argues that constitutional interpretation should be limited to the specific wording of the document.

Subcommittee — smaller, more specialized committees which are organized and operate under the authority of standing committees.

Subnationalism — identification with small ethnic and regional groups within a nation.

Subsidy — an economic benefit given by the government to an individual, business or group that engages in behavior deemed beneficial by policymakers; subsidy payments can take the form of direct cash payments, tax credits or tax deductions.

Suffrage — the right to vote; see *Franchise.*

Sunset clause — a provision or clause inserted in legislation to declare its expiry date; most legislation does not contain such clauses as the intention is that laws will be permanent, at least until subsequent modification or repeal.

Sunset provisions — expiration dates written into some federal programs; Congress can renew the program if it is satisfied that the program is achieving its objectives.

Sunshine laws — laws that require government agencies to hold public proceedings on a regular basis.

Superdelegate — a party leader or elected official who is automatically granted delegate status for the national convention; superdelegates do not have to be chosen in primaries.

Super Tuesday — a term used to describe primary elections held in a large number of states on the same day.

Supplemental Security Income — a federal program that provides a minimum income to seniors and the disabled who do not qualify for social security.

Supply-side economics — the economic theory that when the supply side of the economy (the producers, capitalists) is taxed less and subject to less regulation, it creates more profit (and taxes on that increased profit); even at a lower rate, it should be equivalent to or even surpasses the original tax; the apotheosis of SSE is the flat rate income tax); see *Trickle-down economics.*

Supremacy clause — the part of Article VI of the Constitution that specifies that the federal Constitution, and laws passed by the federal government, are the supreme law of the land.

Supremacy doctrine — the doctrine that national law takes priority over state law; included in the Constitution as the *Supremacy Clause.*

Surplus — the amount by which the available funds exceed spending during a fiscal year.

Swing — how electoral results change between elections (e.g., "There has been a 15% swing toward the Democrats in this district since the 2001 election").

Swing voter — voters who are not loyal to any particular party but who swing from one party to another according to circumstances at the time.

Symbolic speech — actions that are intended to convey a belief.

Syndicalism — early 20th-century revolutionary political doctrine whereby the means of production are taken over in a general strike by workers' unions, who then effectively take over the government.

System of government — how power is distributed among different parts and levels of the state.

T

Talk radio — a radio format featuring a host who interviews guests; often very partisan.

Tammany Hall — The New York headquarters of the Democratic Party in the 19th century which became notorious for political corruption.

Tax credit — a reduction in one's tax burden designed to help certain people.

Tea Party — a grassroots American political movement (not a political party) advocating adherence to the Constitution as well as reining in alleged excessive taxing and spending by the government; the term derived by advocates sending tea bags (symbolizing the Boston Tea Party) to congresspersons who had a reputation for supporting large spending bills.

Temporary Assistance to Needy Families — a federal welfare program that provides money to low-income families.

Term limit — a legal prohibition against running for a political office after holding it for a prescribed number of years or terms.

Terrorism — the use of violent tactics with the aim of creating fear and destabilizing a government; frequently targets civilians.

Theocracy — government controlled by the church/priesthood or a proclaimed living god (e.g., ancient Egypt and modern-day Iran).

Think tank — a non-government, non-profit research institute comprised of scholars and physical scientists generally dedicated to the advocacy of (and finding rationales for) some broad political, economic or social belief.

Third party — in American politics, any political party other than the Democrats and Republicans.

Three-fifths compromise — a compromise between the Northern and Southern states at the Constitutional Convention stipulating that slaves would be counted as 3/5 of a person for purposes of representation and taxation.

Totalitarian — a government that wishes to subordinate the individual to the state by controlling not only all political and economic matters but also the attitudes, values, and beliefs of its population.

Totalitarian government — a regime in which the government controls every facet of life.

Total war — a highly destructive total war in which combatants use every resource available to destroy the social fabric of the enemy.

Tragedy of the commons — the concept espousing the impracticality of communally owned resources such as grazing land or ponds for fishing, etc.; individuals acting independently will maximize their benefits at the expense of others, thus in time depleting the common resource;

---

alternatively, where resources are privately owned there is an incentive to moderate their exploitation so as to preserve for the owner's further use.

Transfer value — in preferential-voting proportional-representation elections a winning candidate's surplus votes are transferred to the next available candidate; this is achieved by transferring all of the ballot papers at a fraction of their value.

Transnational — something that lies beyond the boundaries of a nation-state or consists of several nation-states.

Treason — crime committed against one's country (e.g., spying for an enemy nation).

Treaty — legally binding agreement between two nations; United States treaties are generally negotiated by the President or Secretary of State and must be ratified by the Senate.

Trial balloon — a novel idea put forward (or "floated") but not embraced by a politician to gauge its popularity.

Trickle-down economics — an attempt to improve the economy by providing big tax cuts to businesses and wealthy individuals (the supply side); these cuts encourage investment and entrepreneurship which then create jobs so; allegedly, the effect will be felt throughout the economy; see *Supply-side economics*.

Trojan horse — an organization with an innocuous or "motherhood statement" type title intended to gain public acceptance to introduce programs, funding or legislation of a more partisan nature than one is led to believe.

Trustee — a representative who bases their decision not on public opinion but on what they believe is right or best.

Trustee representation — a type of representation in which the people choose a representative whose judgment and experience they trust; the representative votes for what they think is right, regardless of the opinions of the constituents.

Two presidencies — the distinction between the president's roles in domestic and foreign policymaking; presidents generally have more discretion in the foreign policy arena.

Turkey farm — a government agency or department of less than priority status, staffed primarily with political appointees and other patronage hires.

Turnout — the percentage of enrolled citizens who vote.

Two-party-preferred — the final tally for the two most popular candidates or parties of all the votes (regardless of whether they may have been first, second or third choices) in single-member preferential voting systems.

Tyranny of the majority — when the majority violates the rights of the minority; a concept first coined in the nineteenth century by French writer Alexis de Tocqueville and embraced by John Stuart Mill, who claimed that even democracies had limitations because minority rights could be forfeited in the pursuit of popular causes; possible solutions to such tyranny could be a constitutionally entrenched bill of rights, proportional representation or a democracy divided up into a federation where people of different beliefs and values could gravitate to separate geographical areas that maintained their distinct laws and practices.

U

Unconventional participation — a political activity that, although legal, is considered inappropriate by many people; includes demonstrations, boycotts, and protests.

Underemployment — when people who seek work can only find part-time jobs.

Unemployment — when not everyone who wants a job can find one.

Unfunded mandate — a mandate for which the federal government gives the states no money.

Unicameral — government with a single-house legislature (e.g., France, Sweden, South Korea, New Zealand).

Unilateral — a state acting alone in the global arena.

Unipolar — an international system with a single superpower dominating other states.

Unitary system — a system of government where power is concentrated in the hands of the central government.

Unity — the idea that people overwhelmingly support the government and share certain common beliefs, even if they disagree about particular policies.

Universe — the group of people about which a research survey is trying to generalize when conducting a public opinion poll.

Useful idiot — description for people of influence who support a cause they fail to understand the full ramifications of and end up being exploited by the leaders of that cause; originally attributed to Lenin (although research has failed to confirm this) in describing western personalities such as H.G. Wells, George Bernard Shaw, Paul Robeson and journalist Walter Duranty, who visited the USSR during times of famine, were allowed to visit only selected areas and then returned home giving glowing reports of the new "workers' paradise."

Utilitarianism — consequentialist philosophy originally espoused by the 18th-century writer Jeremy Bentham, whereby the best policy is that which gives the greatest happiness to the greatest number.

User fee — a fee charged by the government to do certain things (e.g., paying a toll to use a tunnel).

V

Veto — Latin for "I forbid," the power of the president to stop a bill passed by both houses of Congress if they disapprove of it for any reason; see *Line item veto* and *Pocket veto*.

Veto message — a message written by the president and attached to a bill they have vetoed; explains the reasons for the veto.

Veto override — if the president vetoes a bill, Congress may override the veto by a two-thirds majority vote in both houses; the bill would then become law, the president's objections notwithstanding.

Virginia Plan — a plan at the Constitutional Convention to base representation in the legislature on population.

Voter turnout — the percentage of citizens who vote in an election.

Voting behavior — a term used to describe the motives and factors that shape voters' choices.

Vote of no confidence — in parliamentary systems, where the executive can only continue to serve at the behest of the majority of the legislature, a vote of no confidence (generally by the lower house) would be a death knell for the current administration; unless another coalition of parties could form a majority it would precipitate an election.

Voting Rights Act — a law passed in 1965 that banned discrimination in voter registration requirements.

W

War Powers Resolution — passed by Congress in 1973, the War Powers Resolution demands that the president consults with Congress when sending troops into action; also gives Congress the power to force the withdrawal of troops.

Washington community — the "inside the beltway" group that closely follows politics and constantly evaluates the relative power of politicians.

Watchdog journalism — journalism that attempts to hold government officials and institutions accountable for their actions.

Watergate — hotel in Washington, D.C. that was home to the Democratic Party's campaign headquarters, which were broken into by operatives of the Richard Nixon campaign of 1972; the resulting scandal, known as "Watergate," led to Nixon's resignation.

Watermelon — derogatory term for a Green politician or supporter who allegedly is more concerned with pushing socialist policies than with the environment ("green on the outside but red in the center").

Weberian model — the model of bureaucracy developed by sociologist Max Weber that characterizes bureaucracy as a rational and efficient means of organizing a large group of people.

Welfare — the term for the set of policies designed to help those in economic need.

Welfare state — the term to describe the government or country that provides aid to the poor and help to the unemployed.

Westminster — the location of the British houses of parliament; a name for a system where, among other attributes, the executive is divided between an "above-politics" head of state and a chief executive appointed by the legislature, a career rather than politically-appointed senior public service sector and a bicameral parliament.

Wets and dries — terms used in British Conservative Party politics since the Thatcher era to describe the moderates and the hardliners; "wet" originated from British public school vernacular to describe those perceived as weak as being "soppy;" the Canadian equivalent is a "Red Tory."

Whip — political party official in a legislative body charged with the duty of encouraging party members to vote with their parties on key pieces of legislation; a parliamentary party disciplinary officer who ensures that their party members do the right thing, such as being in attendance for certain crucial votes; the notice sent by political parties to legislative members.

Whistleblower — a person who reports wrongdoing in a government agency.

White House staff — the people with whom the president works every day.

White primary — the practice of political parties only allowing whites to participate in their primaries.

Winner-take-all — an electoral system in which the person with the most votes wins everything (and everyone else loses); most states have winner-take-all systems for determining electoral votes.

Wonk — someone engrossed in the technicalities of some aspect of public policy.

Writ — in electoral terms, a writ is a document commanding an electoral officer to hold an election and contains dates for the close of rolls, the close of nominations, the polling day and the return of the writ; the issue of a writ triggers the electoral process.

Writ of *certiorari* — the legal document, issued by the Supreme Court, that orders a lower court to send a case to the Supreme Court for review.

Writ of habeas corpus — (literally to "produce the body") is a court order to an individual (e.g., prison warden) or agency (institution) holding someone in custody to deliver the imprisoned individual to the court to determine whether the custodian has lawful authority to detain the prisoner.

Writ of mandamus — a judicial order directing a government official to perform a duty of their office.

Y

Yellow journalism — journalism that focuses on shocking, sordid, sometimes near-libelous stories to sell newspapers.

Z

Zeitgeist — German for "the spirit of the time," the prevalent beliefs and attitudes of a place or country at any particular period.

Image Credits

Chapter 1

Thomas Hobbes, English philosopher, and political theorist.
Wright, John Michael. Thomas Hobbes. C. 1669-1670. Oil on canvas. National Portrait Gallery, London. Wikimedia Commons.

Locke (left) and Montesquieu (right), French Enlightenment philosophers.
Sir Godfrey Kneller. *Portrait of John Locke.* 1697. Oil on canvas. Hermitage Museum, St. Petersburg. Wikimedia Commons.
French School. *Portrait of Montesquieu.* 1728. Oil on canvas. Palace of Versailles, Versailles. Wikimedia Commons.

Rousseau (left) & Paine (right), French Enlightenment philosophers.
Quentin De La Tour, Maurice. *Portrait of Jean-Jacques Rousseau.* Late 18th Century. Pastel on paper. Musée Antoine-Lécuyer, Saint-Quentin. Wikimedia Commons.
Milliere, August, George Romney, and William Sharp. *Thomas Paine.* c. 1876. Oil on canvas. National Portrait Gallery, London. Wikimedia Commons.

Drafting the Declaration of Independence.
Pratt, Mara L. *American's Story for America's Children: The Early Colonies.* Boston: D.C. Heath & Company, 1901.

Portraits of Daniel Shays and Job Shattuck, leaders of the Massachusetts "Regulators."
"Shays' Rebellion." The Portraits of Daniel Shays and Job Shattuck, Leaders of the Massachusetts "Regulators" 1787. Smithsonian Institution: National Portrait Gallery, Washington, D.C. *Bickerstaff's Boston Almanack.* Bickerstaff, 1787. Wikimedia Commons.

James Madison (left) and Edmund Randolph (right).
Bryant, William Cullen, and Sydney Howard Gay. *A Popular History of the United States.* New York: Charles Scribners' Sons, 1881.
Brumidi, Constantino. *Portrait of Edmund Randolph.* 19th century. Wikimedia Commons.

William Paterson, Supreme Court justice and pioneer of the New Jersey Plan

Sharples, James, Gregory Stapko, Thomas Addis Emmet, and Max Rosenthal. *Portrait of William Paterson (1745–1806) When He Was a Supreme Court Justice (1793–1806).* 1794. Oyez: IIT Chicago-Kent College of Law, Illinois Institute of Technology. *The History of the Supreme Court of the United States.* 1902. Wikimedia Commons.

Title page of the Federalist Papers by Alexander Hamilton, James Madison, and John Jay.
Hamilton, Alexander, James Madison, and John Jay. *The Federalist: A Collection of Essays, Written in Favour of the New Constitution, as Agreed upon by the Federal Convention, September 17, 1787.* Vol. 1. New York: J. and A. McLean, 1787. *America's Story from America's Library.* The Library of Congress. Wikimedia Commons.

Alexander Hamilton, political theorist and author of the Federalist Papers.
Bryant, William Cullen, and Sydney Howard Gay. *A Popular History of the United States.* New York: Charles Scribners' Sons, 1881.

Seals of the House of Representatives (left) and Senate (right).
The United States. Congressional Relations. U.S. Government Publishing Office. *U.S. Government Publishing Office.* By U.S. Federal Government. Federal Digital System. Wikimedia Commons.
The United States. Senate. *United States Senate.* By Congress. Internet Archive. Wikimedia Commons.

Chief Justice John Marshall of the McCulloch v. Maryland case.
Inman, Henry. *John Marshall.* 1832. Oil on canvas. Library of Virginia, Richmond, Virginia. Wikimedia Commons.

Thomas Jefferson, U.S. president, and political theorist.
Scott, David B. *A School History of the United States.* New York: Harper & Brothers, 1883.

Supreme Court building.
The United States Department of Agriculture. *Supreme Court Building in Washington, DC.* By Ken Hammond. Wikimedia Commons.

Plato, philosopher of ancient Greece.
Raphael. *The School of Athens (detail).* 1509. Fresco. Stanza Della Segnatura, Palazzi Pontifici, Vatican, Rome. Wikimedia Commons.

Constitutional Convention of 1787.
Juengling, Frederick, and Alfred Kappes. *The Convention at Philadelphia, 1787.* 19th Century. New York Public Library: Mid-Manhattan Picture Collection, New York. *Our First Century.* N.p.: R.M. Devin, 1881. Wikimedia Commons.

Chapter 2

The First Federal Congress, 1789, where the Bill of Rights was created.
Executive Office of the President of the United States. *U.S. Capitol – The First Federal Congress, 1789.* 1973–1974. Oil on canvas. Great Experiment Hall Cox Corridors. Wikimedia Commons.

Aristotle, ancient Greek philosopher.
Anzenbacher, Arno. *Engraving of the Philosopher Aristotle.* Picture Archive of the Austrian National Library, Vienna. *Introduction to Philosophy.* Freiburg and Herder. Wikimedia Commons.

U.S. President Dwight D. Eisenhower.
The United States General Services Administration. National Archives and Records Administration. National Archives. *Photograph of Dwight D. Eisenhower.* Wikimedia Commons.

General Washington in the American Revolution.
Lossing, Benson J. Our Country. New York: Johnson and Bailey, 1895. Wikimedia Commons.

Presidential portrait of George W. Bush.
Sanden, John Howard. *The Official Portrait of George W. Bush, 43rd President of the United States (2001–2009).* 2012. The White House Historical Association, Washington, D.C. *John Howard Sanden: American Portrait Painter.* Wikimedia Commons.

U.S. President Franklin Delano Roosevelt.
Franklin D. Roosevelt. 1940. *National Archives and Records Administration*, Hyde Park, New York. Wikimedia Commons.

U.S. Secretary of State Hillary Clinton.
The United States. United States Department of State. *U.S. Secretary of State Hillary Rodham Clinton Meets with Japanese Foreign Minister Katsuya Okada at the Waldorf Astoria Hotel during the 64th Session of the UN General Assembly in New York City, New York.* Wikimedia Commons.

U.S. Senator of Vermont, Bernie Sanders.
United States Senate. *Sanders Square.* 2015. Wikimedia Commons.

Portrait of Hitler at an SS meeting during the German occupation of WWII.
Belgian Flemish Nationalist Politician (VNV), Writer and Poet Ward Hermans (1897–1992) as a Speaker at a Meeting of the General SS Flanders in Ghent, during the German Occupation in World War II, Above Him Large Portrait of Hitler. 1941. National Archives, The Netherlands. *Nationaal Archief.* Wikimedia Commons.

Occupy Wall Street poster.
Cochran, Seth. *A "We Are The 99%" Poster Created by an Occupy Wall Street Group.* 2011. Wikimedia Commons.

Stephen Colbert at the 71st Peabody Awards.
Krusberg, Anders. *71st Annual Peabody Awards Luncheon Waldorf Astoria Hotel.* 2012. Peabody Awards. Wikimedia Commons.

Electoral College map of the 2012 United States presidential election.
Skidmore, Gage. "Electoral College Map for the 2012 United States Presidential Election." 2012. Wikimedia Commons.

Friends of NRA logo.
Greene, Jeremy. *New Friends of NRA Logo as of December 2011.* Digital image. *Friends of NRA.* Wikimedia Commons.

Nineteenth Amendment, passed in 1920.
United States. National Archives and Records Administration. *The Charters of Freedom.* The U.S. National Archives and Records Administration. Wikimedia Commons.

U.S. voting booths.
Buckawicki, Mark. *The Polling Station of Ward 1.* 2013. Nashua, New Hampshire. Wikimedia Commons.

Watergate Complex.
United States. U.S. Department of Justice. National Archives and Records Administration. *Record Group 21: Records of District Courts of the United States, 1685–1991. Gerald R. Ford Library & Museum "The Watergate Files" Exhibit.* Wikimedia Commons.

Canadian Prime Minister Justin Trudeau.
Radio Television Malacañang (RTVM). *Justin Trudeau and Benigno Aquino III at the APEC Philippines 2015 (cropped for Use in Election Infoboxes).* 2015. Asia-Pacific Economic Corporation. Wikimedia Commons.

Seal of the Supreme Court of the United States.
United States. United States Federal Court. *Seal of the Supreme Court of the United States.* 2008. Wikimedia Commons.

Civil Rights movement protest.
Wolfson, Stanley. *Photograph Shows Marchers Carrying Banner "We March with Selma!" on Street in Harlem, New York City, New York.* 1965. Library of Congress, Washington, D.C. *New York World Telegram & Sun.* Wikimedia Commons.

Seattle Ministerial Conference in 1999.
Seattle Ministerial Conference November 30–December 3, 1999. 1999. Switzerland. *World Trade Organization.* Wikimedia Commons.

Civil Rights leader Martin Luther King Jr.
Reyneau, Betsy G. *Portrait of Dr. Martin Luther King, Jr.* National Archives and Records Administration: Donated Collections: Records Group 200. *Teachers' Resources.* National Archives. Wikimedia Commons.

Campaign poster for William J. Bryan, American politician.
Williams, Neville. *Campaign Poster for William J. Bryan.* c. 1900. Campaign poster. Library of Congress, Washington, D.C. Wikimedia Commons.

Chapter 3

Logo of the Republican Party of the United States of America. Abbreviation GOP stands for "Grand Old Party." By Republican Party (http://gop.com/) [Public domain], via Wikimedia Commons.

The official logo of the United States Democratic Party.
By United States Democratic Party [Public domain], via Wikimedia Commons.

The official logos of the Libertarian party of the United States and the Green Party of the United States.
By Libertarian Party of the United States [Public domain], via Wikimedia Commons.

The official logo of the Green Party of the United States.
By Green Party of the United States (http://www.gp.org/rebranding-campaign) [Public domain].

Thomas Jefferson, founder of the Democratic Republicans.
Beach, Chandler B., A.M., and Frank Morton McMurry, Ph.D., eds. *The New Student's Reference Work for Teachers, Students, and Families.* Chicago: F.E. Compton, 1914. Wikimedia Commons.

Andrew Jackson, presidential candidate of 1824.
Beach, Chandler B., A.M., and Frank Morton McMurry, Ph.D., eds. *The New Student's Reference Work for Teachers, Students, and Families.* Chicago: F.E. Compton, 1914. Wikimedia Commons.

Theodore Roosevelt (left) and William Howard Taft (right),26th and 27th Presidents of the United States.
Theodore Roosevelt. [Public domain], via Wikimedia Commons. *William Howard Taft.* Library of Congress Prints and Photographs online collection. [Public domain], via Wikimedia Commons.

Ross Perot, an American businessman.
United States. Department of Veterans Affairs. *Ross Perot at the United States Department of Veterans Affairs.* 2008. Wikimedia Commons.

1916 Democratic Party National Convention.
The 1916 Democratic Party National Convention Held at the St. Louis Coliseum in St. Louis, Missouri. 1916. Library of Congress, Washington, D.C. Wikimedia Commons.

Presidential candidate Rick Santorum campaigning for Iowa Caucus, January 2012.
By *IowaPolitics.com* (http://creativecommons.org/licenses/by-sa/2.0), via Wikimedia Commons.

United States Electoral College map. Copyright by Sterling Test Prep.
Al Gore, American politician and environmentalist.
Al Gore, Former Vice President of the United States. c. 1994. *American Forces Radio and Television Services.* Wikimedia Commons.

Political cartoon shows the newly drawn Massachusetts State Senate district of South Essex created by the legislature to favor the Democratic-Republican Party candidates of Governor Elbridge Gerry over the Federalists (1812).
By Elkanah Tisdale (1771-1835) (often falsely attributed to Gilbert Stuart). Originally published in the *Boston Centinel*, 1812. [Public domain], via Wikimedia Commons.

American Medical Association headquarters building in Chicago, Illinois.
Crocker, J. IBM Building, Chicago, IL, USA. 2004. Wikimedia Commons.

Justice Anthony Kennedy, author of the Supreme Court's decision in Citizens United v. Federal Election Commission.
Collection of the Supreme Court of the United States. *Anthony Kennedy, Associate Justice of the Supreme Court of the United States.* Oyez: IIT Chicago-Kent College of Law. Wikimedia Commons.

Logo for the 24-hour news channel, CNN.
Turner Broadcasting, Inc. *Digital image.* 2015. Wikimedia Commons.

U.S. Federal Communications Commission Inspector General badge.
Federal Communications Commission. Digital image. *Office of the Inspector General. Federal Communications Commission.* Wikimedia Commons.

Chapter 4

Roosevelt signs the declaration of war against Japan in 1941, starting America's involvement in WWII.
Rowe, Abbie. *United States President Franklin D. Roosevelt Signing the Declaration of War against Japan, in the Wake of the Attack on Pearl Harbor.* 1941. National Archives and Records Administration, Washington, D.C. Wikimedia Commons.

President Ronald Reagan and Vice President George H. W. Bush, both issued many signing statements. President Ronald Wilson Reagan and Vice President George Herbert Walker Bush Work in the Oval Office of the White House, July 20, 1984. 1984. Executive Office of the President of the United States, Washington, D.C. Wikimedia Commons.

President Franklin Delano Roosevelt at his fourth inaugural address.
Photograph of President Franklin D. Roosevelt Delivering his Fourth Inaugural Address. 1945. National Archives and Records Administration: Harry S. Truman Library, Independence, Montana. Wikimedia Commons.

2008 Republican Presidential candidate John McCain.
United States. Congress. *John McCain (R-AZ), United States Senator.* By Code of Federal Regulations. Wikimedia Commons.

U.S. President Gerald Ford.
United States. *Gerald Ford, Official Presidential Photograph.* Executive Office of the President of the United States. *Gerald R. Ford Presidential Library and Museum.* By David Hume Kennerly. National Archives and Records Administration. Wikimedia Commons.

U.S. Senate in session during the impeachment trial of President Bill Clinton.
Floor Proceedings of the U.S. Senate, in Session during the Impeachment Trial of Bill Clinton. 1999. *C-SPAN Archives.* Wikimedia Commons.

Founding members of the Congressional Black Caucus.
U.S. Congress. Founding Members of the Congressional Black Caucus. Black Americans in Congress. Office of the Clerk, U.S. House of Representatives. Wikimedia Commons.

Logo for the U.S. Senate Select Committee on Intelligence.
Digital image. U.S. Government, 2013. Wikimedia Commons.

Supreme Court building.
Architect of the Capitol. *U.S. Capitol – Sunny Afternoon at the Supreme Court.* 2012. U.S. Capitol, Flickr. Wikimedia Commons.

Seal of the United States Court of Appeals for the First Circuit.
U.S. Government. Digital image. District of Columbia Court of Appeals Seal. 2015. Wikimedia Commons.

Members of the Warren Court, who made the unanimous decision for Brown v. Board of Education.
United Press International Telephoto. *The Members of the Warren Court.* 1953. Library of Congress, Washington, D.C. Wikimedia Commons

Max Weber, German sociologist.
1894. *Live Journal.* Live Journal, Inc. Wikimedia Commons.

President Lyndon B. Johnson at the University of Michigan commencement in 1964, where he made his first public reference to his Great Society policies.
LBJ Great Society Speech. University of Texas Photography Lab, Austin. Wikimedia Commons.

Assassination of President James Garfield.
Berghaus, A., and C. Upham. *An Engraving of James A. Garfield's Assassination.* 1881. *Frank Leslie's Illustrated Newspaper. Images of American Political History.* Wikimedia Commons.

Seal of the C.I.A. United States Federal Government.
Digital image. *Cornell University Law School.* Cornell University, 1950. Wikimedia Commons.

President Ronald Reagan.
American Forces Radio and Television Service. *Official Portrait of President Ronald Reagan.* 1981.
University of Texas: Ronald Reagan Presidential Library and Museum. Wikimedia Commons.

Montesquieu, French political theorist.
Bayard, Émile-Antoine. *Portrait of Montesquieu.* 1889. *Album of the Centenary: Great Men and Great Events of the French Revolution.* By Augustin Challamel and Desire Lacroix. Paris: Jouvet & Cie, 1889. Wikimedia Commons.

President Richard Nixon.
Richard M. Nixon, Ca. 1935–1982. National Archives and Records Administration: Still Picture Records Section, Special Media Archives Services Division. Department of Defense. Department of the Army. Office of the Deputy Chief of Staff for Operations. U.S. Army Audiovisual Center. Wikimedia Commons.

Abraham Lincoln with his cabinet.
Carpenter, Francis Bicknell. *First Reading of the Emancipation Proclamation of President Lincoln.* 1864. Oil on canvas. United States Capitol: West Staircase, Senate Wing, Washington, D.C. Wikimedia Commons.

U.S. President Barack Obama with Canadian Prime Minister Stephen Harper.
United States. White House. Executive Office of the President of the United States. *Barack Obama, President of the United States of America, with Stephen Harper, Prime Minister of Canada.* By Pete Souza. The White House: President Barack Obama. Wikimedia Commons.

Logo for the Gallup Corporation, one of the main polling firms of the U.S.
Gallup, Inc. This is the standard logo for Gallup, Inc. Digital image. Wikimedia Commons.

President John F. Kennedy meets with representatives from the NAACP: Dr. E. Franklin Jackson and Bishop Stephen G. Spottswood.
Knudsen, Robert. *President John F. Kennedy Meets with Representatives from the National Association for the Advancement of Colored People (NAACP). Dr. E. Franklin Jackson, President of Washington, D.C. NAACP Branch; Bishop Stephen G. Spottswood, Chairman of NAACP Board of Directors; President Kennedy; Arthur B. Spingarn, Former NAACP Vice-President. Oval Office, White House, Washington, D.C.* 1961. White House Photographs Collection. John F. Kennedy Presidential Library and Museum, Boston. Wikimedia Commons.

Internal Revenue Service Building on Constitution Avenue in Washington, D.C.
U.S. Department of the Treasury. *IRS Building on Constitution Avenue in D.C.* Wikimedia Commons.

Logo of the Federal Communications Commission.
United States. Federal Communications Commission. Office of Engineering and Technology. *Understanding the FCC Regulations for Computers and Other Digital Devices.* By U.S. Government. 1996. Print. Ser. 62. Wikimedia Commons.

Painting of Thomas Jefferson (leader of the anti-federalists) and Alexander Hamilton (author of The Federalist Papers) with George Washington in the Capitol building.
Architect of the Capitol, and Constantino Brumidi. *US Capitol – George Washington with Thomas Jefferson and Alexander Hamilton.* 1872. Oil on plaster. Capitol Building Room S-213, Washington, D.C. Wikimedia Commons.

Seal of the U.S. Bureau of Indian Affairs.
Department of the Interior. *Seal of the U.S. Department of the Interior, Bureau of Indian Affairs (1824).* Digital image. 2012. Wikimedia Commons.

Chapter 5

Official logo of the Executive Office of the President of the United States
Public domain.

Official logos of some U.S. Federal agencies.
Public domain.

Guantanamo Bay map.
Public domain via Wikimedia Commons.

President Bush signs the Homeland Security Appropriations Act of 2004.
United States. Department of Homeland Security. White House. By Tina Hager. Washington, D.C. 2003. Wikimedia Commons.

U.S. President Bill Clinton signs the Defense of Marriage Act in 1996.
Public domain (government works).

President Bush signs the Patriot Act.
Draper, Eric. *President George W. Bush Signs the Uniting (and) Strengthening America (by) Providing Appropriate Tools Required (to) Intercept (and) Obstruct Terrorism (USA PATRIOT) Act, Anti-Terrorism Legislation, in the East Room Oct. 26.* 2001. Washington, D.C. *The White House.* Wikimedia Commons.

Leaders of the Civil Rights March on Washington (1963).
August 28, 1963. By Unknown or not provided author (U.S. National Archives and Records Administration) [Public domain], via Wikimedia Commons.

Counter Terrorist Unit seal for the Department of Homeland Security.
United States. Department of Homeland Security. Counter Terrorist Unit. *CTU.* By U.S. Department of Homeland Security. Wikimedia Commons.

President Roosevelt signs the Tennessee Authority Act, part of the New Deal.
United States Tennessee Valley Authority. *United States President Franklin D. Roosevelt Signs the T.V.A. Act, Which Established the Tennessee Valley Authority.* 1933. *Tennessee Valley Authority.* Wikimedia Commons.

The Federal Reserve headquarters in Washington, D.C.
By Dan Smith (http://creativecommons.org/licenses/by-sa/2.5)], via Wikimedia Commons.

President Barack Obama and Vice President Joe Biden meet with members of the National Security Council in 2014.
Souza, Pete. Washington, D.C. *The White House Flickr.* Wikimedia Commons.

The USS Arizona burning after the Japanese attack on Pearl Harbor on December 7, 1941.
U.S. Navy. 1941. National Archives and Records Administration, Washington, D.C. Wikimedia Commons.

Saddam Hussein, Iraqi dictator and terrorist shortly after his capture (2003).
Armed Forces Radio and Television Service, 2003. Washington, D.C. Wikimedia Commons.

The Joint Chiefs of Staff photographed in the Joint Chiefs of Staff Gold Room, more commonly known as The Tank, in the Pentagon on December 14, 2001. From left to right are: U.S. Air Force Chief of Staff Gen. John P. Jumper, U.S. Marine Corps Commandant Gen. James L. Jones Jr., Vice Chairman of the Joint Chiefs of Staff Gen. Peter Pace, U.S. Marine Corps, Chairman of the Joint Chiefs of Staff Gen. Richard B. Myers, U.S. Air Force, U.S. Army Chief of Staff Gen. Eric K. Shinseki, U.S. Navy Chief of Naval Operations Adm. Vern E. Clark.
By Mamie Burke [Public domain], via Wikimedia Commons.

President Lyndon B. Johnson signs the Economic Opportunity Act.
U.S. Government. 1964. LBJ Presidential Library, Austin, TX. Wikimedia Commons.

Official logo of the Environmental Protection Agency.
Public domain.

President George W. Bush signs the No Child Left Behind Act.
Morse, Paul. *Visiting Hamilton High School in Hamilton, Ohio, Jan. 8, 2002, President George W. Bush Signs into Law the No Child Left Behind Act.* 2002. Executive Office of the President of the United States. *The White House.* Wikimedia Commons.

Barack Obama signing the Patient Protection and Affordable Care Act at the White House.
Souza, Pete. 2010. Executive Office of the President of the United States. *Nancy Pelosi Flickr.* Wikimedia Commons.

Pro-Life March for Life in Washington D.C. in 2008, protesting Roe v. Wade.
Martin, Eric. *Pro-Life, March For Life 2008 U.S. Capitol, U.S. Supreme Court, Washington, D.C., Constitution Avenue.* 2008. Wikimedia Commons.

President James Madison, co-author of The Federalist Papers.
James Madison, Half-length Portrait, Seated, Facing Right, with Documents in Hand. 1828. Pendleton's Lithography. Library of Congress, Washington, D.C. Wikimedia Commons.

A same-sex couple is celebrating overturning of DOMA in San Francisco in 2013.
Dombrowski, Quinn. *Mommy, Mama, and Baby Georgie.* 2013. Wikimedia Commons.

President Obama discusses health care reform in a speech to Congress.
United States. White House. Executive Office of the President of the United States. *The White House: President Barack Obama.* By Pete Souza. United States Federal Government. Wikimedia Commons.

First Lady Michelle Obama on the Ellen DeGeneres show.
Kennedy, Chuck. *First Lady Michelle Obama and Ellen DeGeneres Dance during a Taping of "The Ellen DeGeneres Show" Marking the Second Anniversary of the "Let's Move!" Initiative.* 2012. Official White House Photo, Burbank, California.

President Barack Obama votes on the 2012 Presidential Election Day.
United States. White House. Executive Office of the President of the United States. *United States President Barack Obama Casts His Ballot during Early Voting in the 2012 U.S. Election at the Martin Luther King Jr. Community Center in Chicago, Illinois.* By Pete Souza. Chicago, Illinois. 2012. Wikimedia Commons.

President Obama receives an update on the Affordable Care Act.
United States. The White House. Executive Office of the President of the United States. By Pete Souza. 2014. Wikimedia Commons.

Seattle recall petitions in 1910.
Presenting Recall Petitions against Seattle, Washington Mayor Hiram Gill. The Recall Election Took Place February 1911. 2010. Seattle Public Library: Seattle Room. McClure's. 1911. Wikimedia Commons.

Chart of the Iron Triangle theory.
Diagram of an Iron Triangle in Government. Digital image. 2004. Wikimedia Commons.

Chapter 6

Slave auction in America.
Ellis, Edward S. *The Youth's History of the United States.* New York: The Cassell Publishing Company, 1887.

William Lloyd Garrison, leader of the abolitionist movement.
American Abolitionist William Lloyd Garrison, Three-quarter-length, Seated. National Archives and Records Administration. Wikimedia Commons.

U.S. Colonel Robert E. Lee.
Vannerson, Julian. *Portrait of Gen. Robert E. Lee, Officer of the Confederate Army.* 1864. Library of Congress: Prints and Photographs Online Catalog, Washington, D.C. Wikimedia Commons.

Medals that commemorate the leaders of the desegregation of public schools that led directly to Brown v. the Board of Education.
United States. United States Mint. Authorized by Public Law 108–180, *This Medal Commemorates Reverend Joseph A. DeLaine, Harry and Eliza Briggs and Levi Pearson for Their Contributions to the Nation as Pioneers in the Effort to Desegregate Public Schools That Led Directly to the Landmark Desegregation Case of Brown Et Al. v. the Board of Education of Topeka Et Al.* By Charles L. Vickers and Donna Weaver. 2003. Print. Wikimedia Commons.

Suffragettes Elizabeth Cady Stanton (left) and Susan B. Anthony (right).
Elizabeth Cady Stanton (seated) with Susan B. Anthony (standing). c. 1900. Library of Congress: Prints and Photographs Division, Washington, D.C. Wikimedia Commons.

Feminist and suffragette Victoria Woodhull.
Victoria Claflin Woodhull Martin (1838–1927). 1880. Everything Paweks Online Magazine. Wikimedia Commons.

Eleanor Roosevelt (left) and Esther Peterson (right) of the Presidential Commission on the Status of Women.
Eleanor Roosevelt and Esther Peterson (President's Commission on the Status of Women). 1962. National Archives and Records Administration: Franklin D. Roosevelt Library, Hyde Park, New York. Wikimedia Commons.

A COINTELPRO document outlining the FBI's plans to 'neutralize' activist Jean Seberg for her support of the Black Panther Party.
Held, Richard W. *A COINTELPRO Document Outlining the FBI's Plans to 'neutralize' Jean Seberg for Her Support for the Black Panther Party.* 1970. Pink Noise Studio. Wikimedia Commons.

President George H. W. Bush signs the Americans with Disabilities Act of 1990.
1990. The White House Historical Association, Washington, D.C. Wikimedia Commons.

U.S. Supreme Court Justice William Rehnquist.
Oakes, Robert S. *Justice William Rehnquist.* 1972. Library of Congress, Washington, D.C. Wikimedia Commons.

Politician and activist Harvey Milk.
Nicoletta, Daniel. *Harvey Milk Filling in for Mayor Moscone for a Day in 1978.* 1978. Wikimedia Commons.

Elbridge Gerry, American politician, and Anti-Federalist.
Bogle, James, and John Vanderlyn. *Elbridge Gerry (1744–1814), American Statesman.* 1861. Monmouth College. Wikimedia Commons.

Eugene Debs, political activist.
University of Iowa Libraries: Redpath Chautauqua Collection: Special Collections Department, Iowa City, IA. Wikimedia Commons.

James Madison, fourth President of the United States.
Stuart, Gilbert. *James Madison.* c. 1821. Oil on panel. National Gallery of Art: Gallery 60 A, Washington, D.C. Wikimedia Commons.

The burning of Washington during the War of 1812.
Capture and Burning of Washington by the British. 1876. Wood engraving. Library of Congress: American Memory, Washington, D.C. Wikimedia Commons.

Throwing tea overboard during the Boston Tea Party.
Stephens, Alex H. *A Comprehensive and Popular History of the United States.* Chattanooga: Hickman and Fowler, 1882.

House Committee on Un-American Activities.
Harris, and Ewing. *While Newsmen Take Notes, Chairman Dies of House Committee Investigating Un-American Activities, Proofs and Reads His Statement Replying to President Roosevelt's Attack on the Committee.* 1938. Library of Congress: Prints and Photographs Division, Washington, D.C. Wikimedia Commons.

Sandra Day O'Connor, American jurist, and Supreme Court Justice.
American Jurist Sandra Day O'Connor (b. 1930), Justice of the Supreme Court of the United States. c. 1981–1983. Library of Congress: Prints and Photographs Division, Washington, D.C. Wikimedia Commons.

Guard tower at Abu Ghraib Prison.
United States. U.S. Army. *Local Host Images.* By Michael J. Carden. 2005. Wikimedia Commons.

U.S. Justice Arthur Goldberg.
Arthur Goldberg, U.S. Supreme Court Justice, and UN Ambassador. Lyndon B. Johnson Library Collection. Wikimedia Commons.

U.S. President Lyndon B. Johnson.
Okamoto, Yoichi. *Portrait of President Lyndon B. Johnson.* 1969. University of Texas: LBJ Presidential Library. Wikimedia Commons.

Print celebrating the passage of the Fifteenth Amendment to the United States Constitution.
Kelly, Thomas. *The Fifteenth Amendment.* 1870. Hand-colored lithographs. Library of Congress: Prints and Photographs Division, Washington, D.C. Wikimedia Commons.

Congressman John A. Bingham, a principal framer of the Equal Protection Clause of the Fourteenth Amendment.
Representative John A. Bingham of Ohio, Principal Framer of the Fourteenth Amendment. Congressman John Bingham of Ohio Was the Principal Framer of the Equal Protection Clause. Rep. John A. Bingham. Library of Congress: Prints and Photographs Division, Washington, D.C. Wikimedia Commons.